CW00840053

Translational Action and Intercultural Communication

Edited by

Kristin Bührig, Juliane House
and Jan D. ten Thije

St. Jerome Publishing
Manchester, UK & Kinderhook (NY), USA

Published by
St. Jerome Publishing
2 Maple Road West, Brooklands
Manchester, M23 9HH, United Kingdom
Telephone +44 (0)161 973 9856
Fax +44 (0)161 905 3498
stjerome@compuserve.com
http://www.stjerome.co.uk

InTrans Publications
P. O. Box 467
Kinderhook, NY 12106, USA
Telephone (518) 758-1755
Fax (518) 758-6702

ISBN 978-1-905763-09-2 (pbk)

© Kristin Bührig, Juliane House and Jan D. ten Thije 2009

All rights reserved, including those of translation into foreign languages. No part of this publication may be reproduced, stored in a retrieval system or transmitted in any form or by any means, electronic, mechanical, photocopying, recording or otherwise without either the prior written permission of the Publisher or a licence permitting restricted copying issued by the Copyright Licensing Agency (CLA), 90 Tottenham Court Road, London, W1P 9HE. In North America, registered users may contact the Copyright Clearance Center (CCC): 222 Rosewood Drive, Danvers MA 01923, USA.

Printed and bound in Great Britain by
T. J. International, Padstow, Cornwall, UK

Typeset by
Delta Typesetters, Cairo, Egypt
Email: hilali1945@yahoo.co.uk

British Library Cataloguing in Publication Data
A catalogue record of this book is available from the British Library

Library of Congress Cataloging-in-Publication Data
Translational action and intercultural communication / edited by Kristin Bührig, Juliane House, and Jan D. ten Thije.
p. cm.
Includes bibliographical references and index.
ISBN 978-1-905763-09-2 (pbk. : alk. paper)
1. Translating and interpreting. 2. Intercultural communication. I. Bührig, Kristin. II. House, Juliane. III. Thije, Jan D. ten.

P306.2.T747 2009
418'.02--dc22

2008055389

Translational Action and Intercultural Communication

Edited by Kristin Bührig, Juliane House and Jan D. ten Thije

Translation and interpreting studies and intercultural communication have so far largely been treated as separate disciplines. *Translational Action and Intercultural Communication* offers an overview of a range of different theoretical and methodological approaches to examining the hitherto largely ignored connection between the two research strands.

Drawing on three key concepts ('functional equivalence', 'dilated speech situation' and 'intercultural understanding'), this interdisciplinary volume attempts to interrelate the following thematic strands: procedures of mediating between cultures in translational action, problems of intercultural communication in translational action, and insights into intercultural communication based on analyses of translational action.

The volume features both contrastive papers and papers which investigate communicative events *in actu*. The analyses presented deal with a variety of genres and types of interaction, including children's books, speech acts in dramatic text, popular science and economic texts, excerpts from intercultural university encounters, phatic talk, toast giving and medical communication.

Acknowledgments

We would like to thank Daniel Spielmann for formatting the chapters.

Our gratitude also goes to the anonymous readers of each chapter for their comments and suggestions

Kristin Bührig, Juliane House and Jan D. ten Thije
January 2008

Table of Contents

Acknowledgements

1. Introduction

Translational Action and Intercultural Communication

KRISTIN BÜHRIG
University of Hamburg, Germany

JULIANE HOUSE
University of Hamburg, Germany

JAN D. TEN THIJE
Utrecht University, The Netherlands

The aim of this volume is to investigate the relation between intercultural communication and translational action, and to provide a theoretically and methodologically sound basis for research into this relation. Although there have been previous attempts to provide such a link (Schäffner and Adab 1995; Snell-Hornby *et al.* 1995; Katan 1999/2004), we believe that, given the growing importance of the two fields, it is essential to develop a more explicitly integrative and interdisciplinary theoretical framework.

In the past, attempts to combine the fields of translation studies and intercultural communication studies have unfortunately failed to place this linkage on a firm linguistic basis. To provide such a basis is therefore what the contributions in this volume try to do. Further, intercultural communication research has in the past been mainly concerned with cases in which participants fail to understand one another. In our view, the more important issue is however to reconstruct linguistic structures that enable understanding (cf. Bührig and ten Thije 2006). Therefore, it is a focus on understanding in intercultural communication which characterizes the approach taken here. As it happens, intercultural understanding is also the basis for the single most important concept underlying translation theory: namely functional equivalence. We regard functional equivalence as the presupposition for achieving a comparable function of a text or discourse in another cultural context. Consequently, intercultural understanding can be considered as the success with which the linguistic-cultural transposition has been undertaken, measurable by the degree to which functional equivalence is achieved, i.e., whether and to what degree concrete text/discourse functions in a concrete situation are fulfilled reciprocally (cf. House 1977, 1997, 2006a, 2006b). On this (integrative) view, then, intercultural misunderstanding can be regarded as simply a failure to realize functional equivalence.

The connection between functional equivalence and intercultural understanding can further be accounted for with reference to the concept of the 'dilated speech situation' ('die zerdehnte Sprechsituation') (Ehlich 1983, 1984). According to Ehlich, the prime characteristic of a 'text' is that it is an 'agent of transmission' which derives from the fact that speaker and hearer are not at the same place at the same time. And it is a text's functioning as a sort of 'messenger' which then enables the hearer to receive the speaker's linguistic action, although the production situation and the reception situation diverge in terms of time and place. Through such a 'transmission' undertaken by a text, the original speech situation becomes 'dilated'. Since speakers know that their utterances will be 'passed on', they adapt their formulations accordingly, i.e., a speaker makes a 'text' out of his or her linguistic action. Texts are therefore not limited to the written medium, but can also exist in oral form.

The concept of the 'dilated speech situation' is relevant for intercultural communication research and translation theory in both oral and written communication: Both interpreting and translation are characterized by a specific rupture of the original speech situation, which results from the linguistic barrier between speaker and hearer or between an author and his or her readers. And it is only with the help of an interpreting or translating person that this linguistic barrier between speaker (member of culture 1) and hearer (member of culture 2) or author and reader can be bridged. For the case of interpreting, Bührig and Rehbein (2000) assume the existence of what they call an 'internally dilated speech situation', a situation where the primary communication partners are co-present but are unable to communicate without the translational action of the interpreter, who manages to bridge the linguistically conditioned rupture.

The person doing the translating thus passes on the linguistic action in L1 (Situation 1) to the L2 addressees (Situation 2). This procedure is not without consequence for the transmitted linguistic action. While monolingual texts already show signs of being prepared for transmission, this is particularly true of translated texts, because they are exposed to a double transmission process. The linguistic action in the L2 in the interpreting process is also subject to this translation-specific text construction. For instance, homileïc (phatic) discourse such as small talk often shows a distinct transition from discursive L1 action to a more textual L2 action. Institutional communication, on the other hand, is characterized by the fact that the L1 action realized by representatives of the institution is often already marked as an oral text, which can be dissolved in the interpreting act (Bührig 2001; Bührig and Meyer 2004).

Along with the dilation of the speech situation as a prime feature of translation and interpreting, these two activities are also characterized by a process of linguistic-cultural reflection geared towards the L2 recipient.

On account of this inherent target-oriented reflective feature, all translational constellations can also be said to have a potential for intercultural communication and intercultural understanding related to processes of reflection upon functional equivalence. This will be described in greater detail in the various discursive and textual structures presented in the analyses in this volume.

The three key concepts of 'functional equivalence', 'dilated speech situation' and 'intercultural understanding' mentioned above constitute a framework within which to discuss the linkage between the two disciplines of translation studies and intercultural communication, aimed for by and through the papers in this volume. In what follows, we will select from each of the six contributions relevant theoretical notions that can help concretize the three key concepts informing this volume.

For **Juliane House**, it is the concepts of 'cultural filter', 'overt translation' and 'covert translation' which are of fundamental importance, both for the work she presents and as key concepts of this volume. If we connect the concept of a 'cultural filter' with the notion of the 'dilated speech situation', we realize that the 'cultural filter' refers in fact to a means of text production with which cultural standards and expectation norms holding in speech situation 1 in culture 1 and speech situation 2 in culture 2 are systematically taken account of. An example of such a means of text production would be the parameter of content-orientation versus addressee-orientation that can be interpreted as facilitating understanding via either explicating knowledge for the reader or leaving the reader to infer knowledge on his or her own.

The production process in the case of an 'overt translation' is a particularly good example of the double dilation of the speech situation: here the reader simultaneously resorts to his or her knowledge about culture 1 and his or her knowledge about culture 2. We can thus say that the distinction 'overt'/'covert' basically refers back in principle to different text production mechanisms via different backward linkages to the original text in speech situation 1 and the type of knowledge presupposed in this situation (culture 1). In the case of a 'covert translation', the reader does not know that he or she is reading a translated text. This effect is achieved through the use of special text production mechanisms, i.e., through a cultural filter with which the dilation of speech situation 1 to speech situation 2 can be overcome, such that it is no longer so perceived by the reader, who, in trying to understand the text, now merely resorts to his knowledge of culture 2.

Heidrun Gerzymisch-Arbogast takes up the dimension 'orientation towards content versus orientation towards addressees', which is part of the (German-English) 'cultural filter' suggested by House (1997, 2006c). She does this with reference to an analysis of German scientific introductions and their English counterparts. The different text production mechanisms which she describes on the basis of her contrastive English-German analysis can clearly also be related to the concept of the dilated speech situation. In concrete terms, Gerzymisch-Arbogast uses topic-maps to show how addressee orientation and content-orientation are achieved via filling, or leaving empty, connections between the topics handled in the texts. The different topic structures which she reconstructs are used to measure the degree to which topic connectivity as a component of functional equivalence is achieved. The reconstructed topic structures also show that different, culturally conditioned demands are made on recipients' processes of text understanding and interpretation.

Alexandra Kallia uses a discourse completion test (DCT) for measuring cultural differences in the realization of two speech acts, requests and suggestions, in a number of different communicative situations (cf. Blum-Kulka *et al.* 1989). In this research design it is first of all the researcher who establishes functional equivalence between the speech act realizations in the different languages. Subjects are supposed to fill in blanks provided in the DCT, which were anticipated to involve the employment of a 'cultural filter'. As opposed to how a text traditionally overcomes the dilated speech situation, reception and production roles which a subject adopts overlap in this research. The analysis of the speech act realization in the different languages involved reveals which conventions are followed through the use of a cultural filter.

Antje Wilton investigates oral data in a non-professional homileic (phatic) interpreting situation: humorous small talk occurring at the dinner table. This constellation of translational action can be described – in the sense of Bührig and Rehbein (2000) – as an internally dilated speech situation. Another characteristic of the data examined by Wilton is the fact that the multilingual participants take over the task of interpreting without previous agreement or any previous brief. They are therefore both primary interactants and interpreters. In their role as interpreters they move outside of the interaction situation. The analysis shows that the creation of functional equivalence leads to a sort oscillation between these different speech roles and creates a role conflict for participants. Furthermore, the reconstructed difficulties in transferring humour can be interpreted as resulting from the internally dilated speech situation.

Jan D. ten Thije also reconstructs the internal dilation of the speech situation. In his case, a non-professional interpreter helps overcome the linguistic barrier (between English and Russian) which arises during interpreting humorous teasing in toasting situations at an international research meeting. Ten Thije focuses on the self-retreat of the interpreter. The self-retreat is an extreme result of the discursive handling of the interpreter's role conflict which stems from the fact that he transmits the utterances of the original speakers and at the same time is an autonomous participant in the interaction. Proposals are discussed that assign translational actions of the interpreter to the continuum depending on his or her action space. At one end of the continuum the interpreter is regarded as a so-called *translation machine*; at the other end he or she is considered to be an equal participant in the interaction. The constellation of the self-retreat of the interpreter has not been extensively addressed before in the literature but can be reconstructed with respect to this continuum. The analysis also reveals how interpreters reflect on and act upon the achievement of functional equivalence in the tripartite discourse structure. The author concludes that the distinction between 'professional' and 'non-professional' interpreters is actually questionable.

Kristin Bührig investigates discourse in hospitals in which *ad hoc* interpreters are employed in order to enable communication and understanding between (German-speaking) doctors and (Portuguese- and Turkish-speaking) patients. In her analysis, Bührig examines the way in which the 'cultural apparatus' (Rehbein 2006) emerges step by step. She investigates which speech acts within the internally dilated speech situation serve as starting points for a reflection on participants' actions and how this reflection process is being communicated. She further examines which strategies are used to render these reflections functionally equivalent in the target language. Such a procedure illuminates instances of cultural action which can point to possibilities of optimizing institutional communication.

In summary and to conclude, the individual contributions in this volume, based as they are on the notions of 'functional equivalence' and the 'dilated speech situation', all point to certain concepts that are essential for the reflection process inherent in intercultural understanding: 'Cultural filters' exhibit the degree of explicitness with which the transfer of knowledge is conducted for intercultural understanding; the gaps and/or the gap-filling in the topic maps show the degree to which coherence and cohesion is achieved for intercultural understanding; the 'perspectivizing apparatus' and the 'cultural apparatus' are different discursive realizations of the reflection process characterizing intercultural understanding.

This conceptual summary shows how productive an interdisciplinary theoretical discussion between translation studies and intercultural communication research can be, and how the development of a joint integrative framework can open up many new perspectives for future transdisciplinary research.

References

Blum-Kulka, Shoshana, Juliane House and Gabriele Kasper (eds) (1989) *Cross-Cultural Pragmatics: Requests and Apologies*, Norwood, NJ: Ablex.

Bührig, Kristin (2001) 'Interpreting in Hospitals', in S. Cigada, S. Gilardoni and M. Matthey (eds) *Communicare in Ambiente Professionale Plurilingue*, Lugano: USI, 107-119.

------ and Bernd Meyer (2004) 'Ad-hoc Interpreting and Achievement of Communicative Purposes in Doctor-patient-Communication', in J. House and J. Rehbein (eds) *Multilingual Communication*, Amsterdam & Philadelphia: John Benjamins, 43-62.

Bührig, Kristin and Jochen Rehbein (2000) *Reproduzierendes Handeln. Übersetzen, simultanes und konsekutives Dolmetschen im diskursanalytischen Vergleich*, Arbeiten zur Mehrsprachigkeit • Reihe B • 6.

Bührig, Kristin and Jan D. ten Thije (eds) (2006) *Beyond Misunderstanding. Linguistic Analyses of Intercultural Communication*, Amsterdam & Philadelphia: John Benjamins.

Ehlich, Konrad (1983) 'Text und sprachliches Handeln. Die Entstehung von Texten aus dem Bedürfnis nach Überlieferung', in Jan Assmann, Aleida Assman and Christoph Hardmeier (eds) *Schrift und Gedächtnis. Beiträge zur Archäologie der literarischen Kommunikation*, München: Fink, 24-43.

------ (1984) 'Zum Textbegriff', in A. Rothkegel and B. Sandig (eds) *Text – Textsorten – Semantik, Linguistische Modelle und maschinelle Verfahren*, Hamburg: Helmut Buske, 9-25.

House, Juliane (1977/1981) *A Model for Translation Quality Assessment*, Tübingen: Narr.

------ (1997) *Translation Quality Assessment: A Model Re-visited*, Tübingen: Narr.

------ (2006a) 'Deutsch und Englisch als Wissenschaftssprachen', in Peter Colliander and Doris Hansen (eds) *Übersetzer und Übersetzerkulturen*, München: Meidenbauer, 91-122.

------ (2006b) 'Text and Context in Translation', *Journal of Pragmatics* 38(3): 338-58.

------ (2006c) 'Communicative Styles in English and German', *European Journal of English Studies* 10(3): 249-67.

Katan, David (1999/2004) *Translating Cultures. An Introduction for Translators, Interpreters and Mediators*, Manchester: St. Jerome Publishing.

Schäffner, Christina and Beverly Adab (1995) 'Translation as Intercultural Communication – Contact as Conflict', in Mary Snell-Hornby, Zuzana Jettmarová and Klaus Kaindl (eds) *Translation as Intercultural Communication. Selected Papers from the EST Congress – Prague 1995*, Amsterdam & Philadelphia: John Benjamins, 325-339.

Thije, Jan D. ten (2006) 'The Notion of *Perspective* and *Perspectising* in Intercultural Communication Research', in Kristin Bührig and Jan D. ten Thije (eds) *Beyond Misunderstanding. Linguistic Analyses of Intercultural Communication*, Amsterdam & Philadelphia: John Benjamins, 97-153.

2. Moving across Languages and Cultures in Translation as Intercultural Communication

JULIANE HOUSE
University of Hamburg, Germany

Abstract. *In this paper I want to do three things: first, I want to briefly discuss the roles that cultural studies and linguistic approaches to translation play in translation studies. I will argue that one way of bridging the widening rift between the two camps is to make use of functional approaches to analyzing text and discourse. Functional approaches offer themselves as mediating tools because they take account of the context of linguistic units, which means that they necessarily consider the embeddedness of linguistic units in cultural contexts and can thus serve as a useful instrument for looking at translation as intercultural communication. Secondly, I will give an example of such a functional-contextual approach to translation which includes the operation of two distinct types of translation. This approach will be exemplified in the third part of this paper. Fourthly and finally, I will briefly discuss a recent phenomenon which may endanger the nature of translation as intercultural communication and reduce it to an instrument for linguistic-cultural colonization.*

1. Culturally-oriented versus linguistically-oriented translation studies

In recent decades, we have seen a shift in translation studies from linguistically oriented approaches to culturally-oriented ones. Some decades ago there was an even spread between those scholars who leaned towards viewing translation as an operation on languages and those who leaned towards viewing it as a cultural procedure. It is probably fair to say that today the majority of translation researchers have come to view translation as first and foremost a cultural procedure. This view is epitomized in frequently heard statements such as "one does not translate languages but cultures" or "communicating across linguistic borders means bridging culture". How did this shift come about? Translation studies, I would suggest, is here simply following a general trend in the humanities and social sciences, whose contents and methodologies have over the past decades been substantially influenced by post-modernist, post-colonial, feminist and other socio-politically and philosophically motivated schools, and translation and intercultural studies are no exception in this regard (see, for example, Venuti 1995; von Flotow 1997; Robinson 1997).

However, it is neither advisable nor necessary to divide the field into linguistic and cultural concerns. This can be avoided by taking account of culture as intimately linked with language, following for instance the model set a long time ago by various linguistic schools, such as the Prague school of linguistics, British contextualism and systemic functionalism, German functional pragmatics – schools which conceive of language as primarily a social phenomenon, which is naturally and inextricably intertwined with culture. In these and other socio-linguistically and contextually-oriented approaches, language is viewed as embedded in culture such that the meaning of any linguistic item can only be properly understood with reference to the cultural context enveloping it. Since in translation 'meaning' is of particular importance, it follows that translation cannot be fully understood outside a cultural frame of reference. Adherents of such an integrative view of language and culture (cf. for instance House 2002b; Koller 2004; Steiner 2004) consider translation as a particular type of socio-cultural practice, and they also hold that translation is, at its core, a linguistic procedure. Such an integrative view means that we can be able to bridge the gap between 'the two cultures', the cultural studies-oriented view of translation and the linguistics-oriented view of translation. To do this, we will have to first discuss in greater detail what is meant by 'culture', and whether it is legitimate to use the concept 'culture' which is today seen by many to fly in the face of a shifting multiplicity of value systems and signifying practices.

2. What is 'culture'?

'Culture' has been the concern of many different disciplines from philosophy, sociology, anthropology, literature to latter day cultural studies, and the definitions offered in these fields vary according to the particular frame of reference invoked. Two basic views of culture have however emerged: the humanistic concept of culture and the anthropological one. The humanistic concept of culture captures the 'cultural heritage' as a model of refinement, an exclusive collection of a community's masterpieces in literature, fine arts, music etc. The anthropological concept of culture refers to the overall way of life of a community, i.e., all those, explicit and implicit designs for living which act as potential guides for the behaviour of its members. Culture in the anthropological sense of a group's dominant and learned sets of habits, as the totality of its non-biological inheritance, involves presuppositions, preferences and values – all of which are, of course, neither easily accessible nor verifiable.

Four analytical levels on which culture has been characterized can be differentiated: the first one is the general human level, along which human beings biologically and societally differ from animals. Human beings, unlike animals, are capable of creatively shaping and changing the environment into which they are born. The second level is the societal level, culture being the unifying, binding force which enables human beings to position themselves vis-à-vis systems of government, domains of activities, religious beliefs and values in which human thinking expresses itself. The third level corresponds to the second level but captures various societal and national subgroups according to geographical region, social class, age, sex, professional activity and topic. The fourth level is the personal, the individual one relating to the individual's guidelines of thinking and acting. This is the level of cultural consciousness, which enables a human being to be aware of what characterizes his or her own culture and makes it distinct from others.

Based on these levels, i.e., integrating human, social and individual views of culture, the concept of culture can then be informally defined as whatever a person needs to know or believe in order to operate in a manner acceptable to its (i.e. a society's) members. Culture in this sense is not anything material; rather it refers to the behaviour of its members. The important and recurrent aspects of culture are thus the cognitive one guiding and monitoring human actions and the social one emphasizing what is shared by members of a society.

However, along with the rise of post-modernist, post-structuralist, post-colonial and feminist studies in the humanities, the whole notion of culture has come under severe attack (cf. Gupta and Ferguson 1997). The critique formulated here can be summarized as follows: the very idea of 'culture' is an unacceptable abstraction, there are no 'pure cultures', and there are no such things as 'social groups' because these groups are constantly destabilized by external influences, individual idiosyncracies and actions. Cultures themselves are, on this view, mere ideologies, idealized systems simply serving to reduce real differences that always exist between human beings in particular socially and geographically delimited areas. Is the very concept of a 'culture' therefore useless, particularly for an eminently practice-oriented field such as translation? Surely not. In the empirical social sciences, attempts to 'problematize' and 'relativize' the concept of 'culture' have as yet not prevented solid ethnographic descriptions. Moreover, if such criticism were taken to its logical conclusion by social scientists, they would no longer exist.

One recent approach which seems to be particularly well suited to resolving the hotly debated issue of generalization vs. diversification and individualization of cultures is the one advanced by Sperber (1996). Sperber views culture in terms of different types of 'representations' (which may be representations of ideas, behaviours, attitudes etc.). Within any group there exist a multitude of individual 'mental representations', most of which are fleeting and individual. A subset of these representations, however, can be overtly expressed in language and artefacts. They then become 'public representations', which are communicated to others in the social group. This communication gives rise to similar mental representations in others, which, in turn, may be communicated as public representations to others, which may again be communicated to different persons involving mental representations, and so on. If a subset of public representations is communicated frequently enough within a particular social group, these representations may become firmly entrenched and turn into 'cultural representations'. The point at which a mental representation becomes sufficiently widespread to be called 'cultural' is, however, still a matter of degree and interpretation, because there is no clear division between mental, public and cultural representations.

Members of a particular culture are constantly influenced by their society's (and/or some of the society's cultural subgroups') public and cultural representations (with regard to values, norms, traditions, etc.). This influence is exerted most prominently through language used by members of the society in communication with other members of the same and different sociocultural groups. Language as the most important means of intercultural communication, of transmitting information and providing human bonding therefore has an overridingly important position within any culture. Language is the prime means of an individual's acquiring knowledge of the world, of transmitting mental representations and making them public and intersubjectively accessible. Language is thus the prime instrument of a 'collective knowledge reservoir' to be passed on from generation to generation. But language also acts as a means of categorizing cultural experience, thought and behaviour for its speakers. Language and culture are therefore most intimately (and obviously) interrelated on the levels of semantics, where the vocabulary of a language reflects the culture shared by its speakers.

As opposed to this view that language 'reflects' the culture of a social group, the group of ideas that came to be known as 'linguistic relativity' imply the very opposite: language in its lexicon and structure has an influence on its speakers' thinking, their 'worldview' and behaviour. The idea that an individual's mother tongue is an important source of cognitive and behavioural conditioning goes back to German idealistic philosophy and was most prominently formulated by Herder and von Humboldt, who propagated the view that every language, as an a priori framework of cognition, determines the 'Weltanschauung' of its speakers. The spiritual structure that language possesses is assumed to correspond to the thought processes of its users, language being situated at the interface between objective reality and man's conceptualization of it. The relativity postulate put forward in the first half of the 20th century by Edward Sapir and his disciple Benjamin Lee Whorf advanced basically similar ideas. Whorf in particular inferred mental and behavioural differences from differences between languages on the levels of lexis and, in particular, syntax.

The consequence of the Humboldtian and Whorfian postulate for translation is the denial of its theoretical possibility – 'theoretical' because the practice of translation has, of course, been undeniably present and, indeed, thriving from time immemorial. This apparent contradiction can, however, be resolved by pointing out that linguistic relativity – though clearly affecting, in specified areas, some of our cognitive behaviour – can always be counteracted through language itself and its users' creativity, dynamism and flexibility. Further, it is necessary to also link linguistic diversity with external differences of historical, social and cultural background rather than one-sidedly insisting on the overriding importance of a link between cognitive and linguistic differences. If languages are seen to be structured in divergent ways because they embody different conventions, values and experiences, then the importance of what may be called **linguistic-cultural** relativity emerges. Such a notion of relativity is much more relevant for translation (for a detailed discussion see House 2000). Cultural knowledge, including knowledge of various subcultures, has long been recognized as indispensable for translation, as it is knowledge of the application linguistic units have in particular situational and socio-cultural contexts which makes translation possible in the first place. 'Application' here refers to the relation holding between an expression and the cultural situation in which it is used – it is **pragmatic meaning**. In establishing equivalences between L1 and L2 linguistic units in translation, the notion of 'application' is crucial: if sense and reference differ for two linguistic units in translation, it is their application in particular knowable and describable cultural contexts that ensures translatability. Linguistic units, as argued above, can in any case never be fully understood in isolation from the particular cultural phenomena for which they are symbols.

While differences in the 'worldview' of speakers of different languages resulting in different concepts in their minds may not be accessible to translators and communicators, the intersubjectively experiencable application of linguistic units in a particular cultural situation can. And even if cultural distances between languages are great, cultural gaps can, in theory, always be bridged via ethnographic knowledge. Conceptions of language within the broader context of culture, whereby meaning is seen as contextually determined and constructed, are not recent developments, but have a venerable tradition in Russian Formalism, Prague School, systemic functional and functional pragmatic linguistics, as well as American sociology of language, speech act theory and discourse analysis, and they were used to construct a functional theory of translation. Such a broad socio-cultural view of language is appropriate for describing and explaining translation as intercultural communication. I explain what this view of translation involves in the following section.

3. Translation as intercultural communication

In translation a text in one language, the original, is reproduced in another language while keeping the 'meaning' equivalent. Equivalence is the key term here. It characterizes the relationship between the original and its translation, and is constitutive of translation (Koller 2004) in that it enables one to distinguish a translation from other forms of interlingual text production such as adaptations of various kinds (summaries, simplifications for different groups of addressees). Generally speaking, a translation is equivalent with its original if it has a function which is equivalent. The function of a text, which can be defined as the use which the text has in a certain context, consists of two components: an interpersonal and an ideational one (Halliday 1994). These components reflect the undeniable fact that language has two basic uses: to transmit ideas and to link human beings with one another.

In translating, then, a text in one language is replaced by a functionally equivalent text in another language. 'Functional equivalence' can be established by referring original and translation to the *context of situation* which envelops the original and the translation in necessarily different ways, just as the two language systems involved in translation (and the minds of author and translator and reader(s) for that matter) are necessarily different. In order to ensure that original and translation are functionally equivalent, the function of a text, consisting, as mentioned above, of an interpersonal and an ideational functional component, must be kept equivalent. For this, the text is to be analyzed at various levels: **Language** (Linguistic forms), **Register** and **Genre**. The relationship between these levels can be seen in terms of semiotic planes which relate to one another in a Hjemslevian 'content-expression' way, with **Genre** being the content-plane of **Register**, and **Register** being the expression plane of **Genre**. **Register** in turn is the content-plane of **Language**, and **Language** is the expression plane of

Register. **Register** is divided in Hallidayan fashion into **Field**, **Tenor** and **Mode** (cf. also House 1997).

Equivalence of function, however, differs markedly in two empirically derived types of translation, **overt** translation and **covert** translation (House 1977). The distinction between these two types is crucial for any conception of functional equivalence, and also for translation as intercultural communication. It is reminiscent of Schleiermacher's classic distinction between 'einbürgernde' and 'verfremdende Übersetzung', a critical difference being however that the covert-overt distinction suggested here is tied to a well-argued theory of translation. It was first suggested as result of a critical appreciation of approaches (e.g. by Reiss 1971) which accounted for different types of functional equivalence relationships by setting up a source text-linked text typology. Adopting a text typology as a means of trying to gain insight into, and account for, different types of translation equivalence relationships is not fruitful because such an approach presupposes that the nature of a translation is somehow determined by the nature of the source text, while the process of translation is itself a constant. Hence it has been presupposed that if one can successfully classify texts then one shall have successfully accounted for differences in translation, and the theoretical problems surrounding them. As opposed to this line of thinking, a **translation typology** seems to be stronger in explanatory adequacy when it comes to describing and judging the different processes of translation involved in handling culture- specific phenomena in the two language communities. In other words, the claim is that in order to resolve the crucial conflict in translation between universality and culture specificity, a distinction of two basic translation types, **overt** and **covert** translation, can prove insightful.

This distinction, as mentioned above, harks back to Friedrich Schleiermacher's two famous methods of translating which he characterized as two ways of being 'einbürgernd' (roughly: enculturating) in the target context. In his speech 'Über die verschiedenen Methoden des Übersetzens' delivered in 1813, Schleiermacher characterized these two methods as follows:

> Entweder der Übersetzer lässt den Schriftsteller möglichst in Ruhe und bewegt den Leser ihm entgegen, oder er lässt den Leser möglichst in Ruhe und bewegt den Schriftsteller ihm entgegen. (1973:55)
> (Either the translator leaves the author in peace as much as possible and moves the reader towards him, or he leaves the reader in peace as much as possible and moves the author towards him.)

The point I wish to make here is that Schleiermacher, in characterizing the latter method', which in my terminoloy is an **overt** translation, does

NOT, as is often erroneously claimed (for instance famously by Venuti 1995, who uses the term 'foreignizing' in this context) speak of 'verfremdend' (literally: making strange) but of "dem Bestreben des Übersetzers, den Ton der Sprache fremd zu halten" (the translator's attempt to keep the tone of the language strange) and to make sure that a feeling, "dass sie Ausländisches vor sich haben, auch auf seine Leser fortzupflanzen" (that they have something foreign, 'outlandish' in front of them also lives on in the readers') (1973:55). So Schleiermacher does not at all – as the propagators of the so-called functional school of translation (e.g. Reiss and Vermeer 1984; Nord 1997) are wont to claim – refer to a category of effect or purpose (skopos). Schleiermacher refers to the nature of the linguistic forms and their particular arrangement in the translated text. The language of the translation is for Schleiermacher a language which links the original's language with foreign (and strange) elements. The translation resulting from this hybridization procedure, as we would say today, has "die Spuren der Mühe aufgedrückt" (the traces of labour imposed; 1973:45), and it turns out to be a text, which is in some sense very close to its original, but critically – because of this very closeness – is not at all similar and not really comparable. And this is exactly where twentieth-century translation theorists have taken up from. So we read for example in Walter Benjamin's important writing about the nature of translation:

> Es ist daher ... das höchste Lob einer Übersetzung nicht, sich wie ein Original ihrer Sprache zu lesen. Die wahre Übersetzung ist durchscheinend, sie verdeckt nicht das Original, steht ihm nicht im Licht ... (1972:9).
> (It is therefore not the highest praise of a translation to read like an original in its language. The true translation is shining through, it does not cover up the original, does not stand in its light ....)

And Ortega y Gasset, another original thinker on translation, goes as far as saying that in cases where the author is brought across to the language of the new readers, we are not dealing with translation in its proper sense. Strictly speaking, says Ortega y Gasset (1965), we are here not dealing with a translation but an imitation or a circumlocution of the original text. It is only when we tear the reader away from his linguistic habits and force him to throw himself into the mind of the original author that a translation proper comes into being. In this case genuine linguistic and cultural transfer takes place – we have here a true meeting of languages, cultures and contexts, of transfer in the classical conception by Uriel Weinreich (1953) as a result of a contact situation, which can lead to deviations and innovations of the target cultural norms through the influence of a foreign language. In overt translation, transfer is often strongly noticeable, as an incompatibility of linguistic and cultural norms. So the original is not at all lost – original and translation are in a certain way both present. They are – to borrow a term from genetics – phenotypically hybrid, i.e., they are translations which keep their hybrid nature visible on the textual surface. For translation theory and the conception of translation as intercultural communication, this characterization of overt or phenotypically hybrid is particularly important because it illuminates the important point that in a certain type of translation one is explicitly NOT considering the effect or purpose of a translation, but rather the linguistic-cultural means, revealed in textual analysis, with which this effect may (or may not!) be achieved. It is well known that in linguistic theory considerations of the so-called perlocutionary effect have long been abandoned because of the difficulties of establishing exactly what that effect is. Any fixation onto the effect of a text is thus equally unfruitful, and in essence reductionist.

To sum up, one can make a distinction between overt and covert translation. One may hypothesize that in these translation types a different kind of intercultural communication will take place between texts as representatives of two cultures. Let us therefore look in greater detail at these two types.

An **overt** translation is, as the name suggests, very visibly, very overtly a translation, not as it were a second original, hence its target culture addressees are quite 'overtly' not being directly addressed. In an overt translation, the original is tied in a specific way to the culture enveloping it; it has independent status in the source culture, and is both culture-specific and pointing beyond the source culture because the original text – independent of its source language origin – is also of potential general human interest. In a word: it also evidences 'universality'; source texts that call for an overt translation have an established worth or value in the source culture – and potentially in other cultures. In their universality, they are often 'timeless' as works of art and aesthetic creations; for instance, they transcend any distinct historical meaning. Although timeless and transmitting a general human message, such texts that call for overt translation are also and at the same time culture-specific because they often reflect a particular *état de langue*, or a geographical or social variety and because they have independent status in the language community through belonging to the community's cultural products. Many such texts are literary texts and can be characterized by their fictional nature, i.e., they are situationally abstract in that they do not immediately refer to a unique historical situation. Fictional texts describe a kind of 'fictive reality' which is, in every reception by an individual reader, newly related to the specific historical reality in the concrete situation in which the reader finds him- or herself. The message in a fictional text is entirely emic, text-contained, i.e., the message presupposes no wider context so that everything necessary for its interpretation is to be found within the message itself – and this is what gives the literary text its independent, indeed its culturally universal feature. This self-sufficiency might also explain why such texts can more easily be transferred in toto through space, time and cultures – and this despite the fact that those texts may well be heavily marked for culture-specific regional or social varieties.

An overt translation is embedded in a new speech event in the target culture: it operates in a new frame, a new 'discourse world'. An overt translation is thus a case of 'language mention' resembling a quotation or citation. An original and its overt translation are equivalent at the levels of **Language /Text** and **Register** as well as **Genre**. At the level of the individual textual function, however, 'true' functional equivalence is not possible. At best, an equivalence of a 'removed' nature can be achieved: its function is to enable access to the function which the original has (had) in its discourse world or frame. As this access must of necessity be realized in the target linguaculture via the translation, a switch in the discourse world becomes necessary, i.e., the translation operates in its own discourse world, and can thus reach only the aforesaid 'second level equivalence', featuring a sort of 'topicalization' of the original's textual function. Paradoxically, this type of functional equivalence is achieved through an equivalence at all the three analytical levels, i.e., **Language/Text**, **Register** and **Genre**, which together facilitate the co-activation of the source text's frame and discourse world. It is through this co-activation of both discourse worlds and frames that members of the target cultural and linguistic community are put in a position to 'eavesdrop', as it were, i.e., they are enabled to appreciate the function the original text has, albeit at a – linguistic and cultural – distance. In tackling an overt translation, the translator must therefore quite 'overtly' produce a text that allows the new audience to gain an impression of, and 'feel' for, the cultural impact that the original text has on source culture members, permitting them to observe and be worked upon by the original text. In the case of overt translation, we can speak with some justification of genuine cultural transfer. Transfer is here understood in Weinreich's (1953) sense as a result of a contact situation which leads to deviations from the norm of the target language/culture through the influence of another language and culture. This means that in overt translation, cultural transfer is often noticeable as a (deliberately) jarring difference (in Benjamin's sense) and deviation of the translation from target cultural norms.

The situation is very different in the case of **covert** translation. A covert translation is a translation which enjoys the status of an original text in the receiving culture. The translation is covert because it is not marked pragmatically as a translation at all, but may, conceivably, have been created in its own right. A covert translation is thus a translation whose original, in terms of status, or uniqueness, is not particularly tied to the target culture. An original and its covert translation are – one might say – 'universal' in the sense that they differ 'only' accidentally in their respective languages. The original is not culture specific, but rather of potentially equal concern for members of different cultures. While it is thus clear that certain texts designed for 'ready consumption', ephemeral and transitory texts, such as e.g. instructions, commercial circulars, advertisements and other 'pragmatic texts' such as journalistic and scientific texts, are not culture-bound, it is the covert type of translation (normally) required by such texts which presents much more subtle and intricate cultural translation problems than overt translation. In order to meet the needs of the new addressees in their cultural setting, the covert translator must take different cultural presuppositions in the two cultures into account.

In covert translation the translator must re-produce or re-create an equivalent speech event and reproduce or represent in the translation text the function the original has in its linguistic-cultural framework, i.e., 'real' functional equivalence is aimed at, and often achieved in covert translation. A covert translation operates quite 'overtly' in the different frame and discourse world set up by the target culture without, however – and this is in fact the critical difference between overt and covert translation – wishing to co-activate the discourse world in which the original had unfolded. Covert translation is thus at the same time psycholinguistically less complex than overt translation and more deceptive. Covert translation often results in a very real cultural distance from the original text, since the original is transmuted in varying degrees, and it is the translator's task to 'cheat', as it were, and to remain hidden behind this feat of deception regarding the origin of the text produced. Since true functional equivalence is aimed at, changes at the levels of **Language/Text** and **Register** may, if necessary, be freely undertaken, and the result may be a very different text, which is why covert translations are often received as though they were original texts.

In order to achieve this 'originality' in covert translation, the translator employs a so-called 'cultural filter'. With the use of this filter, the translator can make systematic allowances for culture specificity, accommodating for differences in socio-cultural norms and differences in conventions of text production and communicative preferences. This 'cultural filter' is thus the means with which the translator **compensates** for culture specificity. The cultural filter is often so expertly integrated into the fabric of the text that the seams do not show. Since the notion of cultural filter is crucial not only for covert translation, but also for problems of culture transfer and compensation, it is dealt with more extensively in the next section.

4. Cultural filtering in translation as intercultural communication

In the course of analyses of a corpus of texts and their translations (German-English, English-German), which were classified as belonging to the broad functional categories 'interpersonal' and 'ideational' (Halliday 1994), I found (House 1977) that the translator had evidently placed what I called a 'cultural filter' between the source and target texts. The translator viewed the source text, as it were, through the glasses of a target culture member. If the source text and the target text are to have truly equivalent functions, then the translator – in order to meet the needs of the target culture addressees in their specific cultural setting, and in order to achieve an effect equivalent to the one the source text has had – must take relevant cultural presuppositions in the two language communities into account, and these presuppositions are linked most frequently to the interpersonal functional component for which values along the dimensions of **Tenor** and **Mode** are particularly important. Thus whenever a text has a well-marked interpersonal functional component, the employment of the cultural filter is both particularly important and complicated, as one is here dealing with assessments and adjustments of social role relationships, social attitudes, author's personal stance, involvement etc. – phenomena that are notoriously difficult to diagnose, describe and translate. Despite this difficulty, it is important to point out that in any cultural filtering, actually existing and verified differences of the socio-cultural norms and presuppositions of cultural knowledge to be taken into account should ideally be based on the results of empirical cross-cultural research (see below). An application of a cultural filter which lacks any intersubjectively verifiable evidence leads to the production of a covert version which amounts to a culturally inadequate translation.

A glance at the rich anecdotal literature on translation describing numerous 'exotic' cultural oddities may lead one to believe that there are, indeed, many crucial cultural differences complicating the translation process. However, on closer examination, most of the impressive examples of cultural differences are found to be drawn from comparisons of a European language and languages of South East Asia or American Indian languages, where the socio-cultural differences are obviously remarkable. As concerns translations between European languages, however, it seems sensible to endorse the attitude taken by Koller (2004), who points out that cultural differences should not be exaggerated, since – as is well known by practising translators – expressions referring to culture-specific political, institutional, socio-economic, historical and geographical phenomena, which can only be understood in the particular 'cultural situation' in which they are embedded, and which consequently lack a corresponding expression in the target culture, can nevertheless be translated by means of certain compensatory mechanisms. Koller lists a number of standard translational procedures for overcoming such cultural translation problems, such as using loan words or loan translations, adaptations, explications, commentaries, definitions and paraphrases. All these procedures have venerable traditions in ethnographic research and, of course, in the rich tradition of bible translations.

Elevating concrete, mundane and material differences between cultures, such as differences in safety regulations or shopping routines, to the rank of impenetrable cultural and translation barriers, as is unfortunately done in some contemporary translation studies (in particular in German functional translation theory), is both unnecessary and bordering on the ludicrous. One should not forget that, as de Waard and Nida rightly point out

> all peoples share more cultural similarities than is usually thought to be the case. What binds people together is much greater than what separates them. In adjustments to the physical environment, in the organization of society, in dealing with crucial stages of life (birth, puberty, marriage, and death), in the development of elaborate ritual and symbolism, and in the drive for aesthetic expression ... people are amazingly alike. Because of all this, translating can be undertaken with the expectation of communicative effectiveness. (1986:43f)

Despite this universality of the *conditio humana*, there are subtle if crucial differences in cultural preferences, mentalities and values that need to be known to the translator when he or she sets out to produce a covert translation and apply a cultural filter. Such knowledge should be based on empirical research into language pair-specific cultural differences, the assumption being that research into culturally determined communicative preferences in two discourse communities can give more substance to the concept of a cultural filter than mere intuition and tacit native-speaker knowledge and understanding. In the following, an example of such research involving English and German discourse will be outlined.

5. Substantiating the notion of a cultural filter

Over the past three decades, a series of German-English contrastive pragmatic analyses were conducted within larger projects in which the discourse of German and English native speakers was compared (for a summary of the various studies, see House 2006). Subjects were students at British and German universities as well as experts in various professional contexts. The data was collected in open, self-directed dyadic role-plays, often followed by retrospective interviews, discourse completion tests combined with a variety of meta-pragmatic assessment tests, as well as naturalistic interactions between German and English native speakers, comparative analyses of original texts and their translations, field notes, interviews, diary studies, and the examination of relevant background documents. The analyses were conducted on one of the following three levels:

(1) On the most 'superficial' level, a comparison was made of *tokens* that correspond pragmatically in the two language communities, given the different systems of selection holding for the various *types* in the two communities.
(2) On a 'deeper' level, norms of expectation with regard to certain illocutionary acts, their sequencing and their effects were taken into account.
(3) On an even 'deeper' level, the socio-cultural functions of the analytic categories were investigated, i.e., their respective positions were examined along sociolinguistic parameters such as +/- power, +/- social distance, as well as the resulting types of politeness, formality and so on.

The following pragmatic and discursive phenomena were investigated in the various studies: speech acts, discourse strategies, realization of certain discourse phases, gambits and modality markers (see House 2006 for a detailed discussion of this work). The analyses yielded a series of individual results, which together provide converging evidence that points to a set of more general hypotheses about the nature of German-English cultural differences: in a variety of everyday situations and discourse types, German subjects tend to interact in ways that are more direct, more explicit, more self-referenced and more content-oriented; they were also found to be less prone to resort to using verbal routines than Anglophone speakers. This pattern of cross-cultural differences that has emerged from these German-English contrastive-pragmatic analyses can be displayed along the following five dimensions:

Directness	↔	Indirectness
Orientation towards Self	↔	Orientation towards Other
Orientation towards Content	↔	Orientation towards Persons
Explicitness	↔	Implicitness
Ad-hoc-Formulation	↔	Use of Verbal Routines

Along these hypothesized dimensions, German speakers were found to give preferences to positions on the left hand side. It must be emphasized that we are dealing here with continua or clines rather than clear-cut dichotomies, and that these continua reflect tendencies rather than categorical distinctions. By hypothesizing dimensions of cross-cultural difference in discourse orientations which add substance to the notion of a cultural filter, it is also implicitly suggested that language use is linked to culture and mentality, and that linguistic differences in the realization of discourse phenomena may be taken to reflect deeper differences in cultural preference patterns and expectation norms at a conceptual-cognitive and emotive level.

These tendencies are confirmed in studies by a number of different researchers, such as Clyne (1987, 1994), Luchtenberg (1994), Agar (1992) and many others, who posited linguistically and culturally conditioned differences in the organization of information (linear versus convoluted or hierarchical, reader versus writer orientation, focus on content versus focus on addresses, and so on); cf. also Mauranen (1993) and Duszak (1994), who support the assumption made here that there exist culturally conditioned differences in communictive styles. Support for the hypothesis relating to these culturally conditioned preferences and textual conventions also comes from translation scholars: see Göpferich (1995), who found differences between German more 'serious', content-related, and English interpersonally-oriented, persuasive product descriptions, and Schmitt (1995), who pointed to a stronger 'routinization' in English traffic and other signs as opposed to a greater variation in formulations in a comparable German domain, as well as Kusch and Schröder (1989), who found a stronger focus on content in science texts in German as opposed to comparable English texts; and finally Fandrych and Graefen (2005), who reported on similar differences in German and English academic writing.

Koller (personal communication) has suggested that it is necessary to differentiate between a linguistic and a genuinely cultural filter. The types of pragmatic differences in the presentation of a certain state of affairs which the above dimensions refer to are really language-related. Genuine cultural filtering would take place when for instance cultural ('material') conventions are filtered or substituted in the act of translation, when for instance, to take a simple example, the convention of drinking tea in England is substituted in a German translation by drinking coffee and eating pieces of cake, or when the English 'Veterans' Day' turns into 'Volkstrauertrag' (National Mourning Day) in a German translation. However, since the type of filtering which I posit for covert translation often involves both linguistic and cultural phenomena, and since a clear-cut separation is impossible, one would really have to speak of a linguistic-cultural filter. For the sake of brevity, I will continue to use the term 'cultural filter' with the understanding that it does include linguistic filtering.

Having characterized overt and covert translation and the nature and use of cultural filtering involved in covert but not in overt translation, we will now look at some examples which show that both the application of a cultural filter and covert and overt translation, respectively, are fraught with difficulties and invoke different problems of intercultural communication.

6. Exemplifying the notion of translation as intercultural communication

6.1 Children's books

There has been massive one-sided translation from English into German in this genre for the past few decades. In the majority of the cases examined in corpus-based studies (House 2001, 2004), these translations have undergone heavy cultural filtering, such that the role of children in the family, the educational styles of the parents as well as the entire tenor of these books were changed to a considerable degree. The following examples are evidence of this trend (backtranslations into English – in brackets – are mine).

Example (1)[1]

(Meeting a friend)
Seeing that something was expected of it, the bear stood up and politely raised its hat.

Der kleine Bär stand plötzlich auf und lüftete seinen Hut.
(The little bear stood suddenly up and lifted its hat.)

Example (2)

(Bankdirector to Paddington)
I do hope you won't close your account, Mr Brown.

Ich hoffe, Du wirst weiterhin Kunde unserer Bank bleiben.
(I hope you will continue to be our bank's customer.)

Example (3)

(Mr Brown offers Paddington some biscuits)
I'm sorry they haven't any marmalade ones, but they were the best I could get.

---

[1] Examples (1) to (4) are excerpted from: Michael Bond, *A Bear called Paddington*, London, 1958, and *Paddington unser kleiner Bär* (Paddington our little bear), München, 1968 (translated by Brigitte von Mechow and Peter Kent)

Hier gibt es eben nichts mit Marmelade.
(Here is simply nothing with marmalade.)

Example (4)
(Paddington in a shop)
(Mr Gruber) took Paddington into his shop and after offering him a seat ...

Dann zog er den kleinen Bären in den Laden "Setz dich!" sagte er..
(Then he pulled the little bear into the shop. 'Sit down!' he said.)

In examples (1) to (4) cultural filtering occurs along the parameters of directness versus indirectness, and content orientation versus addressee orientation. The question we must ask however is whether such filtering as well as the fact that we have here cases of covert translation in the sense defined above are indeed legitimate strategies in the genre of children's books – a genre which is not only literary in the usual sense of the word, but also one for which an educational objective is constitutive. We must further ask whether one should not give preference to an overt translation here, which would – to use Walter Benjamin's words – allow the original 'durchscheinen' (to shine through) such that it is not hidden by the new text, which would not 'stand in its light' – ihm "nicht im Licht steht", as Benjamin (1972:9) has put it. Since it is in my opinion an important function of translations of children's books to broaden their young readers' mental horizon, to lead children into a new and foreign discourse world and to stimulate their curiosity for things alien to them, everything speaks for an overt translation – a type of translation which I have characterized as one in which real cultural transfer and intercultural communication is permitted to take place. In examples (1) to (4) such intercultural communication is not possible – and judging from my corpus (52 translations from and into English) these are not isolated cases. Worse still, in these examples, changes along the dimension of directness of the linguistic actions also lead to changes in politeness. My analyses of several Paddington books and their German translations show that the changes undertaken are indeed systematic such that the tenor of the English originals is invariably more polite.[2]

Given that it is after all a Teddy bear who is treated with exquisite politeness in the English Paddington books – a marked situation in an English environment as well – a humorous tone results, which is also lost in the German translation. This is particularly noticeable in example (2), where

[2] I cannot elaborate on the role politeness plays in translation here and refer the reader to House (1998; 2006).

the description of the hat lifting as 'polite' is simply left out in German. This may be a small point, however if – as is the case here – we are dealing with a pattern of such interventions into the original text, it gains in importance.

With the loss of politeness and seriousness in the case of the description of Paddington we find a further characteristic of the German translation of the Paddington books – and other translations as well – namely, infantilization and sentimentalization. We can see this in example (1), where 'the bear' is rendered as "der kleine Bär" (the little bear), sometimes even "unser kleiner Bär" ('our little bear'), which can be taken as an indication that the conception of children and their role in a family has been transformed.

Remarkable in (2) is also the fact that Paddington is addressed in German with the familiar form 'Du'. While there is of course no equivalent expression in English, it would have been more appropriate to use the non-familiar 'Sie-Form' in German, given the characterization of Paddington as a dignified, serious and respectable person. The more familiar form 'Du' also manipulates the figure of Paddington into a more sentimentalized one bereft of seriousness. That a bank director addresses a teddy bear with exquisite politeness as in example (2) creates a sense of humour which is lost with the loss of politeness and distance.

In examples (3) and (4) we also notice a loss of indirectness and politeness. The speech act of apology in (3) in the original is transformed into an assertion. The speech act 'offer' in the English original is transformed in the translation into a much more direct 'order' (cf. here the analyses in Blum-Kulka *et al.* 1989; House 1989), which also amounts to a reduction of politeness in Mr Gruber's utterance. This again is no isolated instance; many similar examples exist that provide evidence of the tendency towards greater directness in the German translations and thus of the application of a cultural filter.

In example (5), we can see filtering along the dimension of explicitness-implicitness. Here we are dealing with a narrative in which 'Mrs Xmas' saves Xmas when Father Xmas falls ill. In the German translation nearly every paragraph is filled with additional details about the seriousness of the crisis, the purpose of which is to blow up Mrs Xmas' achievements in an attempt to emphasize female independence and competence.

Example (5)[3]

> *"Just look at you" cried Mrs Xmas "You're all covered in spots. However will I finish making all these presents by myself? I'd better hurry up and find the reindeers".*

[3] Source: Penny Ives, *Mrs Christmas*, London, 1990, and *Morgen kommt die Weihnachtsfrau* (Tomorrow Comes Mrs Xmas), Hamburg, 1990 (translated by Ishel Eichler).

> *"Sieh Dich nur an!" rief die Weihnachtsfrau, "Du bist ja krank. Überall die Pusteln. Wie soll ich denn ganz allein die vielen Geschenke fertigkriegen?" Der Weihnachtsmann schloss nur müde die Augen, er war sogar zu schwach, eine Antwort zu geben. "Das muss ich diesmal tatsächlich alleine schaffen. Weihnachten kann schliesslich nicht einfach ausfallen", murmelte die Weihnachtsfrau. "Erst mal geh ich zu den Rentieren,die brauchen ihr Futter."*
> ("Just look at you!" called Mrs Xmas "You are ill! Red spots everywhere! How shall I get all these presents ready on my own?" Father Xmas merely shut his eyes, he was even too weak to give an answer. "So this time I will have to manage all on my own. After all, Xmas cannot simply be cancelled", mumbled Mrs Xmas. "First of all I'll go to the reindeers, they need their food".)

Example (5) shows how in the German translation possible questions which the reader might have with reference to the circumstances, motivations, thoughts and actions of the participants represented in the text are explicitly verbalized, whereas these questions are left implicit in the original, where the reader is left to infer these details him- or herself. This explicitness is again not an isolated case, there are many more examples of this feature (cf. House 2006).

Example (6) shows an ideologically motivated shift from the original:

Example (6)

> Finally she put on her red suit and hat. No one would recognize her now.
>
> *Am nächsten Morgen war es soweit: schon früh stand die Weihnachtsfrau auf, zog sich den roten Mantel an und setzte sich die Mütze an. Der Weihnachtsmann bekam noch einen Abschiedskuss.*
> (Next morning it began: early on Mrs Xmas got up, put on her red coat and hat. Father Xmas received a goodbye kiss.)

Note that in (6) the sentence "No one would recognize her now" is NOT translated. My hypothesis is that it is undesirable in the context of feminist ideology that a strong woman is not recognized as such.

One last example from my children's book corpus again shows how the original is being deliberately modified due to ulterior motives:

Example (7)[4]

> (One of the Herdmann children has an experience of Christian enlightenment)
> *She had walked into the corner of the choir-robe cabinet, in a kind of daze – as if she had just caught onto the idea of God, and the wonder of Christmas.*
>
> *Sie war in ihrer Benommenheit gegen den Schrank mit den Gesangbüchern gelaufen.*
> (In her daze, she had walked against a cupboard with the hymn books.)

In example (7) the allusion to God and the miracle of Xmas is NOT translated, and also the title of the book omits mention of the book being about Xmas. Instead, the title and indeed the entire translation emphasize the rebellious nature of the family portrayed, because such a rebellion against authorities seamlessly fits the ideology which pervades the entire translation. Thus for instance, the exclamation "My God" is not translated with the directly equivalent 'Mein Gott' (frequent in German), but rather with the expletive "Verdammt" (Damned).

The tendency discovered in the German translations to embellish the story told in the English originals and to superimpose certain ideologies onto it is typical of the translations in my corpus.

In sum, the above analyses of the covert translations of children's books have all revealed that substantial cultural filtering along the dimensions of cultural difference discussed above had taken place. As we have seen, the consequence of such filtering is not only that target culture readers are confronted with a text familiar to them from an equivalent target genre, but also that the very presence of the filter blocks the reception of different, potentially strange cultural conventions and values – which may not be desirable in the context of this particular genre. An overt translation mode might be more appropriate. This does not mean, however, that overt translation is the generally preferred option with literary text. Let us look at how overt translations of other literary texts – despite the fact that they do not feature cultural filtering – similarly impede intercultural communication as they do not allow the strangeness of a foreign text to 'shine through' in the new text and in a different language.

---

[4] Source: Barbara Robinson, *The Best Christmas Pageant Ever*, New York, 1972, and *Hilfe die Herdmans kommen* (Help the Herdmanns Are Coming), Hamburg, 1972 (translated by Nele and Paul Maar).

6.2 Other literary texts

In the following two texts we will look at two overt translations where, as mentioned above, cultural transfer and shining through phenomena should in principle be possible. The two translations in examples (8) and (9) are however still cases of overt translations as there is no cultural filtering detectable.

Consider now example (8).

Example (8)[5]

> *"Everything very nicely done, Mr Russell," said Mrs Venables. "Yes'm?" said Mr Russell. "Very glad you think so, 'm. We done what we could to the best of our ability." "I'm sure," said Mrs Venables, "that if his own people had been there, they couldn't have wished for anything nicer". "No'm", agreed Mr Russell, much gratified, "and it's a pity they couldn't a-been present, for there's no doubt a handsome funeral is a great comfort for them as is left. Of course, it ain't so grand as a London funeral would be" – He glanced wistfully at Wimsey. "But much nicer", said Winsey in a ridiculous echo of Mrs Venables. "You see, it has so much more of the personal touch." "That's very true", said the undertaker, much encouraged. "Why I dessay these London men get as much as three or four funerals every week....".*
>
> *"Sie haben das alles sehr nett gemacht, Mr Russell", sagte Mrs Venables. "Ja, Madam?" antwortete Mr Russell. "Es freut mich, daß Sie das sagen, Madam. Wir haben nach besten Kräften getan, was wir konnten"."Ich glaube bestimmt", sagte Mrs Venables "daß seine eigenen Angehörigen es sich nicht schöner hätten wünschen können, wenn sie hier gewesen wären"."Sicher nicht, Madam", pflichtete Mr Russell ihr sehr zufrieden bei, "und schade ist es, dass sie nicht da sein konnten, denn so ein schönes Begräbnis ist für die Hinterbliebenen immer ein großer Trost. Natürlich sind unsere Beerdigungen nicht so prachtvoll wie vielleicht in London" – Mit einem erwartungsvollen Blick zu Wimsey. "Dafür aber viel netter", plapperte dieser Mrs Venables nach. "Hier hat noch alles so etwas Persönliches." "Sehr wahr" pflichtete*

[5] Source (detective novel): Dorothy Sayers, *The Nine Tailors*, London, 1934; translated as *Der Glockenschlag* by Otto Bayer 1978, Reinbek: Rowohlt.

> *der Bestattungsunternehmer ihm sichtlich erleichtert bei. "Na ja, die Leute in London haben sicher jede Woche drei oder vier Beerdigungen..."*
> ("You have done everything *very* nice, Mr Russell", said Mrs Venables. "Yes, Madam? It makes me glad that you say this, Madam. We have done with all our might what we can. I certainly believe that his own relatives could not have wished it more beautiful, if they had been here". "Certainly not, Madam", Mr Russell very contentedly concurred with her "and it is a pity that they could not be there, for such a nice funeral is always a great consolation for the bereaved. Of course our funerals are not as magnificent as may be in London" – with an expectant glance to Wimsey. "But for this much nicer", this one prattled after Mrs Venables. "Here everything has still something personal." "Very true" the funeral undertaker concurred with him visibly relieved. "Well, the people in London certainly have three or four funerals every week...".)

In excerpt (8), we can see that large stretches of the dialogues in the original text which are marked for regional and social varieties as well as register-specific colloquiality are not and indeed cannot be rendered equivalently in the translation as there are no equivalent dialects and/or registers in the receiving linguaculture. Differences which derive from *sui generis* intracultural and intralinguistic variation are in principle untranslatable (cf. House 1973). In excerpt (8) we witness an interaction between the gentleman detective Lord Peter Wimsey, the village undertaker Mr Russell and the Rector's wife Mrs Venables, with the speech of the latter characters being marked by both strongly regional and social varieties, and this is in marked contrast to the speech of the aristocratic detective. This interesting and well-crafted linguistic spectrum cannot be equivalently reproduced in the German translation, which here consists of a constructed linguistic neutrality devoid of dialectal traces. From this it also follows that the type of intercultural communication facilitated here is very different from the type of communication enabled by the covert translations in examples (1) to (7) above. Despite the apparent mismatches in the dialectal variation between source and target linguacultures, the original is left largely intact because no equivalent speech event is created, nor is one intended. Intercultural communication is then only possible on the level of the textual content, which allows the new readers to learn about incidents in the foreign culture through their description, but not on the level of language, where we see that the text has been moved into what one may call 'Third Space' (Bhabha 1994).

Let us now look at another case of an overt translation where the foreignness of the original is not carried over into the new text, this time however for a different reason. Extract (9) is taken from a contemporary novel by booker prize winner Kiran Desai.[6]

In extract (9) we witness the failure of the protagonist, an English-educated Indian judge, to teach his wife the (ex)colonial language English and the consequences of this failure.

Example (9)

"What is this?" he asked holding up the bread roll. Silence. "If you can't say the word, you can't eat it". More silence. He removed it from her plate. Later that evening, he snatched the Ovaltine from her tentative sipping. "And if you don't like it, don't drink it." He couldn't take her anywhere and squirmed when Mrs Singh waggled her finger at him and said: " Where is your wife, Mr Patel? None of this purdah business, I hope?" In playing her part in her husband's career, Mrs Singh had attempted to mimic what she considered a typical English woman's balance between briskly pleasant and firmly no-nonsense, and had thus succeeded in quashing the spirits of so many of the locals who prided themselves on being mostly nonsense.

"Was ist das?", fragte er und hielt das Stück Brot hoch. Schweigen. "Wenn Du das Wort nicht weißt, darfst du es nicht essen". Noch mehr Schweigen. Er nahm es ihr vom Teller. Später am Abend entriss er ihr die Ovomaltine, bevor sie vorsichtig daran hatte nippen können. "Wenn du es nicht magst, dann trink es auch nicht." Er konnte sie nirgendwo hin mitnehmen und wand sich, wenn Mrs Singh den Finger hob und sagte: "Wo ist denn Ihre Frau, Mr. Patel. Das ist doch hoffentlich nicht so ein purdah-Zeugs?" Um ihre Rolle in Mr Singhs Karriere spielen zu können, hatte Mrs Singh versucht, sich ganz in das zu verwandeln, was sie für eine typische Engländerin hielt, freundlich forsch und allem Unsinn abgeneigt, und so hatte sie viele der Einheimischen niedergewalzt, die stolz auf ihren Unsinn waren.

("What is that?" he asked and held the piece of bread up. Silence. "If you don't know the word, you're not allowed to eat it". More silence. He took it from her plate. Later in the evening he snatched the ovaltine from her before she had been able to take a careful nip.

---

[6] Kiran Desai, *The Inheritance of Loss*, London, 2006; translated by Robin Detje as *Erbin des verlorenen Landes* (Heiress of a Lost Country), Berlin Verlag, 2006.

> "If you don't like it, then don't drink it". He could take her nowhere with him and he squirmed, when Mrs Singh lifted her finger and said: "Where is your wife, Mr Patel? That is hopefully not such a purdah stuff?" In order to be able to play her role in Mr Singh's career, Mrs Singh had tried to completely change into what she assumed was a typical Englishwoman, friendlily pushy and averse to all nonsense, and so she had mowed down many of the natives who were proud of their nonsense.)

The translated excerpt in (9) shows that the translator has attempted to mimic the language of the original and even leaves – as does the original – foreign words in the text to get the original's linguistic profile across. However, due to differences in the expression potential of the two languages, the translation fails to match the sophisticated and original style of the original: for example, "he snatched the Ovaltime from her tentative sipping" is very different from the more neutral and pedestrian 'He snatched the Ovaltine from her before she had been able to take a careful sip'. Further, the expressiveness of the lexical items "squirmed", "waggled her finger" and "firmly non-nonsense" is far from being matched in the stilted German wordings "wand sich", "den Finger hob" and "allem Unsinn abgeneigt". In line with the expression potential of the German language, the translation is replete with so-called *Modalpartikeln* (modal particles) with which subtle shades of meaning are expressed – meanings which, as these linguistic means do not exist in English and not in this original text, are freely added by the translator (e.g. "noch", "denn"). In both these cases we are confronted with the impossibility of achieving full stylistic equivalence: a one-to-one match of the expressive potential of the two language systems is simply impossible here.

Phenomena such as the ones described above are so intimately interwoven with the source language and cultural community that they cannot easily cross over to a new language and culture. This type of intralingual and intercultural variation seems to be one of the phenomena where intercultural communication finds its limits, where 'shining through' is impossible to achieve.

The two examples (8) and (9) above show that even in cases of overt translation, where the original text is not subjected to cultural filtering, intercultural communication in the sense that the new text allows the original to 'shine through' is not always facilitated, either because intralingual and intracultural variation prevents it or because of an incompatibility of the two linguistic systems involved. In cases such as these the limits of translatability – in the sense of what Koller (2004) has called 'translation proper' – seem to have been reached.

6.3 Economic and popular science texts

In both economic and popular scientific texts, one can detect many instances of cultural filtering. We will again look at some cases of English-German translation and the way they exhibit filtering along the dimensions of communicative preferences described above.

Example (10) belongs to the genre of Annual Report. Exemplars of this genre are today issued by multinationals in large numbers. They tend to appear first in English and are later translated into many different languages. Here we will look again at cases of English originals and their German translation.

Example (10)[7]

> *We believe our first responsibility is to the doctors, nurses and patients, to mothers and fathers and all others who use our products.*
> *In meeting their needs everything we do must be of high quality*
> *...Our suppliers and distributors must have an opportunity to make a fair profit*
> *...Everyone must be considered as an individual!*
>
> *Allem voran steht unsere Verantwortung gegenüber den Ärzten, Krankenschwestern, Patienten, aber auch gegenüber Müttern, Vätern und all den Menschen, die unsere Produkte verwenden oder unsere Dienste in Anspruch nehmen.*
> *Die Erfüllung ihrer Ansprüche erfordert von uns stets ein hohes Qualitätsniveau.*
> *...Unseren Lieferanten wie auch unseren Abnehmern sollen wir die Möglichkeit geben, einen angemessenen Gewinn zu erzielen.*
> *...Jeder von ihnen ist als Individuum zu achten.*
> (Above everything else there is our responsibility to mothers, fathers and all the people who use our products or our services. Fulfilling their demands requires from us always a high level of quality.
> ... Our suppliers as well as our distributors we shall give the opportunity to achieve an adequate profit .... Everyone of them is to be honoured as an individual.)

The formula "I believe" in the English original in example (10) is not translated with an equivalent formula in the German text. This omission is not trivial and has serious consequences: the credo-formula "I believe"

[7] Source: Our Credo. Miller and Miller Annual Report 1986; Unser Credo Geschäftsbericht 1986 (Names anonymized).

suggesting a pseudo-religious affirmation is genre-constitutive as it substantially contributes to the text function of convincing addressees of the 'mission' of the company, suggesting also a personal conviction on the part of the text producer which is strategically designed to be infectious for the addressees, such that they are converted to also become 'believers'. The modal verb "must", which in the English original also functions as emphasizer of a subjectively felt internalized obligation, is not rendered analogously in German. Rather, the (modal) verbs "erfordern" (require), "sollen" (shall), "sein ..zu" (be ... to), etc. are used, all of which deviate from the core meaning of the modal "must" and rather express external obligations.

Consider also extracts (11) and (12) which are examples of popular scientific texts:

Example (11)[8]

> *It is important to note that whereas all Neanderthals made Mousterian tools, not all Mousterian toolmakers were Neanderthals.*
>
> *Alle Neanderthaler stellten Werkzeuge der Moustérien-Kultur her, aber nicht alle Werkzeugmacher des Moustérien waren Neanderthaler.*
> (All Neanderthals made tools of the Mousterian culture, but not all toolmakers were Neanderthals)

Example (12)[9]

> *The fluid that surrounds a fetus in the uterus can now be examined for the prenatal detection of genetic disorders, yet the procedure is being performed for only a tenth of the parents most in need of it.*
>
> *Das Fruchtwasser, in dem das Ungeborene schwimmt, enthält Zellen, die sich vom Fetus abgelöst haben. Führt man eine Kanüle in die Fruchtblase ein, die den Fetus umgibt, so kann man eine Probe des Fruchtwassers entnehmen, die enthaltenen Zellen auf Fehler in der Erbinformation untersuchen und damit bereits beim Ungeborenen Erbkrankheiten nachweisen.*

---

[8] Source: Erik Trinkaus and William H. Howells, 'The Neanderthals', *Scientific American*, December 1979, p. 94, and 'Die Neanderthaler', *Spektrum der Wissenschaft*, February 1980, p.80

[9] Source: Fritz Fuchs, 'Genetic Amniocentesis', *Scientific American*, June 1980, p. 37, and 'Diagnose von Erbkrankheiten beim Ungeborenen' (Diagnosis of Genetic Diseases in the Unborn), *Spektrum der Wissenschaft*, August 1980.

(The amniotic fluid, in which the fetus swims, contains cells which have been detached from the fetus. If one inserts a syringe into the amniotic sac which surrounds the fetus, one can take out a sample of the amniotic fluid, examine the cells contained therein regarding errors in the genetic information and thus find out about genetic diseases already in the unborn.)

In example (11) we notice that the phrase "It is important to note that..." is not rendered at all in the translation. The effect of this omission is that readers of the German text are not as involved as readers in the original in that they are not alerted to something they should pay attention to, as they are in the English text. Since there is no system constraint that explains not rendering this phrase, we can assume that this is a case of cultural filtering.

While the English original in example (12) presents information in a compressed manner, the German translation spreads out many details that are not contained in the original. Note also that – despite the provision of all these details – there is no reference to those human beings for whom an amniocentesis might be relevant. A consequence of this is that the opportunity for involving readers is foregone. Once again the translator may have followed German textualizaion conventions holding for this genre.

Examples (11) and (12) come from medical popular scientific texts, which generally aim at imparting scientific insights and developments in the field of medicine to lay readers in an easily intelligible form, such that readers' interest in the subject matter is stimulated. The German popular science texts follow an implicitly more 'serious' (often also pedagogic) norm, and they are culturally filtered to fit indigenous norms of the relevant receiving genre. Genuine intercultural communication is blocked through the operation of this cultural filter. The translation is a German text just like any monolingual and monocultural text in the same genre.

In the preceding sections we have seen that in both overt and covert translation intercultural communication can become problematic: in overt translation intralingual variation or system constraints may prevent the production of a text where the original 'lives on' and is allowed to 'shine through'. Instead, the translation is moved to what may be called Third Space – neither here nor there, neither source nor target culture. In covert translation it is cultural filtering which was seen to interfere with true cultural transfer and the provision of knowledge of foreign cultural conventions and preferences.

Phenomena such as these may however now be in a process of change through the dominant influence of English in its role as global *lingua franca*. I discuss this development in the next and final session.

7. On the changing nature of translation as intercultural communication through the influence of global English

In the course of today's increasing globalization and internationalization processes in science, politics, culture and economics, there is also a rising demand for texts which are simultaneously meant for, and addressed to, recipients in many different linguistic and cultural communities. In other words, an increasing number of texts are needed which are either translated (mostly covertly) or produced immediately as 'comparable texts' in different languages. In the past, translators and text producers tended to routinely apply a cultural filter in such cases, with which the cultural specificity in the particular target text was taken into account. However, the worldwide political, economic, scientific and cultural dominance of the English language, especially in its function as a global *lingua franca*, has been given added momentum through the revolution in information and communication technologies. As a result, a tendency towards 'cultural universalism' and 'cultural neutralism' – which is really a drift towards Anglo-American norms – seems to have been set into motion. In the decades to come, the conflict between cultural universalism and culture specificity in the presentation of a specific subject matter and, with this, the demands on text production by global information and marketing strategies on the one hand and local, particular textualization conventions on the other hand, will become ever more marked, given the unstoppable spread of English in many domains of modern life. And whereas cultural filtering in covert translation was common in the past, it is now plausible to hypothesize that in the future much less cultural filtering will occur, and many more 'culturally universal' or 'culturally neutral' translation texts will be routinely produced, which are in reality carriers of anglophone West-European/ North-Atlantic cultural norms (cf. Baumgarten *et al.* 2004; House 2006).

Recent exemplars of German translations of English popular science and business texts show that such Anglophone influence on indigenous German norms has indeed occurred in the areas of subjectivity and addressee orientation in recent years (Nuyts 2001; Smith 2002; Baumgarten and Probst 2004). This suggests an adaptation of German communicative norms to Anglophone norms in the sense described above.

Extract (13) is a telling example taken from the millennium edition of the twin journals *Scientific American* and *Spektrum der Wissenschaft:*

Example (13)[10]

> *Nevertheless, I am convinced that the decades-old dream of a useful, general-purpose autonomous robot will be realized in the not too distant future. The machines will be capable of carrying out simple chores, such as vacuuming, dusting, delivering packages and taking out the garbage. By 2040, I believe, we will finally achieve the original goal of robotics and a thematic mainstay of science fictions: a freely moving machine with the intellectual capabilities of a human being. In light of what I have just described as a history of largely unfulfilled goals in robotics, why do I believe that rapid progress and stunning accomplishments are in the offing?*
>
> *Den bisherigen Misserfolgen zum Trotz bin ich davon überzeugt, dass der jahrzehntelange Traum eines autonomen Allzweckroboters in nicht allzu ferner Zukunft wahr werden wird. Immerhin werden sie einfache Dinge tun können wie Böden putzen oder Müll wegbringen. Bis zum Jahre 2040 werden wir dann, so denke ich, das grosse, auch in der Science Fiction vielbesungene Ziel erreicht haben: eine frei bewegliche Maschine mit den geistigen Fähigkeiten eines menschlichen Wesens. Wie komme ich zu diesem Optimismus, in krassem Widerspruch zur bisherigen Entwicklung?*
> (Despite the previous unsuccessful attempts I am convinced that the deceades-old dream of an autonomous all-purpose robot in the not too distant future will come true. They will be able to do at the very least simple things such as cleaning floors or taking out the garbage. By the year 2040 we will, I believe, have reached the great goal which has also been much sung in Science Fiction: a freely moving machine with the intellectual capabilities of a human being. How do I arrive at such an optimism, in stark contradiction of the previous development?)

The fact that the author uses the personal pronouns "ich" (I) and "wir" (we) in the German text is a new development which points to Anglophone influence in the the area of subjectivity. Note, further, that there is an increase in addressee orientation through the use of the rhetorical question designed to simulate a dialogue with the reader ("Wie komme ich zu diesem Optimismus?", 'How do I arrive at such optimism?'). And the German text – like its English model – now also contains elements of spoken language

[10] Source: Hans Moravecs, 'Rise of the Robots', *Scientific American*, December 1999, p. 86, and Hans Moravecs, 'Die Roboter werden uns überholen' (The Robots Will Overtake Us), *Spektrum der Wissenschaft*, January 2000, p. 72.

(cf. the insert "So denke ich", 'So I think').

In the following short extract taken from an economic text we can also see how closely the German translation follows its English source text.

Example (14)[11]

> *....in the past year, we can see that we have built strong positions in the leading agricultural producing and consuming regions of the world*
>
> *...daher können wir feststellen, dass wir eine starke Position in den führenden landwirtschaftlichen Erzeuger- und Verbraucherregionen der Welt aufgebaut haben.*
> (...thus we can state that we have built up a strong position in the leading agricultural producing and consuming regions of the world.)

Example (14) shows that the use of the personal pronoun "wir" (we), which was formerly shunned in German letters to shareholders (impersonal and passive constructions were the rule), has now also entered the German genre of letters to shareholders via the many translations from English into German. And this demise of cultural filtering has now also seeped into the production of original German letters to shareholders, missions and visions as recent work by Böttger (2007) has shown.

What can we make of this development? Does the influence of Anglophone text conventions and preferences on German norms in such influential genres as scientific and economic texts result in a change from formerly genotypical covert translation to a type of phenotypical translation which is really a new form of overt translation? Overt NOT in the sense of a 'shining through' of the original, of a dialogue between two linguacultures, and of the life of something foreign inside another cultural tradition, but in a totally new sense of a conquest of one tradition by another more influential, more powerful one.

While the influence of the English language in the area of lexis (so-called 'Anglicisms') has long been acknowledged and bemoaned by many, Anglophone influence at the levels of pragmatics and discourse has hardly been recognized, let alone rigorously researched. The effect of the trend towards cultural universalism and neutralism in certain genres in many languages and cultures of the world is, however, an important research area for the next millennium. What is needed in this area is clearly research into the means of analyzing problems that so far have no name. One of the global

---

[11] Source: Letter to shareholders ADM 2001.

aims of such research would also be to try to close the gap between the two cultures – the linguistic camp and the cultural studies camp described at the beginning of this article, since we are here dealing with a cultural phenomenon that needs to be explored with the rigorous analytic means provided by linguistics.

Rules of discourse, conventions of textualization and communicative preferences often remain hidden and act stealthily at a deeper level of consciousness. This does not mean, however, that they are less powerful and persuasive. On the contrary. Once we have all internalized 'universal' communicative conventions and cultural values (to which we will be exposed ever more frequently), it may be difficult, indeed, to appreciate multilingualism, multiculturalism and culture-specificity.

References

Agar, Michael (1992) 'Review of Werner Holly Politikersprache', *Language in Society* 21: 158-60.

Baumgarten, Nicole, Juliane House and Julia Probst (2004) 'English as a lingua franca in covert translation processes', *The Translator* 10(1): 83-109.

Baumgarten, Nicole and Julia Probst (2004) 'The interaction of spokenness and writtenness in audience design', in Juliane House and Jochen Rehbein (eds.) *Multilingual Communication*, Amsterdam: Benjamins, 63-86.

Benjamin, Walter (1972) 'Die Aufgabe des Übersetzers', in Walter Benjamin *Gesammelte Schriften Bd. IV/1,* Frankfurt/Main: Suhrkamp.*Vorwort des Übersetzers zu der Übersetzung von Charles Baudelaire Tableaux Parisien*, 9-21.

Bhabha, Homi (1994) *The location of culture,* London: Routledge.

Blum-Kulka, Shoshana, Juliane House and Gabriele Kasper (eds) (1989) *Cross-Cultural Pragmatics*, Norwood, NJ: Ablex.

Böttger, Claudia (2007) *Lost in Translation? Analysing the role of English as the lingua franca of multilingual business communication,* Hamburg: Kovac.

Clyne, Michael (1987) 'Cultural Differences in the Organization of Academic Texts: English and German', *Journal of Pragmatics* 11: 211-47.

------ (1994) *Intercultural Communication at Work. Cultural Values in Discourse,* Cambridge: Cambridge University Press.

Duszak, Anna (1994) 'Academic Discourse and Intellectual Styles', *Journal of Pragmatics* 21: 291-393.

Fandrych, Christian and Gabriele Graefen (2002) 'Text commenting devices in German and English academic articles', *Multilingua* 21: 17-43.

Flotow, Luise von (1997) *Translation and Gender*, Manchester: St. Jerome.

Göpferich, Susanne (1995) 'Textsorten und Translationsprobleme', in Wolfgang Börner and Klaus Vogel (eds) *Der Text im Fremdsprachenunterricht*, Bochum: AKS Verlag.

Gupta, Akhil and James Ferguson (eds) (1997) *Culture, Power, Place: Ethnography at the End of an Era*, Durham, NC: Duke University Press.

Halliday, Michael A.K. (1994) *An Introduction to Functional Grammar*, London: Arnold, second edition.

House, Juliane (1973) *Theoretical Aspects of Translation*, Washington, DC: ERIC.

------ (1977/1981) *A Model for Translation Quality Assesment*, Tübingen: Narr, first and second edition.

------ (1989) 'Politeness in English and German: The functions of *please* and *bitte*', in Shoshana Blum-Kulka, Juliane House and Gabriele Kasper (eds) *Cross-Cultural Pragmatics*, Norwood, N.J.: Ablex, 96-122.

------ (1997) *Translation Quality Assessment: A Model Revisited*, Tübingen: Narr.

------ (1998) 'Politeness and Translation', in Leo Hickey (ed.) *The Pragmatics of Translation*, Clevedon: Avon, 54-71.

------ (2000) 'Linguistic Relativity and Translation', in Martin Puetz and Marjolijn Verspoor (eds) *Explorations in Linguistic Relativity*, Amsterdam: Benjamins, 69-89.

------ (2001) 'How do we know when a translation is good?', in Erich Steiner and Colin Yallop (eds) *Exploring translation and multilingual text production*, Berlin: Mouton de Gruyter, 127-61.

------ (2002a) 'Maintenance and Convergence in Covert Translation English-German', in Bergljot Behrens, Catherine Fabricius Hansen, Hilde Hasselgard and Stig Johansson (eds) *Information Structure in a Cross-Linguistic Perspective*, Amsterdam: Rodopi, 199-213.

------ (2002b) 'Universality versus culture specificity in translation', in Alessandra Riccardi (ed.) *Translation Studies. Perspectives on an Emerging Discipline*, Cambridge: Cambridge University Press, 92-111.

------ (2004) '*Linguistic aspects of the translation of children's books*', in Harald Kittel, Armin Frank, Norbert Greiner, Theo Hermans, Werner Koller, José Lambert and Fritz Paul (eds) *Translation-Übersetzung-Traduction. Bd. 1. Handbücher zur Sprach- und Kommunikationswissenschaft*, Berlin: Mouton de Gruyter, 1296-321.

------ (2006) 'Communicative Styles in English and German', *European Journal of English Studies* 10(3): 249-67.

Koller, Werner (2004) *Einführung in die Übersetzungswissenschaft*, Heidelberg: Quelle & Meyer, seventh edition.

Kusch, Martin and Hartmut Schröder (1989) 'Contrastive Discourse Analysis', in Martin Kusch and Hartmut Schröder (eds) *Text -Interpretation-Argumentation*, Hamburg: Buske, 79-92.

Luchtenberg, Sigrid (1994) 'A Friendly Voice to Help You vs Working Through Your Manual. Pragmatic Differences between American and German Software Manuals', *Journal of Pragmatics* 21: 315-19.

Mauranen, Anna (1993) *Cultural Differences in Academic Rhetoric*, Fankfurt/Main: Lang.

Nord, Christiane (1997) *Translating as a Purposeful Activity,* Manchester: St.Jerome.

Nuyts, Jan (2001) 'Subjectivity as an evidential dimension in epistemic modal expressions', *Journal of Pragmatics* 33: 383-400.

Ortega y Gasset, José (1965) *Miseria y Esplendor de la traducción. Glanz und Elend der Übersetzung*, München: Langewiesche-Brandt.

Probst, Julia (2003) 'Strategien der Adressatenorientierung in englischen und deutschen populärwissenschaftlichen Texten', in Johannes Eckerth (ed.) *Empirische Arbeiten aus der Fremdsprachenerwerbsforschung*, Bochum: AKS Verlag, 265-86.

Reiss, Katharina (1971) *Möglichkeiten und Grenzen der Übersetzungskritik*, München: Hueber.

------ and Hans J.Vermeer (1984) *Grundlegung einer allgemeinen Translationstheorie*, Tübingen: Niemeyer.

Robinson, Douglas (1997) *Translation and Empire. Postcolonial Theories Explained,* Manchester: St. Jerome.

Schleiermacher, Friedrich (1973 [1813]) 'Ueber die verschiedenen Methoden des Uebersezens', in Hans-Joachim Störig (ed.) *Das Problem des Übersetzens*, Darmstadt: Wissenschaftliche Buchgesellschaft, 38-70.

Schmitt, Peter A. (1995) 'Warnhinweise in deutschen und englischen Anleitungen: Ein interkultureller Vergleich', *Fremdsprachen Lehren und Lernen* 24: 197-222.

Smith, Carlota (2002) 'Perspective and point of view: Accounting for subjectivity', in Bergljot Behrens, Catherine Fabricius Hansen, Hilde Hasselgard and Stig Johansson (eds) *Information structure in a cross-linguistic perspective*, Amsterdam: Rodopi, 63-80.

Sperber, Dan (1996) *Culture: A Naturalistic Approach*, Oxford: Blackwell.

Steiner, Erich (2004) *Translated Texts: Properties, Variants, Evaluations*, Frankfurt/Main: Lang.

Venuti, Lawrence (1995) *The Translator's Invisibility*, London: Routledge.

Waard, Jan de and Eugene A. Nida (1986) *From One Language to Another. Functional Equivalence in Bible Translating*, Nashville: Nelson.

Weinreich, Uriel (1953) *Languages in Contact*, New York: Linguistic Circle of New York.

3. Text Topics and Their Intercultural Discourse Variation

A Sample Analysis Using Text Maps

HEIDRUN GERZYMISCH-ARBOGAST &
DOROTHEE ROTHFUß-BASTIAN
Saarland University, Germany

Abstract. *The article proposes a methodological tool for describing the topic structure of texts and their potential intercultural variation. After positioning topic structures within the field of interculturally varying discourse patterns, the problems inherent in text topic identification and representation are briefly outlined. On the basis of this discussion, the notion of text map and the procedure for establishing text maps is introduced and exemplified with a sample analysis of a passage from the introductory chapters of the English Introduction into Psychology by William James (1890/1975) and the German Grundriss der Psychologie by Wilhelm Wundt (1896). The analysis exemplifies the procedure of establishing text maps; its potential value is heuristic. After visualizing the text topic structures contrastively, their differences are presented and discussed. On the basis of the parameters yielded in the analysis it is suggested that text maps provide a verifiable methodological tool for larger-scale empirical studies into the nature and scope of varying topic and discourse structures.*

1. Intercultural differences in discourse patterns and the role of text topics

Variations in discourse patterns have been much discussed in intercultural communication and pragmatics (e.g. Kaplan 1966; Galtung 1985; Agar 1992; Clyne 1994; Luchtenberg 1994; Ventola 1995a, 1995b; House 1996 1998, 1999; Bührig 2004),[1] and House's suggestion of scalar differences between English and German conversational attitudes has been widely accepted for written academic texts. House differentiates five dimensions along which differences in discourse patterns can be identified and described: German speakers tend to be more direct, self-oriented, content-oriented, and explicit while English speakers lean towards indirectness, orientation

[1] With reference to translation, cf. also Gerzymisch-Arbogast (1993, 1997, 2003a); see also Buhl (1999).

towards the other, addressee orientation, implicitness and the use of routine formulas (House 1999:49). The linguistic manifestations of these dimensions are described using lexico-semantic, syntactic and pragmatic categories (e.g. Baumgarten 2003). The selection and development of topics in texts is generally recognized as playing an important role when it comes to describing discourse structure (Clyne 1994). But although topic structure (or information sequencing as the broader term) has generally been accepted as an important dimension when describing potentially varying discourse patterns using such broad terms as 'linear' or 'digressive' (Clyne 1994), theoretical and methodological deficits of the theme/rheme notions have so far impeded larger-scale empirical studies into the nature of intercultural differences in the topic structures of texts. It is therefore suggested here that the concept of text maps provides an operationalizeable instrument to depict and visualize topic structures in texts and as such lends itself to functioning as a comparative standard when interculturally contrasting topic structures in discourse patterns.

Against the background of House's dimension of content versus addressee-orientation, it is assumed that the more or less content-oriented nature of utterance topics in a text contributes to a more or less content- or addressee orientation in texts, which can then be described and illustrated by the way utterance topics are developed in discourse. The resulting (contrastive) text topic patterns as dimensions of discourse are visualizeable as text maps which enhance understanding the organization of texts around concepts and lend themselves to in-depth analysis and comparison. Text maps are thus considered an operationalizeable indicator for the degree of content-orientation vs. addressee-orientation in texts, as will be exemplified and illustrated by the sample analysis in section 4. Preceding this application and illustration, the theoretical status of text topics and the problems of their identification and representation will be briefly discussed in the following section.

2. Text topics and their representation

2.1 Theme identification

Generally speaking, that which is known or given in sentences or utterances is called **theme** and that which is not known, the new elements, are called **rheme**. For **theme**, **topic** or **given information**, and for **rheme, comment** or **focus** or **new information** are also used.[2]

---

[2] For an overview of terms, see Gerzymisch-Arbogast (2003b).

The many theme-rheme definitions so far suggested in the literature can be classified according to the kind of criteria they apply. These criteria can be differentiated as sentence-internal, text-internal and situation-specific:

- Sentence-internal criteria for the differentiation of theme and rheme are:[3]
  □ subject vs. predicate or
  □ logical subject vs. predicate or
  □ that which is presupposed vs. that which is asserted.

- Text-internal criteria are:[4]
  □ previously mentioned in the text or contextually bound or
  □ under question in context or retrievable from context

- Situation-specific criteria, i.e. criteria related to a speaker and hearer in an utterance are:[5]
  □ present in the awareness of the participants at the time of utterance or
  □ identifiable by the hearer from the perspective of the speaker or
  □ (expressed as a metaphor): on stage/off stage.

A comparative analysis of the merits and shortcomings of these approaches can be found in Mudersbach (2003). What is relevant here is that none of these approaches considers the following:

> (1) the functional interrelationship between these criteria (e.g. the text-internal criterion **previously mentioned** and the speaker/hearer criterion **identifiable by the hearer**) or
> (2) the inferred world knowledge that interacts with the verbalized message in the selection and development of topics.

With respect to (1) this means that topic structures cannot be described by syntactic, semantic, text or situation categories alone and in isolation but that pragmatic categories need to be used for their description, interrelating the communicative constellation between a speaker and a hearer in a given situation verbalized in the text. Such (interrelated) pragmatic categories include, for example, the information constellation of the communicative

---

[3] Authors who use sentence-internal criteria include Allerton (1978), Chomsky (1971), Daneš (1970), Gundel (1977), Halliday (1967/68), Hockett (1958), Lyons (1977), de Beaugrande and Dressler (1981), and recently Musan (2002).
[4] See Daneš (1974), Fries (1971), Halliday (1970, 1974), Sgall (1974, 1975a, 1975b, 1976), Sgall et al (1973).
[5] See Allerton (1978) and Chafe (1976).

partners and their respective stock of knowledge and attention focus.[6]

Topics (for the purpose of establishing text maps as used in the sample analysis in section 4) are therefore identified by using Mudersbach's pragmatic model (Mudersbach 1981; for an application, see Gerzymisch-Arbogast 1987).

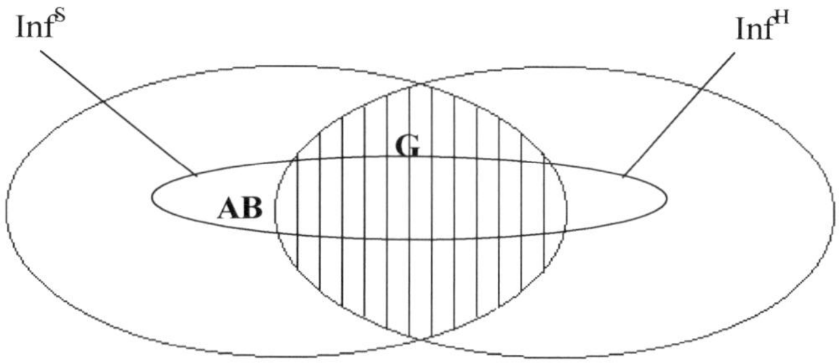

Figure 1. Pragmatic Parameters in Theme-Rheme Identification (Inf/S = Information stock of speaker; Inf/H = information stock of hearer; G = overlapping information stock of communicating partners, AB = focus of attention of speaker and hearer)

With respect to (2), it is generally accepted that successful communication depends to a large extent on implicit (world) knowledge, inferences and individual hypotheses. Topics can therefore be assumed to contain a substantial amount of inferred knowledge, and topic identification needs to take this into account. None of the above sentence-, text- or situation-specific criteria for topic identification allows for the interplay of explicit and implicit knowledge, however. Describing topic structures in texts therefore needs to depict the interrelationship of the knowledge stock implicit in a speaker/hearer constellation, their (overlapping) world knowledge and focus of attention in a given situation (Gerzymisch-Arbogast 1985, 1987, 1994b, 2003b; Mudersbach 2003). Comparing and structuring speaker/hearer stocks of (implicit) information is theoretically based on the principles of communicator and individual semantics (**Kommunikatensemantik**, Mudersbach 1984).

[6] A detailed pragmatic analysis of the theme-rheme distribution in an utterance (as exemplified in Gerzymisch-Arbogast 1987:131ff) is required, unless the language system calls for an obligatory theme indicator – as for example '-wa' in Japanese, cf. Kuno (1972) – or a corresponding rheme indicator.

2.2 Theme representation

Once utterance topics are identified, their sequential development or progression in texts can be represented graphically in various forms (Daneš 1970; Gerzymisch-Arbogast 1987). While several types of theme progressions as suggested by Daneš (1970) are representable by linear graphs, **thematic gaps** (the least developed progression type in Daneš 1970), which presuppose world knowledge and seem to resemble what is otherwise understood by inferences (Bellert 1970) or implications (Dressler 1973) or hypotheses (Mudersbach 1983), resist representation by linear graphic depiction. Their representation is possible by leksemantic networks, i.e. text maps. World knowledge hypotheses are not included in the traditional set-up of semantic networks (de Beaugrande & Dressler 1981). Within leksemantic networks (Mudersbach 1983; Gerzymisch-Arbogast 1996) they are characterized as those relationships between concepts (or arguments) in a text that are not connected explicitly but need an implicature for establishing connectivity with other relationships in a text. Thus, while losing the linear description parameters (e.g. the semantic relations between a sequence of topics), leksemantic networks provide transparency of how world knowledge relationships interact with verbalized information in the text as so called concretizations. This is the *added* value of text maps, as illustrated in the structural graph in Figure 2: the partial network in the box shows that the set of relations inside the box is unconnected with the rest of the relations that make up the text and require a (world knowledge) hypothesis to establish connectivity (for a classification of hypotheses, see section 4 below).

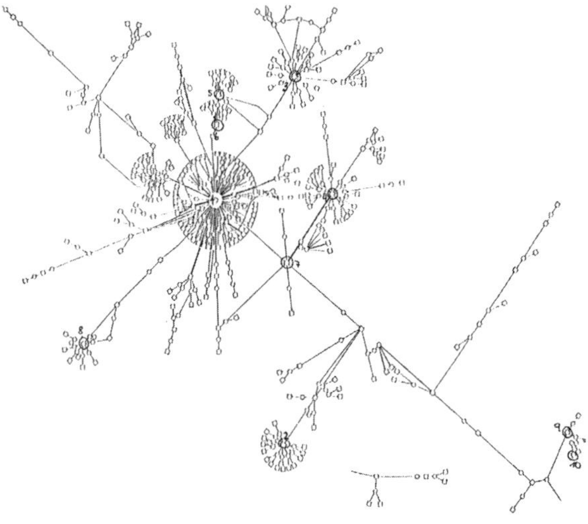

Figure 2. Text Map – Connected Relations plus 'Island' (structural graph)

3. Text Maps as visualizations of discourse structure

Text Maps[7] can thus be described as a particular kind of semantic networks, visualizing the complexity of all relations in a text, including world knowledge hypotheses. They consist of:

(1) the complete inventory of verbalized utterances in a text, organized as relations
and
(2) individual, potentially reader-specific hypotheses[8] necessary to understand a text as a coherent whole.

A text is thus represented as a relational network, consisting of the utterances of a text and the potential implicatures that are needed (by the individual reader) to understand the text as a coherent whole. The hypotheses may be classified as intra-textual (endogenous) and extra-textual (exogenous) and lend themselves to making the individual interpretation of a text transparent and accessible for description and analysis (see section 2.3).

While semantic networks have been well-established since 1968 in the description of meaning in computational linguistics,[9] they have proved problematic in depicting text structure,[10] mainly due to a mix of heterogeneous (metalinguistic) categories used in their set-up and description. Text Maps, by contrast, depict text structure as natural language utterances in the form of relations, which may be connected or not connected and thus (via the unconnected relations) make a text open for individual interpretation. The degree of connectivity (connected relations vs. unconnected relations, i.e. **islands**) of a text determines its degree of **coherence** or, in more general terms, its degree of openness for interpretation through individual hypotheses.

---

[7] The concept of **Text Map** is identical with the semantic network representations based on the leksemantic meaning concept as depicted in Gerzymisch-Arbogast (1994a, 1996) and Gerzymisch-Arbogast and Mudersbach (1998). It should not be confused with the concept of **Topic Map** used in the domain of artificial intelligence research (cf. especially Lobin 2001). Without going into too much detail here it should nevertheless be pointed out that the concept of **Text Map** only serves the purpose of visualizing text structures, in contrast to the concept of **Topic Map** which also includes the representation of knowledge structures on a sytems level.

[8] Hypotheses are virtually the same as **inferences**, **implications**, **presuppositions**.

[9] For an overview, see Mehl (1993), Leinfellner (1994).

[10] The semantic networks introduced by de Beaugrande and Dressler in 1981 have found little acceptance in the text linguistic literature, mostly due to their heterogeneous descriptive categories and set-up.

3.1 Establishing Text Maps[11]

Conceptually, the text maps as they are presented here proceed from the leksemantic meaning concept as proposed by Mudersbach (1983). In contrast to the traditional bilateral concept of meaning as an inseparable entity of *signifiant* and *signifié* (de Saussure 1916), leksemantics was developed with the intention of describing contextual meaning (Mudersbach 2002:53). The concept uses the idea of interrelated meaning relations on various levels of depth in the analysis and has been extensively described for its use in translation studies (Gerzymisch-Arbogast 1994 a, 1994b, 1996, 1999; Gerzymisch-Arbogast and Mudersbach 1998; Gerzymisch-Arbogast *et al.* 1999) so that we can limit ourselves to a broad outline of the following sequence of steps when extracting semantic networks from natural-language texts:

Step 1: Segmentation of the text into utterances.

Step 2: Transformation of natural language utterances into relations and preparation of data entry forms (if the analysis is computerized)

Step 3: Enter relations into data bank (with simultaneous listings of lexical arguments and relators), including possible hypotheses

Step 4: Analysis of connectedness of relations, including the quantity and quality of arguments, relators and hypotheses

Step 5: Establishing Text Maps by graphically centering all arguments and the connecting relations (including the hypotheses) around the concept (argument) which enters into the largest number of relations in the text. A coherent, multi-level sample text map is graphically depicted in Figure 4.

Presupposed in representing texts as text maps is the hypothesis that natural language utterances can be translated into relations consisting of at least one argument (usually a NP) and one relator (usually a VP). Text maps are constructed by interpreting a natural language utterance, for instance ‘Professors read books’, as a two-valency relation consisting of the concepts ‘professors’ and ‘books’ and connected by the relator ‘read’. The formal representation and visualization of ‘Professors read books’ would thus be depicted as in Figure 3.

---

[11] Due to restrictions on space, the procedure can only be roughly outlined here. For further details, see Gerzymisch-Arbogast (1996) and Gerzymisch-Arbogast and Mudersbach (1998).

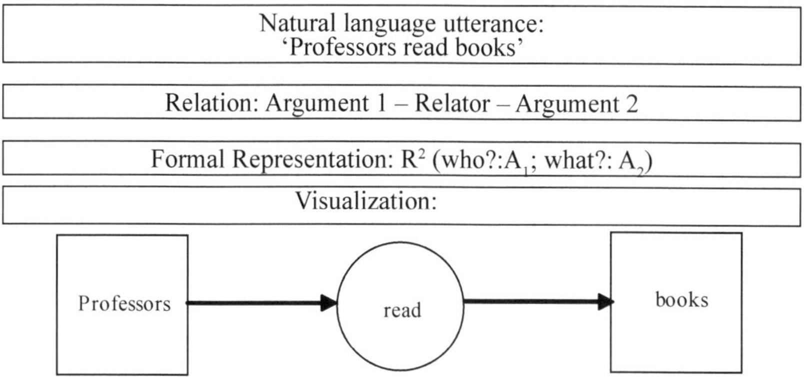

Figure 3. Transformation of a natural language utterance into a relation (Gerzymisch-Arbogast 1994a:64)

The segmentation of a text into utterances and the listing of all utterances in a text – represented as relations – yields a linear representation of a text (Gerzymisch-Arbogast 1999:84ff). On the basis of this linear representation (see Appendix), it is possible to determine which arguments in the text are connected with each other, which arguments form **islands** and into how many relations an argument enters in a text. The text used to exemplify the analysis here is a passage from the introductory chapters of the English *Introduction into Psychology* by William James (1890/1975) and the German *Grundriss der Psychologie* by Wilhelm Wundt (1896), reproduced in the Appendix and further discussed in section 4.1 below.

3.2 Visualization

The visualization of text structures as text maps is illustrative of

(1) the connected and unconnected (islands) relations in a text
(2) the topic structure (i.e. quantity and quality of topics).

In the structural example in Figure 4, all relations are connected. Concept B is the central concept (primary topic) binding the largest number of relations; concept A is a secondary topic on a second meaning level of B and constituting several other dependent meaning levels.

Moreover, the sample text map in Figure 4 shows a heavy concentration of arguments (concepts) and relations on a first meaning level around the concept B, with hardly any second meaning (topic) levels. This means that concept B is not highly differentiated (except for its dependent concept) in the text but is treated almost exclusively on a first (i.e. conceptually superficial) meaning level.

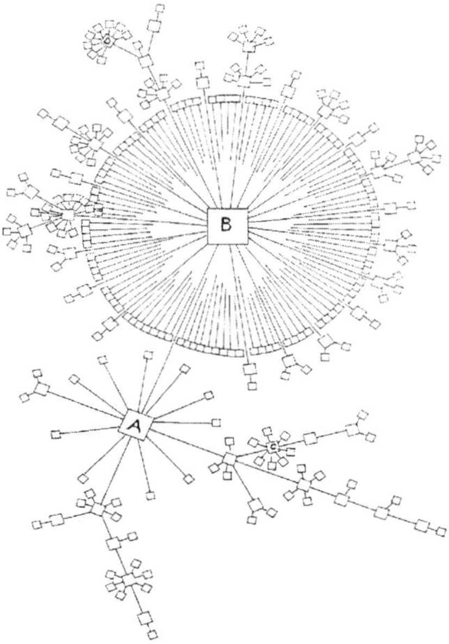

Figure 4. Text Map – Complete Connectivity (Structural Graph)

3.3 Hypotheses

We can differentiate several types of hypotheses. They may be characterized as follows:

- **grammatical hypotheses** are formed by connecting grammatical relationships, e.g. different case or plural endings, subject-verb concordances, etc.
- **semantic hypotheses** are formed by establishing semantic contiguity on a systems level of language (synonymy, hyponymy, whole-part, opposition; Lyons 1977:198ff, 270ff). Semantic hypotheses in the texts under comparison include, for example, *Begriffsbestimmung* and *Definition* (Wundt, utterances 2 & 9); *the associationist school* and *the associationist* (James, utterances 11 & 28).
- **text semantic hypotheses** are formed by establishing co-reference on a text level. Textsemantic hypotheses in the texts under comparison are, for example, *such things as feelings, desires, cognitions, reasonings, decisions* and the co-reference with *the material (James*, utterances 2,3 & 5); *the spiritual faculties of memory* and its co-reference with *its successes* (James, utterances 16 & 22).

- **text external hypotheses** are formed by integrating elements of the reader's world knowledge into the text. These are reader-specific hypotheses which are formed for coherence purposes and may vary across individual readers.

4. Sample analysis

The following sample analysis will represent and compare the topic structures of the German and English text using text maps as an analytical tool. It shows and discusses differences in the organization of topic structures and suggests that the varying quantity and quality of topics is indicative of a stronger **addressee**-orientedness of the topic structure of the English text versus stronger **content**-orientedness in the German text. After describing the text samples (4.1), the 5-step analysis in the extraction of text maps from natural linear texts is shown (4.2) and the topic structures are visualized by text maps (4.3). Problems in the analysis and possible perspectives for further research are then discussed (4.4).

4.1 The text samples

Finding comparable original text (passages) in the language pair under consideration was very difficult. Since translated texts are unacceptable for our purposes, we chose text passages from comparable academic works in English and German. With the introductory paragraphs of William James' *Introduction into Psychology* (1890/1975) and Wilhelm Wundt's *Grundriss der Psychologie* (1896) we were able to establish comparability in terms of academic subject, authority of author, text type (introductory chapters) and approximate time of publication. As a basis for our analysis we took the first two paragraphs of the introductory chapters (German text: 13 sentences; English text: 16 sentences) so that we could reliably say that there were no **previously mentioned** items in the texts. We neglected the diachronic linguistic aspect in view of the fact that we were less interested in the phenomenon of a potential change in language use in favour of the structural organization of the texts. The segmented original text excerpts are given online (http://www.translationconcepts.org/journals.htm).

4.2 The analysis

The analysis was carried out along the 5-step procedure as outlined above (see also Gerzymisch-Arbogast 1999:82ff):

Step 1: Segmentation of text
The text was segmented into utterances. The English text contains 33, the German text 25 utterances.

Step 2: Transformation of natural language utterances into relations
The utterances were transformed into relations in their linear sequence.

Step 3: Data Bank entry
The analysis was carried out manually.

Step 4: Analysis
The analysis covered the following parameters: (a) how many topics were indentifiable in the German and the English texts (topic quantity), (b) how many meaning levels these topics produced (topic quality), (c) how many hypotheses were needed to make the texts coherent (quantity of hypotheses), (d) how these hypotheses were differentiated (quality of hypotheses), and (e) to what extent the relations in the texts were connected (degree of connectivity).

Step 5: Text Maps

(1) Establishing topics:
Table 1 shows that the two texts established 9 (German) versus 16 (English) topics. For the purposes of visualization, the topics 1-9 (G) versus 1-16 (E) were arranged as central arguments with concentric circles featuring those arguments connected with the respective topic. The concentric circles represent the meaning levels of the topic. If an argument on a concentric circle in turn enters into relations with other arguments, it is considered as a secondary (or third – n) topic vis-à-vis the central topic, forming concentric circles as first to n-meaning levels.

(2) Forming hypotheses:
Hypotheses were formed to connect those topics which were not connected by verbalized relations. They vary in type and quantity as shown in Table 1.

(3) Determining the degree of connectivity:
The degree of connectivity was determined by the quota of connected relations vs. unconnected relations (**islands**) (Buengmoom 2001:54, 75ff).

4.3 Comparative visualizations

The visualization of the two text maps illustrate the findings given in Table 1.

4.4 Results and interpretation

The results show that the English text features (1) more topics and thus a greater variety of topics with (2) more 1-meaning-level topics than the German text. The deeper meaning differentiation in the German topic structure suggests that the German text is conceptually more differentiated, i.e. more **content-related**.

4.4.1 Topic structure

The higher quantity of topics in the English text corresponds to a greater variety of topics (*psychology*; *phenomena*; *we*; *the most natural way of unifying the material*; *another way of unifying the chaos*; *faculties*; *any particular cognition or recollection*; *successes <of memory>*; *the soul*; *this*; *we as spiritualists*; *I*; *the self or ego of the individual*; *the associationist schools of ...*; *the associationist*; *something*) versus fewer topics (*zwei Begriffsbestimmungen der Psychologie*; *die metaphysiche Definition*; *die empirische Definition*; *ihr*; *es*; *"innerer Sinn"*; *Naturerscheinungen*; *Vorstellungen*; *die subjektiven Regungen*) with a greater conceptual differentiation on several meaning levels for the German text.

We interpret the greater variety of topics with few meaning levels in the English text (around such concepts as *most natural way of unifying the material; another way of unifying the chaos; faculties; successes; the soul*) versus fewer meaning levels (and less varied) topics (around such concepts as *zwei Begriffsbestimmungen; die metaphysiche Definition; die empirische Definition*) in the German text as indicative of a stronger content-orientedness in the German text versus a greater addressee-orientedness in the English text.

4.4.2 Connectivity degree

Again, the two texts vary in their degree of connectivity: the English text shows more hypotheses than the German text and correspondingly a lower degree of connectivity (E: 43,8%; G: 55,6%). The hypotheses also vary in type with more text-semantic hypotheses in the English text.

5. Summary

For the purposes of this article, the sample analysis has shown that the English and German sample texts vary with respect to their topic structures. Using text maps as an analytical tool, the parameters of (1) quantity and (2) quality of topics, (3) quantity and (4) quality of hypotheses and (5) degree of connectivity were islotated. These parameters lend themselves for use in broader (empirical) analyses of intercultural shifts in topic and text structures. Of course, the findings here are quantitatively not relevant and can only have a heuristic value. They show, however, that topic structures are accessible to systematic description, which is a prerequisite for broader empirical studies. Visualization by text maps is helpful when illustrating the varying topic structures.

	Topic Maps	Wundt	James
1	Topics		
1.1	Quantity of topics	9	16
1.2	Quality of topics		
	3-level topics (consisting of three topic environments)	es (with *Naturerscheinungen* as 2nd and *Vorstellungen* as 3rd level)	psychology (with *phenomena* as 2nd and *we* as 3rd level)
	2-level topics (consisting of two topic environments)	ihr (with "innerer Sinn" as 2nd level)	the associationist (with *something* as 2nd level); most natural way of unifying the material (with *the soul* as 2nd level)
	1-level topics (consisting of one topical environment)	zwei Begriffsbestimmungen der Psychologie; die metaphysiche Definition; die empirische Definition; die subjektiven Regungen	another way of unifying the chaos; faculties; particular cognition or recollection; successes; this; we/spiritualists; I; self/ego of the individual; associationist schools
2	Hypotheses		
2.1	Quantity of hypotheses	5	10
2.2	Quality of hypotheses		
	semantic	5	7
	text semantic	–	3
	text external	–	–
3	Connectivity Degree		
3.1	connected relations	5	7
3.2	unconnected relations	4	9
3.3	degree of connectivity	5:4 (55,6%)	7:9 (43,8%)

Table 1. Comparison of Topics and Hypotheses in English and German Text Maps

References

Primary Literature

James, William (1890/1975) *The Principles of Psychology*, Chicago, London, Toronto: Encyclopaedia Britannica.

Wundt, Wilhelm (1896) *Grundriss der Psychologie*, Leipzig: Engelmann.

Secondary Literature

Agar, Michael (1992) 'Review of Werner Holly 1990. Politikersprache', *Language in Society* 21: 158-60.

Allerton, D.J. (1978) 'The notion of "givenness" and its relations to presupposition and to theme', *Lingua* 44: 133-68.

Baumgarten, Nicole (2003) 'Close or Distant: Constructions of Proximity in Translations and Parallel Texts', in Heidrun Gerzymisch-Arbogast, Eva Hajicova, Petr Sgall, Zuzana Jettmarová, Annelie Rothkegel and Dorothee Rothfuss-Bastian (eds) *Textologie und Translation* (Jahrbuch Übersetzen und Dolmetschen, Bd. 4/II), Tübingen: Gunter Narr, 17-34.

Beaugrande, Robert de/ and Wolfgang U. Dressler (1981) *Einführung in die Textlinguistik*, Tübingen: Niemeyer.

Bellert, Irena (1970) 'On a Condition of the Coherence of Texts', *Semiotica* 2: 344-63.

Buengmoom, Mukda (2001) *Analyse deutscher und thailändischer Fachtexte und ihre Relevanz für das Fachübersetzen Thailändisch/Deutsch. Eine exemplarische Untersuchung auf der Basis der textlinguistischen Parameter Kohärenz, Thema-Rhema-Struktur und Isotopie*, Unpublished Dissertation, Universität des Saarlandes.

Buhl, Silke (1999) 'Gestaltungsprinzipien wissenschaftlicher Texte im Sprachenpaarvergleich Deutsch-Englisch am Beispiel von Einsteins und Russels zur Relativitätstheorie', in Heidrun Gerzymisch-Arbogast, Daniel Gile, Juliane House and Annely Rothkegel (eds) *Wege der Übersetzungs- und Dolmetschforschung* (Jahrbuch Übersetzen und Dolmetschen, Bd. 1), Tübingen: Gunter Narr, 117-41.

Bührig, Kristin (1999) 'Konsekutives Übersetzen Englisch-Deutsch', in Heidrun Gerzymisch-Arbogast, Daniel Gile, Juliane House and Annely Rothkegel (eds) *Wege der Übersetzungs- und Dolmetschforschung* (Jahrbuch Übersetzen und Dolmetschen, Bd. 1), Tübingen: Gunter Narr, 241-66.

------ (2004) '"Che devo dire?" – Möglichkeiten und Hindernisse im scherzhaften Umgang mit Schwierigkeiten der Thema-Rhema-Dynamik in der mehrsprachigen Familienkommunikation', in Juliane House, Werner Koller and Klaus Schubert (eds) *Neue Perspektiven der Übersetzungs- und Dolmetschwissenschaft*, Bochum: AKS.

Chafe, Wallace L. (1976) 'Givenness, contrastiveness, definiteness, subjects and topics', in Charles N. Li (ed.) *Subject and Topic*, New York, San Francisco: Academic Press, 25-55.

Chomsky, Noam (1971) 'Deep structure, surface structure and semantic interpretation', in Danny D. Steinberg and Leon A. Jakobovits (eds) *Semantics. An interdisciplinary reader in philosophy, linguistics and psychology*, Cambridge: Cambridge University Press, 183-216.

Clyne, Michael G. (1994) *Intercultural Communication at Work. Cultural Values in Discourse*, Cambridge: Cambridge University Press.

Daneš , Frantisek (1970) 'Zur linguistischen Analyse der Textstruktur', *Folia Linguistica* 4: 72-73.

------ (ed.) (1974) *Papers on Functional Sentence Perspective*, The Hague: Mouton.

de Saussure, Ferdinand (1916) *Cours de linguistique générale*, Paris: Payot.

Dressler, Wolfgang U. (1973) *Einführung in die Textlinguistik*, Tübingen: Niemeyer.

Firbas, John (1964) 'On defining the theme in functional sentence analysis', *Traveaux linguistiques de Prague* 1: 267-80.

------ (1974) 'Some aspects of the Czechoslovak approach to problems of functional sentence perspective', in Frantisek Daneš (ed.) *Papers on Functional Sentence Perspective*, The Hague: Mouton, 11-37.

------ (1975) 'On the thematic and the non-thematic section of the sentence', in Hakan Ringbom (ed.) *Style and Text: Studies presented to Nils Erik Enkvist*, Stockholm: Skriptor, 317-34.

Fries, Ulrich (1971) 'Textlinguistik', *Textlinguistik und Didaktik* 2: 219-34.

Galtung, Johan (1985) 'Struktur, Kultur und intellektueller Stil. Ein vergleichender Essay über sachsonische, teutonische, gallische und nipponische Wissenschaft', in Alois Wierlacher (ed.) *Das Eigene und das Fremde. Prolegomena zu einer interkulturellen Germanistik*, München: Iudicium, 151-93.

Gerzymisch-Arbogast, Heidrun (1987) *Zur Thema-Rhema-Gliederung in amerikanischen Wirtschaftstexten*, Tübingen: Narr Verlag.

------ (1993) 'Contrastive Scientific and Technical Register as a Translation Problem', in Sue Ellen Wright and Leland D. Wright (eds) *Scientific and Technical Translation*, New York: SUNY, American Translators Association Scholarly Monograph Series. Vol. VI., 21-51.

------ (1994a) *Übersetzungswissenschaftliches Propädeutikum* (UTB Uni-Taschenbücher 1782), Tübingen & Basel: Francke.

------ (1986/1994b) 'Zur Relevanz der Thema-Rhema-Gliederung im Übersetzungsprozeß', in Mary Snell-Hornby (ed.) *Übersetzungswissenschaft: Eine Neuorientierung. Zur Integrierung von Theorie und Praxis*, Tübingen, Basel: Francke, 160-83.

------ (1996) 'Termini im Kontext. Verfahren zur Erschließung und Übersetzung der textspezifischen Bedeutung von fachlichen Ausdrücken', *Forum für Fachsprachenforschung*, Bd. 31, Tübingen: Gunter Narr.

------ (1997) 'Der Leserbezug in Sigmund Freuds psychoanalytischen Schriften im Spiegel der englischen Übersetzungen', in Gerd Wotjak and Heide Schmidt (eds) *Modelle der Translation – Models of Translation*, Festschrift für Albrecht Neubert, Frankfurt/M.: Vervuert, 213-33.

------ (1999) 'Kohärenz und Übersetzung: Wissenssysteme, ihre Repräsentation und Konkretisierung in Original und Übersetzung', in Heidrun Gerzymisch-Arbogast, Daniel Gile, Juliane House and Annely Rothkegel (eds) *Wege der Übersetzungs- und Dolmetschforschung*. (Jahrbuch Übersetzen und Dolmetschen, Bd. 1), Tübingen: Gunter Narr, 77-106.

------ (2001) 'Theme-Rheme Organization (TRO) and Translation', in A.P. Frank, N. Greiner, T. Hermans, H. Kittel, W. Koller, J. Lambert and F. Paul (eds) *Übersetzung - Translation - Traduction. Ein internationales Handbuch zur Übersetzungsforschung*, Berlin, New York: de Gruyter.

------ (2003a) 'Interkulturelle Missverständnisse in Text und Translation. Einige Überlegungen am Beispiel des Englischen und Deutschen', in N. Baumgarten, C. Böttger, M. Motz and J. Probst (eds) *Übersetzen, Interkulturelle Kommunikation, Spracherwerb und Sprachvermittlung - das Leben mit mehreren Sprachen* (Festschrift für Juliane House zum 60. Geburtstag), Zeitschrift für Interkulturellen Fremdsprachenunterricht, Jahrgang 8/2003, Nummer 2.

------ (2003b) 'Die Thema-Rhema-Gliederung in fachlichen Texten', in O.H. Jung and A. Kolesnikova (eds) *Fachsprachen und Hochschule*, Frankfurt u.a.: Lang.

------ and Klaus Mudersbach (1998) *Methoden des wissenschaftlichen Übersetzens*, Tübingen, Basel: Francke.

------, Ingrid Fleddermann, David Horton, Joëlle Philippi, Laura Sergo Bürge, Hildegard Seyl, Catherine von Tsurikov and Klaus Mudersbachet (1999) 'Methodik des wissenschaftlichen Übersetzens', in Alberto Gil, Johann Haller, Erich Steiner and Heidrun Gerzymisch-Arbogast (eds) *Modelle der Translation: Grundlagen für Methodik, Bewertung, Computermodellierung, SABEST - Saarbrücker Beiträge zur Sprach- und Translationswissenschaft*, Frankfurt am Main, etc.: Lang, 287-323.

Gundel, J. K. (1977) *Role of topic and comment in linguistic theory*, Indiana University Linguistics Club (unpublished manuscript).

Halliday, Michael A.K. (1967/68) 'Notes on transitivity and theme in English. Part 1', *Journal of Linguistics* : 37-31; Part 2, *Journal of Linguistics* 3: 177-274; Part 3, *Journal of Linguistics* 4: 153-308.

------ (1970) 'Language structure and language function', in John Lyons (ed.) *New horizons in linguistics*, Middlesex: Pelican, 140-65.

------ (1974) 'The Place of "functional sentence perspective" in the system of linguistic description', in Frantisek Daneš (ed.) *Papers on Functional Sentence Perspective*, The Hague: Mouton, 43-53.

Hockett, Charles F. (1958) *A course in modern linguistics*, New York: The Macmillan Company.

House, Juliane (1996) 'Contrastive Discourse Analysis and Misunderstanding: the Case of German and English', in Monica Hellinger and Ulrich Ammon (eds) *Contrastive Sociolinguistics*, Berlin, New York: de Gruyter, 345-61.

------ (1998) 'Kontrastive Pragmatik und interkulturelle Kompetenz im Fremdsprachenunterricht', in W. Börner and K. Vogel (eds) *Kontrast und Äquivalenz. Beiträge zu Sprachvergleich und Übersetzung*, Tübingen: Narr, 62-88.

------ (1999) 'Zur Relevanz kontrastiv-pragmatischer und interkultureller Diskursanalysen für das Fachübersetzen', in Heidrun Gerzymisch-Arbogast, Daniel Gile, Juliane House and Annely Rothkegel (eds) *Wege der Übersetzungs- und Dolmetschforschung* (Jahrbuch Übersetzen und Dolmetschen, Bd. 1), Tübingen: Gunter Narr, 43-54.

Jakobson, Roman (1959) 'On Linguistic Aspects of Translation', in R. Brower (ed.) *On Translation*, Cambrigde: Harvard University Press, 232-39.

Kaplan, Robert B. (1966) 'Cultural Thought Patterns in Inter-Cultural Education', *Language Learning* XVI(1/2): 1-20.

Kuno, S. (1972) 'Functional Sentence Perspective: A Case Study from Japanese and English', *Linguistic Inquiry* 3: 269-320.

Leinfellner, Elisabeth (1994) *Semantische Netze im Text*, Frankfurt: Lang.

Lobin, Henning (2001) *Informationsmodellierung in XML und SGML*, Berlin: Springer.

Luchtenberg, Sigrid (1994) 'A Friendly Voice to Help You vs Working Through Your Manual: Pragmatic Differences Between American and German Software Manuals', *Journal of Pragmatics* 21: 315-19.

Lyons, John (1977) *Semantics*, Volumes 1 & 2, Cambridge: Cambridge University Press.

Mehl, Stephan (1993) *Dynamische und semantische Netze: Zur Kontextabhängigkeit von Wortbedeutungen*, Sankt Augustin: Infix.

Mudersbach, Klaus (1981) *Ein neues Thema zum Thema "Thema Rhema"*, unpublished manuscript, Heidelberg.

------ (1982) 'Dividuensemantik', in W. Leinfellner, E. Kraemer and J. Schaenk (eds) *Language and Ontology. Proceedings of the 6th International Wittgenstein Symposium*, Kirchberg am Wechsel/Austria, Wien: Hölder-Pichler-Tempsky, 270-73.

------ (1983) 'Leksemantik – eine hol-atomistische Bedeutungstheorie', *Conceptus* XVII(40/41): 139-51.

------ (1984) *Kommunikation über Glaubensinhalte. Grundlagen der epistemistischen Linguistik*, Berlin, New York: de Gruyter.

------ (1989) 'The Theoretical Description of Speaker-Hearer- Hypotheses', in R. Dietrich and C.F. Graumann (eds) *Language Processing in Social Context*, Amsterdam: Elsvier Science Publishers B.V. North-Holland, 77-93.

------ (2002) 'Struktur und Strukturierung in der Lexikologie', in D.A. Cruse, F. Hundsnurscher, M. Job and P.R. Lutzeier (eds) *Lexikologie. Ein internationales Handbuch zur Natur und Struktur von Wörtern und Wortschätzen.* (Vol. I), Berlin, New York: de Gruyter.

------ (2003) 'A new rheme for a given theme'. Heidelberg. Unpublished Manuscript.

Musan, Renate (2002) 'Informationelle Dimensionen im Deutschen. Zur Variation der Wortstellung im Mittelfeld', *ZGL 30*: 198-221.

Sgall, Petr (1974) 'Focus and contextual boundness', in Östen Dahl (ed.) *Topic and comment, contextual boundness and focus, Papiere zur Textlinguistik* 6: 25-51.

------ (1975a) 'On the nature of topic and focus', in Hakan Ringbom (ed.) *Style and Text: Studies presented to Nils Erik Enkvist*, Stockholm: Skriptor, 409-15.

------ (1975b) 'Focus and the question test', *Fol.* 7: 301- 305.

------ (1976) 'Zum Stand der Thema-Rhema Forschung in der Tschechoslowakei', in Wolfgang Girke and Helmut Jachnow (eds) *Theoretische Linguistik in Ost-Europa. Originalbeiträge und Erstübersetzungen*, Tübingen: de Gruyter, 163-82.

------, E. Hajićová and E. Benešová (1973) *Topic, Focus and generative Semantics*, Kronberg Ts.

Ventola, Eija (1995a) 'Englisch als lingua franca der schriftlichen Wissenschaftskommunikation in Finnland und in Deutschland', in H. Kretzenbacher and H. Weinrich (eds) *Linguistik der Wissenschaftssprache*, Berlin: de Gruyter, 353-86.

------ (1995b) 'What's in an Academic Text', in Brita Wårvik, Sanna-Kaisa Tanskanen and Risto Hiltunen (eds) *Organization in Discourse. Proceedings from the Turku Conference*, Anglicana Turkuensia 14: 109-28.

4. A Problem of Pragmatic Equivalence in Intercultural Communication

Translating Requests and Suggestions

ALEXANDRA KALLIA
University of Tübingen, Germany

Abstract. *In this chapter an explicit connection is being made between the realization of certain speech acts in intercultural communication and in covert translation. The author presents an empirical study of the realizations of requests and suggestions elicited via the use of discourse completion tests (DCT) in a number of different communicative situations in English, German, Greek, Italian and Russian. The results of this investigation are then compared with the analyses of literary translations (of novels and plays) involving these same languages. It is shown that it is indeed the case that the culture-specific realizations of requests and suggestions established in the DCT study are also reflected in translatory actions in which a cultural filter has been employed to achieve pragmatic equivalence. Translation is thus a useful diagnostic instrument for revealing crosslinguistic variation in pragmatic choices.*

1. Introduction

Empirical research has shown that there is crosslinguistic variation in the strategies employed for the realization of speech acts. Although the same strategy – i.e. direct or indirect forms that are made up of a certain combination of mood, auxiliaries, performative verbs, particles (negative, interrogative, modal), politeness markers, etc. – may be available in a couple of languages, its crosslinguistic variants may not be equally conventionalized and/or they may not be pragmatically equivalent, i.e. they may not occur in the same situations, as the results of discourse completion tests and role plays with native speakers demonstrate. These linguistic differences reflect cultural differences. Wierzbicka (1991) has discussed how the prevalence of different strategies (e.g. directness rather than indirectness) in different cultures indicates different underlying cultural values like cordiality or deference.

The need to consider cultural diversity in order to achieve equivalence has become an issue in recent approaches to translation. Research of translatory action has shown that in some cases it is both possible and necessary that the translators consider the cultural differences between the source and the target language and adapt the texts they translate to the cultural norms of the target language. This type of translation has been called *covert* by House (1997); its characteristic is that the translator employs a cultural filter in order to retain the function of the original text and provide forms with an equivalent function in the target language.

This paper examines the extent to which culture-specific strategies for the realization of requests and suggestions are found in translation practice and discusses cases in which the choice of a different strategy has been culturally necessary as well as cases in which it has been culturally superfluous. Moreover, it addresses the question of how data from translations can give us insight into the pragmatically equivalent forms for the realization of requests and suggestions by comparing the strategies chosen in the translation to results from empirical studies on the degree of conventionality and politeness of particular strategies in particular languages. The data are collected from novels and plays (source languages: German, English, Russian; target languages: English, German, Greek, Italian, Russian); the empirical studies were conducted with native speakers of the languages in question.

2. The notion of pragmatic equivalence

2.1 Pragmatic equivalence and intercultural communication

The object of pragmatics is utterance rather than sentence meaning (i.e. conventional meaning, lexical meaning). Utterances are realizations of sentences, they are events tied to the participants' time and space. The same sentence produced in different situations is a different utterance every time and can have different meanings.

According to Geis, utterance meaning (what he calls utterance significance, S-meaning) includes two aspects. First, utterances have a *transactional* significance, i.e. "they contribute to the achievement of the transactional effect of the interaction" (Geis 1995:33). The transactional effect is one of the goals participants have when they enter interaction and it corresponds to Searle's (1969) essential condition (Geis 1995:35). Speakers intending to perform a certain speech act can phrase their utterances differently. The transactional significance of an utterance consists of the way it is used to address the felicity conditions (propositional content condition, preparatory condition, sincerity condition) of speech acts.

The second aspect of utterance meaning is its *interactional* significance, the contribution of an utterance to face work.[1] Utterances with the same

[1] Face, a key concept in Brown and Levinson's theory of politeness (Brown and Levinson 1978, 1987) is the "public self image that every member <of a society> wants to claim

transactional significance can differ in terms of style, register and degree of politeness, i.e. they can have a different interactional significance.

Pragmatic equivalence includes both transactional and interactional equivalence. Two utterances are pragmatically equivalent if they can be used in the same context and have the same transactional and interactional effect, i.e. if they realize the same speech act and support the relationship between the participants to the same degree. Pragmatic equivalence is an issue that can be the source of problems in intercultural communication. Early papers on the topic (e.g. Thomas 1983 or Wierzbicka 1985) have pointed out some of the problems that can arise in this context.

An utterance like (1), which is a literal translation from Polish, may be produced by a Polish native speaker in order to offer a seat to a distinguished Australian guest.

(1) Mrs. Vanessa! Please! Sit! Sit!

The equivalent of (1) in Polish is a cordial offer and therefore appropriate in addressing a guest. Its English counterpart, however, sounds like a command – a as Wierzbicka comments, "in fact, like a command addressed to a dog" (1991:27) – and therefore is not pragmatically equivalent. An English native speaker would have used in the given situation a formal offer like any of the ones in (2):

(2) Will you sit down?
Won't you sit down
Would you like to sit down?
Sit down, won't you? (Wierzbicka: ibid)

Further research on the realization of speech acts in different languages (e.g. the Cross Cultural Speech Act Realization Project, CCSARP, reported in Blum-Kulka *et al.* 1989) has shed light on typical cases of misunderstandings in intercultural communication, such as those illustrated above and below, in (3). Searle's (1969) claim for universal rules governing the realization of speech acts has been relativized since "pragmalinguistic conventions have ... been found to differ across cultures" (Barron 2003:26). It has been found that the same speech act (e.g. a request) in the same situation is realized in different ways in different languages. The difference in the forms of realization can be roughly described in terms of

---

for himself" (1987:61) and consists of negative face, the individual's need to be free from imposition, and positive face, the need to be liked and appreciated by other members of society.

directness or indirectness[2] or more specifically in terms of sentence type (declarative, interrogative, imperative), particles (interrogative, e.g. *li* in Russian; negative, e.g. *ne* in Russian, *den* in Greek; or modal e.g. *doch* in German), politeness markers (*please*, *bitte*, etc.) minimizers or diminutives (cf. (2) above and (3) below). A certain strategy may be a possible realization form for the same speech act in a couple of languages but may still not be conventionalized to the same degree in both languages. As Comrie (1984b:282) points out

> ... in English one polite way of getting someone to do something is by asking a yes/no question using either some form of *will* or some form of *can*. In other languages, that is not conventionalized. If you tried it in Russian, the reaction would be 'What is this guy trying to do?'

On the other hand, one conventional neutrally polite strategy for performing requests in Russian is negative questions (cf. Mills 1992 and Comrie 1984a:43). Consider the following question, a direct translation from Russian into English:

(3) Don't you know where X is? (Comrie 1984:30)

Example (3) is an appropriate, 'explicitly polite' way of asking a stranger for information in Russian. The same strategy employed in English in the same situation (approaching a stranger and asking for information) is inappropriate since the speaker "seems to be implying that he has a definite right to elicit this piece of information from <the hearer>, but that he has such a low opinion of <the hearer's> intelligence that he doubts whether <the hearer> will be able to give him the information" (Comrie 1984a:29f.). It is this implication that makes the negative question sound rude in this context. This example shows that the use of a given form in the same situation in two different languages does not necessarily guarantee pragmatic equivalence.

In other words, the literal transfer of a strategy from one language to another may accomplish the same transactional effect (realize the same speech act, e.g. a request or a suggestion) but have a different interactional effect (be more or less polite, more or less formal, etc.). If a speaker is not aware of the interactional significance of strategies in a foreign language and

---

[2] According to the distinction between a direct and an indirect speech act (Searle 1975) or to Brown and Levinson´s (1978, 1987) distinction between bald on record strategies and on record with redress. But cf. also Wierzbicka (1991:88) for objections to the distinction between direct and indirect speech acts.

literally transfers a strategy of the native language to the foreign language with the conviction that he or she is using the pragmatically equivalent form, then the result can be what Thomas (1983) has described as **cross cultural pragmatic failure**.

2.2 Pragmatic equivalence as a goal of translation

The aim of translation is to produce an equivalent text in the target language. The notion of equivalence is, however, relative (cf. Koller 1995). In her Model for Evaluating Translation, House (1997) proposes that the type of equivalence which is called for in a certain act of translation depends on the type of text, and on that basis she distinguishes between two different types of translation: **overt** and **covert** translation. Overt translation is similar to a quotation; the translator tries to preserve the original as much as possible and to make his or her audience aware that the original text was intended for some other audience, members of a different culture, usually at some different point in time. For this reason it should be applied to texts that are source-culture-specific, have "a certain status in the source language community (and therefore) must remain as intact as possible given the necessary transfer and decoding in another language" (House 1997:68).

Covert translation, on the other hand, involves more than just transferring a text from one language to another. The aim of the translator is to reproduce the whole function of the original without letting the audience realize that they are dealing with a translation and not with a text originally produced in the target language. The text is reproduced in such a way as to achieve the same effect on the audience in the target language as it did on the audience in the source language. In order to accomplish this aim, the translator focuses on the pragmatic meaning rather than the semantic meaning of the original text and aims at pragmatic equivalence. Covert translation should be applied on texts that are "not particularly tied to the source language and culture" (House 1997:69). The task of the translator is not only to transfer the text from one language to another but to adjust it to the sociocultural framework of the addressees in the target language. For this purpose, he or she applies a **cultural filter** (cf. House 1997:70ff.) which replaces sociocultural features of the source text with their equivalents in the target culture. Such culturally conditioned differences that the cultural filter is designed to accommodate are found for instance in communicative preferences, mentalities, values, social norms and politeness norms (cf. House 1997:74, 1998:66).

The transformations that such a filter effects are specific for every source language/target language pair. House proposes that the changes and modifications of the pragmatic parameters a translator is allowed or even obliged to make in the process of translation should be determined by the results from empirical surveys in which the two languages in question are compared.

The translation of speech acts is one case in which the application of a cultural filter is necessary if the translator's aim is pragmatic equivalence. The realization of speech acts reflects a culture's values (Wierzbicka 1991). In cultures in which cordiality and affect play a significant role (e.g. Slavic and Mediterranean cultures), direct and positive politeness forms are favoured, whereas cultures in which the individual's autonomy is not to be restricted favour indirect (negative politeness) forms.[3] As a result, the notion of politeness is defined differently in different cultures. For Slavic people politeness means showing affection, for Anglo Saxon showing deference-respect.[4] Consider the following two Polish utterances (from Wierzbicka 1991:51f.):

(4) Wez'jeszcze 'sledzika! Konieczie!
Take some more dear little herring. You must. (lit.: necessarily)

(5) Jureczku, daj me papierosa
George-DIM-DIM, give me a cigarette

The offer in (4) includes an imperative form and a form that expresses obligation; the request in (5) is also realized through an imperative, and therefore they both sound very imposing. However, in Polish both forms are appropriate in performing the respective acts: in the offer in (4) the speaker expresses his or her concern that the hearer gets enough to eat; in the request in (5) use of the imperative implies that the speaker considers the hearer to be his or her friend and that he wants to indicate that there is no social distance between them. Moreover, the diminutives show the speaker's affection towards the hearer (in (5)) and his or her eagerness to give the hearer something which is good for him or her (in (4)). All these features (the expression of affection, of concern and the minimization of social distance) are, according to Wierzbicka, typical for the Polish culture and constitute the notion of politeness in it. If we are to translate (4) and (5) into English so that we get pragmatically equivalent utterances, we need forms that have the same interactional effect, i.e. degree of politeness. Since politeness is associated in English with deference rather than solidarity, the imperatives should be replaced by conventionally indirect forms that are appropriate for requests and offers.

---

[3] Wierzbicka herself proposes abolishing the distinction between direct and indirect speech acts (cf. fn 2).

[4] Similarly, Sifianou (1992) describes the English system of politeness as a negative politeness system that gives prominence to tact, and the Greek system of politeness, on the other hand, as a negative politeness system that emphasizes generosity.

This is exactly the task of the cultural filter: to replace those linguistic features of utterances in the source language that do not have the same interactional significance in the target language. In this case the filter aims at substituting respect for the individual's freedom of action (which is conveyed by conventionally indirect forms like "Won't you have..." or "Can you give me...") for concern and affection which can be embarrassing and are therefore avoided in English.

3. Some results from discourse completion tests

3.1 Requests and suggestions

Requests and suggestions are directive speech acts. In both cases the predicated act will be performed by the hearer (or in the case of some suggestions by the hearer and the speaker together) so they are similar to the extent that in both acts the face threat potential lies in the speaker impeding the hearer's freedom of action (i.e., the hearer's negative face) by telling him or her what to do. On the other hand there is a difference between the two acts that makes them suitable objects for crosscultural comparison: in requests the act is in the interest of the hearer, whereas in suggestions it is in the interest of the speaker, either exclusively or at least partly – cf. Edmondson and House's (1981) distinction between **suggest-for-you** ("Why don't you try a new hairdo?") and **suggest-for-us** ("Let's go to the cinema!"), and Kallia (in preparation). What is happening in suggestions then is that the mere content of the act conveys that the speaker cares for the hearer and by doing so orients to the hearer's positive face, which can make the threat to the negative face involved in the directive nature of suggestions secondary. Brown and Levinson (1978:103) acknowledge the expression of caring about the hearer as a reason to perform a face threatening act (i.e. a suggestion) baldly on record (i.e. in the most direct possible way) rather than with redress or off record.

The relation between the two acts is reflected in the fact that they can be realized by the same forms. To begin with, they can both be realized directly through the imperative. Moreover, typical suggestion forms can be used for the realization of requests. The speaker either includes him- or herself in the performance of the act (inclusive *we*, *let's*) or uses an impersonal construction (*what about...?*) to distract attention from his or her person as beneficiary of the act. To a lesser extent, request forms can be employed for the realization of suggestions. The speaker thus implies that he or she sees the interests of the hearer as his or her own. However, this strategy involves some risk, as Banerjee and Carrell (1988) have found out in an empirical study. Non-native speakers who employed a request form for the realization of a suggestion sounded offensive.

3.2 The empirical study

The data I discuss below are part of a larger empirical study on the realization of requests and suggestions and possible misunderstandings in intercultural communication (Kallia, in preparation). The data were collected by means of a discourse completion test (DCT). The subjects were given a questionnaire with four pairs of situations (see Appendix 1). In every situation there were two participants; by the description of the situation (which was kept minimal so as not to influence the subjects' choices too much), it was obvious that a certain act was relevant. What was occasionally left open, however, was whether the act would be performed by the hearer or the speaker (or both). The two situations of a given pair were identical, with only one difference: in one situation the act would be in the interest of the speaker (the aim being to elicit a request) and in the other in the interest of the hearer (the aim being to elicit a suggestion). The subjects were asked to write down what they thought the speaker would say in each situation; they were not instructed to be specifically polite, however. The DCT was open ended, that is, the subjects were not given the hearer's response to the utterance they were asked to provide so that the subjects had considerable freedom.

All situations were constructed to involve a relatively limited face threat. The reasoning is that the greater the amount of face threat involved in an act the greater the possibility that an indirect strategy or a hint will be employed, even by members of a culture that favours directness. So it is in these acts that the differences across languages can be observed. Moreover, it is more realistic to expect subjects to provide single utterances for the realization of minor rather than major face threatening acts. The greater the face threat involved the more likely that the speaker will use side acts like pre-sequences, apologies and justifications. So I hoped to collect data that reflected actual use, knowing the limitations of DCTs (Beebe and Cummings 1996).

The general weightiness of the acts (W) involved in the situations of the DCT are calculated by using Brown and Levinson's (1978, 1987) formula, i.e. as the sum of three factors: the Power (P) one participant has over the other, Social Distance (D) between the participants and Rating of the imposition involved in the act (R). This gives us the values shown below:

Situation pair 1/2: request (2)/suggestion (1) to open a window (R1) between friends (P 0, D 0)
Situation pair 3/4: request (4)/suggestion (3) to open a window (R1) between strangers (P 0, D 1)
Situation pair 7/8:[5] request (8)/suggestion (7) to make coffee (R2) between friends (P 0, D 0)

[5] Situation pair 5/6 is not included in the present discussion.

I have assigned the values 1, 2 and 3 to show the augmentation of a factor. The rating of the factors is not absolute but comparative in the given situations. The value zero (0) is assigned to indicate absence of the factor in question. So, situation pairs 1/2 and 3/4 differ in the distance between the participants (friends vs. strangers), whereas situation pairs 1/2 and 7/8 differ in the rating of the imposition (opening a window vs. making coffee).

3.2.1 Requests

	Situation 2: P 0, D 0, R1 (window, friends)	Situation 4: P 0, D 1, R 1 (window, strangers)	Situation 8: P 0, D 0, R 2 (coffee, friends)
English	*Could you?* *Would you mind?*	*Could you?* *Would you mind?*	*Do you mind?* *Could I have?* *What about?*
German	Imperative *bitte/ doch* (markers): *Mach bitte/ doch auf!* (Open please) Direct question: *Machst du mal auf?* (Are you opening?) *Würdest du/ kannst du?* (would you/can you?)	*Könnten Sie/ würden Sie* (could you/would you?)	*Könntest du/ kannst du* (could you/can you?) *Wie wäre es*? (How would it be?)
Greek	Imperative: *Anixe!* (Open) Direct question (neg): *(Den) anigis?* (Are(n't) you opening?)	Direct question (neg): *(Den) anigete?* (Are(n´t) you opening?) *Tha sas piraze na?* (Would you mind?)	Direct question (neg): *(Den) kanis?* (Are(n´t) you making?) *Ti les gia* (what do you say about?) Suggestion (1st p. pl.): *As kanume* (Let's make)
Italian	Imperative: *Apri!* (Open) *Potresti* (could you?) *Ti spiace?* (do you mind?)	*Può* (Can you?) *Le dispiace* (do you mind)	Direct question: *Fai?* (Are you making?) Suggestion (1st p. pl.): *Facciamo* (Let's make)
Russian	Imperative: *Otkroj!* (Open)	Imperative: *Otkrojte!* (Open) *Ne mogli by vy* (couldn't you?)	*Ne mogla by vy?* (couldn't you?)

Table 1. Most frequent strategies for the realization of requests

Direct strategies (imperatives, performatives, direct questions)[6]
Conventionally indirect (questioning willingness, ability and suggestory formulae)

Table 1 outlines the most frequent strategies used by native speakers in every situation. I did not compare the strategies quantitatively, since the percentage of occurrence of a strategy is not important for identifying pragmatically equivalent forms. The point here concerns the strategies that can possibly occur in a given situation, according to native speakers. In Situation 2, which has the lowest weightiness value of all (no distance, minimal imposition), only direct strategies are used in Greek and Russian, both direct and conventionally indirect strategies are used in German and in Italian and only conventionally indirect strategies are used in English. In situations 4 and 8, which have a somehow greater weightiness (either because the distance or the imposition has increased), we get conventionally indirect strategies in all five languages and the use of direct strategies is obviously reduced. Russian and Italian subjects seemed to be particularly sensitive to a certain factor and not to the general weightiness of the act. Italians avoided direct strategies when there was social distance between the participants (situation 4), whereas Russians used imperatives in situation 4 but employed conventionally indirect strategies in situation 8, in which there was no distance between the participants but the imposition was greater.

3.2.2 Suggestions

	Situation 1: P 0, D 0, R1 (window, friends)	Situation 3: P 0, D 1, R1 (window, strangers)	Situation 7: P 0, D 0, R2 (coffee, friends)
English	*Why don't you?* *You should*	*You could* *Why don't you?*	*You need* *Do you want?*
German	Imperative: *Mach auf!* (Open)	Imperative: *Machen Sie auf!* (Open)	Imperative: *Trink!* (Drink)
	Warum (why) question	*Sie könnten* (you could)	*Willst du?* (do you want?) *Wie wäre es?* (How would it be?)
Greek	Imperative; *Anixe!* (Open)	Direct question (neg): *(Den) anigete?* (Are(n't) you opening) Imperative: *Anixte!* (Open)	Direct question neg: *Den kanis?* (Aren't you making)
	Giati (why) question (neg)	*Thelete?* (do you want?)	*Thelis?* (do you want?) Suggestion (1st p. pl.): *As kanume* (Let's make)

[6] A question like *Machst du mal das Fenster auf?* (Are you opening the window?) realizes a strategy without a literal equivalent in English, which, however, exists in all the other four languages.

Italian	Imperative: *Apri!* (Open)	*Vuole* (do you want?')	Imperative: *Prenditi* (get yourself) Direct question: *Fai?* (Are you making)
	Vuoi? (do you want?)		suggestion (1st p. pl.): *Facciamo* (Let's make)
Russian	Imperative: *Otkroj!* (Open)	Imperative: *Otkro-jte!* (Open)	Imperative: Sdelaj! (Make!)
	Mozhno (It is possible that)	*Vi mozhete* (you can)	*Nuzhno* (It is necessary that)

Table 2. Most frequent strategies for the realization of suggestions

Again, English speakers were the only subjects that refrained completely from using direct strategies. Greek speakers, as in requests, employed both direct and conventionally indirect strategies. German speakers included direct forms for the realization of suggestions in all three situations, which may mean that they consider suggestions to be less face threatening than requests. The Italian data showed the same distribution of direct and indirect strategies as in requests: no direct strategies occurred in situation 3, in which there is distance between the participants. This confirms the importance of the D factor in Italian. Finally, Russian speakers used direct forms in all three situations. As with the German data, this seems to imply that suggestions are perceived as less face threatening. This is supported by the results from the request situations. In situation 8, in which the R factor was comparatively high, the Russian subjects avoided direct strategies. In the parallel suggestion situation 7, in which the act is in the interest of the hearer, direct forms were employed.

4. The data from literary translation

Having established the pragmatically equivalent forms in these five languages, the next step is to see whether these forms are also found in data taken from translations. The hypothesis is that pragmatically equivalent forms are to be expected since the context in which these forms occur is identical in both languages and the translator has communicative competence (as defined by Canale 1983) in both languages. For my research I chose three English novels, one German novel and three Russian plays and their translations in the other four languages (see Appendix 2), texts that call for covert (rather than overt) translation. Part of the job the cultural filter has to do is, for example, to transfer direct forms to indirect ones (and vice versa), depending on the cultural values of the target culture.

4.1 Direct strategies

According to the results from the DCT, direct forms are not expected to be found in English for either requests or suggestions. Nevertheless, Russian and German imperatives are translated into English as imperatives in the great majority of the requests and suggestions found in the source texts. (In the other three target languages the imperative is acceptable, according to the DCT-results). Examples (6) and (7) are typical cases of requests with low weightiness, realized by a direct form (imperative) in the source language (German in (6) and Russian in (7)) and translated by an imperative in all other languages, including English, in which the pragmatic equivalent would be a conventionally indirect form.

(6) SL German (C):[7] Request P 0 D 0 (S is H's husband)[8] R 1
"Und bring den Aschenbecher mit" (Imp.)

TL English	And *bring* the ashtray (Imp.)
TL Italian	E *porta* il posacenere (Imp.)
TL Greek	Ke *fere* ke to tasaki (Imp.)
TL Russian	i *prichvati* pepelqnicu (Imp.)

(7) SL Russian (S): Request P 0 D 0 (S is H's mother) R 1
"Kostja, zakroj okno!" (Imp.)

TL English	Kostya *shut* the window (Imp.)
TL Italian	Kostja, *chiudi* quella finestra (Imp.)
TL Greek	Kostja, *klise* to parathiro (Imp.)
TL German	Kostja, *mach* das Fenster zu (Imp.)

Quite often the English imperative is modified as in (8) with *please*, or in (9) with a *do*-imperative, presumably in an attempt to get rid of the impolite reading the bare imperative has in English. Note that the R factor is increased in both (8) and (9) compared to (6) and (7). (In (9) the speaker asks her brother, Leonid, to give "him" the money they owe to him.) The interesting thing is that although the translator is probably aware that the imperative in English is not the pragmatically equivalent form (since it sounds more authoritative or impolite) he or she does not choose a different strategy (e.g. a conventionally indirect form) but sticks to the strategy used in the original and tries to modify it, either by using the politeness marker *please* (cf. §4.2 below) or the auxiliary *do* which softens the imperative (Bublitz 1978:190). In (8) it is only in English that a marker like *please* is

[7] See Appendix 2 for the sources of the examples.

[8] I explain the relationship between speaker (S) and hearer (H) in brackets following the D-value.

added. In the other three TLs bare imperatives are used although in the SL *doch*, a modal particle, accompanied the imperative (for the function of *doch* also cf. §4.2 below).

(8) SL German (C): Request P 0 D0 (S is H's brother) R2
"Spiel die Mazurka doch noch einmal." (Imp.)
TL English *Please play* the Mazurka again (Please Imp.)
TL Italian *Suona* ancora una volta quella mazurca (Imp.)
TL Greek *Pexe* mu alli mia fora ti mazurka (Imp.)
TL Russian *Sygraj* mazurku ewe raz (Imp.)

(9) SL Russian (CO): Request P 0 D 0 (S is H´s sister) R2
"Ty daj, Ljeonid...daj" (Imp. Imp.)
English: *Do give* it (i.e. the money) to him Leonid ...
Do let him have it (do-Imp. do Imp.)

Only in few cases are direct strategies translated into English through a conventionally indirect form, so that we get pragmatically equivalent forms. Examples (10)-(15) are the only instances in my whole corpus of data in which we get this difference. A closer look at these examples shows that there are some good reasons that justify the initiative on the part of the translator to employ an altogether different strategy in the target language. In (10) we have a routine situation, a request to speak to someone on the phone. The literal translation of the German utterance (*Please connect me with your daughter*) would have sounded not (only) impolite but (also) unnatural, since the *can I /may I* question is conventionalized for this function in English.

(10) SL German (C): Request P 0 D 1 (S is H's son, but he is pretending to be a stranger) R1
"Verbinden Sie mich bitte mit Ihrer Tochter." (Imp. bitte)
TL English *May I please* speak to your daughter? (May I please)

In (11)-(13) we have acts with increased weightiness. In (11) the request is addressed by a starving man to a baker, in (12), similarly, the request is addressed by a young man who cannot afford to buy a pack of cigarettes to the owner of the shop. In both situations the speaker wants to have non-free goods for free, which increases the size of the imposition R (Thomas 1995:130). In (13) there is both age and status difference between the participants (the speaker is the caretaker's young daughter and the hearer is the elderly owner of the estate). Moreover, the act, i.e., "speaking to the speaker's father", takes some effort since the caretaker is a very authoritative and stubborn person, very difficult to talk to. The increased weightiness makes the shift to conventional indirectness necessary.

(11) SL German (C): Request P 0 D 1 (S and H are strangers) R 3
"Schenken Sie mir ein Brötchen." (Imp.)
TL English *Could you* spare me a roll? (Could you?)

(12) SL German (C): Request P 0 D 1 (S and H are slightly acquainted) R 2
"Schenken Sie mir noch eine Schachtel Zigaretten." (Imp.)
TL English *May I have* a pack of cigarettes, too? (May I have)

(13) SL Russian (S): Suggestion P 0 D 1 (S =young female, H = elderly male, acquainted) R 1
"Govorite s moim otcom sami." (Imp.)
TL English *You'd better* speak to father yourself. I shan't (You'd better)

In the following two examples the weightiness is not increased if we measure it with the three variables proposed by Brown and Levinson. However, in both examples the variable of affect has quite aa high value. In (14), the speaker addresses her old and sick brother. The affect is also demonstrated in the original both with the *-ka* ending, a particle that softens imperatives and makes them more polite (Berger 1998:38f.), and the address form *starik*, literally 'old man'. In (15) the speaker addresses his wife. Slugoski and Turnbull (1988) have also pointed out that affect, the emotional closeness (or distance when there is lack of it), is a variable that possibly determines the degree or type of politeness of an utterance (but cf. Field 1991 for different results when positive affect is combined with familiarity). So we can claim that in examples (14) and (15), like (11)-(13), the choice of a positive politeness form (i.e. the speaker expresses that he knows what is good for the hearer) is motivated by the factor of affection.

(14) SL Russian (CO): Suggestion P 0 D 0 (S is H's younger sister) R 1
"ostavajsja-ka, starik, doma." (Imp.-ka)
TL English *You'd better* stay at home, old thing. (You'd better)

(15) SL German (C): Suggestion P 0 D 0 (S is H's husband) R 1
"Ah, du hast einfach überempfindliche Ohren, nimm was dagegen." (Imp.)
TL English *You'd better* take something for it (you'd better)

4.2 Politeness markers

We have seen in §4.1 how in most cases direct strategies were literally transferred into the TL, even when they are not conventionalized in a given TL, e.g. English. It seems that translators do not feel at liberty to change syntactic and semantic properties of utterances. An area in which translators seem to be operating more freely is the use of politeness markers in translation.

'Politeness marker' is a broad term that includes different kinds of downgraders and upgraders which enhance the politeness effect of an utterance (House and Kasper 1981). I will restrict the discussion here to "optional elements added to an act to show deference to the interlocutor and to bid for cooperative behaviour, e.g. please/bitte" (House and Kasper 1981:166). These words and their counterparts in the other languages (*pozhalujsta* in Russian, *per favore*/*prego* in Italian and *parakalo* in Greek) are prototypically associated with politeness, especially in requests and offers.[9] Politeness markers can be inserted or left out in translation without disturbing the structure of the sentence.

After all, *doch* is a discourse particle that occurs in all sentence types and not just in imperatives and that shows contrast. This is the case in both examples below in which *doch* is employed in the German translation. In (16) the speaker, a middle aged married woman who is in love with the hearer, asks him to take her with him away from her husband even though she knows that the hearer does not love her. In (17) the speaker asks her father, the authoritative caretaker of the estate, to let her husband have a horse so that he can ride back home, even though she knows that the hearer does not allow anyone, not even the owner of the estate, to use the horses for purposes other than the work at the estate.

(16) SL Russian (S): Request P 0 D 1 (S=female, H=male, acquainted) R 3
"Evgenij, dorogoj, nenagljadnyj, vozmite menja k sebje" (Imp.)
TL German Lieber, einziger Jewgeni, *nehmen Sie* mich *doch* zu sich
(Imp. doch) (lit: Evgenij, dear, unique, take me to you)

(17) SL Russian (S): Request P 0 D 0 (S is H's daughter) R 2
"Papa, pozvolq muzhu vziatq loshadq" (Imp.)
TL German Papa, *erlaube doch* meinem Mann, dass er ein Pferd nimmt
(Imp. doch) (lit: Papa, allow my husband to take a horse)

4.3 Conventional Indirectness

The conventionally indirect forms in English have been found to be equivalent to direct forms in the other four languages in acts with low weightiness. In translating conventionally indirect forms the translators seem to be able to employ a direct strategy more readily than the other way round (cf. §4.1). In (18) we get imperatives in German and Greek, in (19) in German

[9] These markers are in fact so closely connected with requests that House (1989) proposes an analysis of *please* and *bitte* as **requestive markers**. Still, the point remains that together with *thank you*/*danke* etc. they are considered the polite thing to say in everyday communication.

and Russian. The conventionally indirect forms employed in the Russian translation in (18) and in the Greek translation in (19) are compatible with the findings from the empirical research, too. In Italian we get conventionally indirect forms in both examples, but this is not unexpected considering how decisive the D factor has been found to be in the data from DCT for both requests and suggestions.

(18) SL English (OE): Request P 0 D 1 (S=detective interrogating H, a witness) R 1
"Mr. MacQueen, *will you* tell me, quite honestly, exactly how you regarded your employer?" (Will you?)
TL German Mr. MacQueen, *sagen Sie* mir *bitte* ganz ehrlich, ob Ihnen Ihr Arbeitgeber sympathisch war. (Imp. bitte)
TL Italian Signor MacQueen, *vuole dirmi* con assoluta franchezza che cosa pensava del signor Ratchett (Do you want?)
TL Greek Kirie Makkuin, *gia peste* mu endelos ilikrina: Pos vlepate ton ergodoti sas? (gia (imp. particle) Imp.)
TL Russian Vy mozhete skazatq...? (Can you?)

(19) SL English (OE): Request P 0 D 1 (S=detective interrogating H, a witness) R 1
"*Will you* write your address down here?" (Will you?)
TL German Und *schreiben Sie* mir *bitte* Ihre Adresse auf. (Imp. bitte)
TL Italian *Vorrebbe avere la bontà* di scrivere qui il suo indirizzo? (Would you want to have the kindness?)
TL Greek *Borite na* grapsete sto harti afto ti diefthinsi sas? (Can you?)
TL Russian *Zapishite pozhalujsta* vas adres (Imp. pozhalujsta)

5. Conclusions

Comparison of the realization strategies for requests and suggestions in translation data reveals an overall tendency on the translators' part to stick to the type of strategy (direct or indirect) used in the SL. Therefore, we cannot claim that a cultural filter is employed. The cultural values of the TL as reflected in the strategies employed for the realization of the speech acts are not taken into consideration. This tendency is especially strong when the strategy in the SL is direct and the pragmatic equivalent in the TL (according to empirical research) would be an indirect one. Nevertheless, the translators quite often insert politeness markers to accompany the direct forms so that interactional equivalence is somehow achieved. The appropriate degree of politeness is conveyed but not necessarily the same degree of style, part of which is colloqualism. It seems that the translators are unwilling to change the type and the structure of a sentence and they try to make up for its inadequate interactional significance by adding politeness markers. This leads to the conclusion that the cultural filter is not consciously employed. Indirect strategies are used only when the general weightiness of the act is increased, so that the direct form would be overtly rude. In other words, the cultural filter is employed in cases of emergency. On the other hand, there is a somehow more frequent tendency to use direct strategies, in a TL that favours directness, for the translation of indirect forms.

Generally, the results from translation data are not reliable quantitatively, i.e. if we are interested in establishing the most frequent strategies employed in a certain language. English translations of German and Russian texts feature numerous imperatives, which are untypical of English original texts. Even if they are modified, for example by *do*, they may not sound rude, but still their frequent occurrence is unnatural. Thus, we cannot claim that we are dealing with covert translation, since the translation does not read as an original. If covert translation is indeed the goal in literary translation then the findings from empirical research should be applied.

However, data from translations are worth considering in those cases where there is a difference in the form employed in the TL, even if this does not happen as a rule. Every instance in which a strategy is changed, a politeness marker is added or left out indicates that the literal translation would not have been pragmatically equivalent. Data from translations thus provide negative evidence for pragmatic equivalence. They help us locate the forms that are so unacceptable in the TL in a given context that the translator takes the liberty to modify them. It is these cases in which the application of the cultural filter is compulsory that can give us insight into cultural differences between a given pair of languages (the TL and the SL).

References

Banerjee, Jacqueline and Patricia L. Carrell (1988) '"Tuck in Your Shirt, You Squid." Suggestions in ESL', *Language Learning* 38: 313-64.

Barron, Anne (2003) *Acquisition in Interlanguage Pragmatics*, Amsterdam: John Benjamins.

Beebe, L.M. and M.C. Cummings (1996) 'Natural Speech Act Data Versus Written Questionnaire Data: How Data Collection Method Affects Speech Act Performance', in Susan M. Gass and Joyce Neu (eds) *Speech Acts across Cultures: Challenges to Communication in a Second Language*, Berlin: Mouton de Gruyter, 65-86.

Beerbom, Christiane (1991) *Modalpartikeln als Übersetzungsproblem. Eine kontrastive Studie zum Sprachenpaar deutsch-spanisch*, Frankfurt a. M.: Lang.

Berger, Tilmann (1998) 'Partikeln und Höflichkeit im Russischen', in Tilmann Berger and Jochen Raecke (eds) *Slavistische Linguistik* 1997, München: Sagner, 29-53.

Blum-Kulka, Shoshana, Juliane House and Gabriele Kasper (eds) (1989) *Crosscultural Pragmatics*, Norwood, N.J.: Ablex.

Brown, Penelope and Stephen C. Levinson (1978) 'Universals in Language Usage: Politeness Phenomena', in E.N. Goody (ed.) *Questions and Politeness*, Cambridge: Cambridge University Press, 56-289.

------ (1987) *Politeness: Some Universals in Language Usage*, Cambridge: Cambridge University Press.

Bublitz, Wolfram (1978) *Ausdrucksweisen der Sprechereinstellung im Deutschen und Englischen. Untersuchungen zur Syntax, Semantik und Pragmatik der deutschen Modalpartikeln und Vergewisserungsfragen und ihrer englischen Entsprechungen*, Tübingen: Narr.

Canale, M. (1983) 'From Communicative Competence to Communicative Language Pedagogy', in Jack C. Richards and Richard W. Schmidt (eds) *Language and Communication*, London: Longman, 2-27.

Comrie, Bernard (1984a) 'Russian', in William S. Chisholm, Jr. (ed.) *Interrogativity. A Colloquium on the Grammar, Typology and Pragmatics of Questions in Seven Diverse Languages*, Amsterdam: John Benjamins, 7-46.

------ (1984b) 'Plenary Session', in William S. Chisholm, Jr. (ed.) *Interrogativity. A Colloquium on the Grammar, Typology and Pragmatics of Questions in Seven Diverse Languages*, Amsterdam: John Benjamins, 255-87.

Edmondson, Willis and Juliane House (1981) *Let's Talk and Talk About It*, München: Urban & Schwarzenberg.

Field, Susan E.O. (1991) *On Saying Unpleasant Things: An Experimental Investigation of Politeness Theory*, Ph.D. Diss., Harvard University.

Geis, Michael L. (1995) *Speech Acts and Conversational Interaction*, Cambridge: Cambridge University Press.

House, Juliane (1989) 'Politeness in English and in German. The Functions of 'Please' and 'Bitte'', in Shoshana Blum-Kulka, Juliane House and Gabriele Kasper (eds) *Crosscultural Pragmatics*, Norwood, N.J.: Ablex, 96-121.

------ (1997) *Translation Quality Assessment: A Model Revisited*, Tübingen: Narr.

------ (1998) 'Politeness and Translation', in Leo Hickey (ed.) *The Pragmatics of Translation*, Clevedon: Multilingual Matters, 54-71.

------ and Gabriele Kasper (1981) 'Politeness Markers in English and German', in Florian Coulmas (ed.) *Conversational Routine*, The Hague: Mouton, 157-86.

Kallia, Alexandra (in preparation) *Directness as a Source of Misunderstanding: The Case of Requests and Suggestions*.

Koller, Werner (1995) 'The Concept of Equivalence and the Object of Translation Studies', *Target* 7: 191-222.

König, Ekkehard (1997) 'Zur Bedeutung von Modalpartikeln im Deutschen. Ein Neuansatz im Rahmen der Relevanztheorie', *Germanistische Linguistik* 136: 57-75.

Mills, Margret H. (1992) 'Politeness in Russian Requests', *Russian Linguistics* 16: 65-78.

Searle, John R. (1969) *Speech Acts: An Essay in the Philosophy of Language*, Cambridge: Cambridge University Press.

------ (1975) 'Indirect Speech Acts', in Peter Cole and John Morgan (eds) *Syntax and Semantics 3: Speech Acts*, NY: Academic Press, 59-82.

Sifianou, Maria (1992) *Politeness Phenomena in England and Greece: A Cross-Cultural Perspective*, Oxford: Clarendon Press.

Slugowski, B.R. and William Turnbull (1988) 'Cruel To Be Kind and Kind To Be Cruel: Sarcasm, Banter and Social Relations', *Journal of Language and Social Psychology* 7: 101-121.

Thomas, Jenny (1983) 'Cross Cultural Pragmatic Failure', *Applied Linguistics* 4: 91-112.

------ (1995) *Meaning in Interaction*, London: Longman.

Wierzbicka, Anna (1985) 'Different Cultures, Different Languages, Different Speech Acts: Polish vs. English', *Journal of Pragmatics* 9: 145-78.

Wierzbicka, Anna (1991) *Cross Cultural Pragmatics. The Semantics of Human Interaction*, Berlin: Mouton de Gruyter.

Appendix 1

Questionnaire for the elicitation of strategies for the realization of requests and suggestions

First Questionnaire

Dear participant,

Below you have 8 situations. In every situation you are asked to write exactly what the person in question would say.
Please do not read all the situations at first but reply to one at a time, in the order they are given.
The length of the utterance you give may vary from one word to several sentences, length is not important, as long as the utterance sounds natural.
It is important for you to understand that we are in no way giving you a mark on your responses. There are no right or wrong answers. Sometimes more than one answer might be appropriate, if you think this is the case. Please feel free to offer alternatives.
Thank you very much for your participation.

Situation 1
John and Christine are sitting in a room. The door and the windows are closed. Christine says: "Oh, dear, it's so warm in here!". John believes that Christine will feel cooler if she opens the window.
John:

Situation 2
John and Christine are sitting in a room. The door and the windows are closed. Christine feels warm and she believes that she will feel cooler if John opens the window.
Christine:

Situation 3
Mr. Peters and Mrs. Moore are sitting in doctor X's waiting room. The door and the windows are closed. Mrs. Moore says: "Oh, dear, it's so warm in here!". Mr. Peters believes that Mrs. Moore will feel cooler if she opens the window.
Mr. Peters:

Situation 4
Mr Peters and Mrs. Moore are sitting in a room. The door and the windows are closed. Mrs. Moore feels warm and she believes that she will feel cooler if Mr. Peters opens the window.

Mrs: Moore:

Situation 5
Thomas has been invited to dinner by his professor and he asked his friend George to come with him to his professor's house. When Thomas goes to pick George up he sees that George is wearing a pair of jeans and a T-shirt. Thomas believes that one should dress formally for such an occasion.
Thomas:

Situation 6
Thomas has been invited to dinner by his professor and he asked his friend George to come with him to his professor's house. When George goes to pick Thomas up he sees that Thomas is wearing a pair of jeans and a T-shirt. George believes that one should dress formally for such an occasion.
George:

Situation 7
Ann and Kathryn are friends and they are studying for an exam at Ann's place. Ann has yawned several times and Kathryn believes that she needs some coffee.
Kathryn:

Situation 8
Ann and Kathryn are friends and they are studying for an exam at Ann's place. Kathryn feels sleepy and she believes that she needs some coffee.
Kathryn:

Appendix 2

Texts (only the ones quoted):

OE ***Christie, Agatha.*** *Murder on the Orient Express.*

Translations
German: *Mord im Orient Express.* ***Scherz Verlag. (transl. by E. van Bebber)***
Italian: *Assassinio sull'orient Express.* ***Oscar Mondadori. (transl. by Alfredo Pitta)***
Russian: *Vostocnij Ekspress.* ***Pravda. (transl. by L.Bjespalovoj)***
Greek: *Eglima sto Expres Orian.* ***Lichnari. (transl. by A. Kiriazi)***

C ***Böll, Heinrich.*** *Ansichten eines Clowns.*

Translations
English: *The Clown.* ***Penguin. (transl by L Vennewitz)***

Italian: *Opinioni di un clown.* ***Aernoldo Mondadori. (transl. by Amina Pandolfi)***
Russian: *Glazami klouna.* ***Progress. (transl. by L. Cernaja)***
Greek: *I apopsis enos kloun.* ***Grammata. (transl. by T. Mastoraki)***

CO ***Cechov, Anton.*** *Vishnevij Sad.*

Translations
German: *Der Kirschgarten. Diogenes.* ***(transl by P. Urban)***
English: *The Cherry Orchard.* ***Dent & Sons. (transl. by S.S. Koteliansky)***
Italian: *Il giardino die ciliegi.* ***Oscar Classici Mondadori. (transl. by G.Guerrieri)***
Greek: *O vissinokipos.* ***Dodoni. (transl. by L. Kallergis)***

S ***Cechov, Anton.*** *Caika.*

Translations
German: ***Die Möwe.*** *Diogenes.* ***(transl by P. Urban)***
English: *The Seagull.* ***Dent & Sons. (transl. by S.S. Koteliansky)***
Italian: *Il Gabbiano.* ***Oscar Classici Mondadori. (transl. by G.Guerrieri)***
Greek: *O glaros.* ***Dodoni. (transl. by L. Kallergis)***

5. Interactional Translation

ANTJE WILTON
University of Erfurt, Germany

Abstract. *In this chapter, a phatic non-professional interpreting event is investigated involving humorous talk between multilingual interactants at the dinner table. Participants in this event interact with one another and, at the same time, assume the responsibility of interpreting spontaneously, i.e. without any previous arrangement having been made. This constellation is thus characterized by the fact that interactants take on a double role as primary interactants and mediators. The results of the analysis show that the interpreters, in their attempt to create functional equivalence, tend to oscillate between these different roles, leading to role conflicts and problems in interpreting humorous talk.*

1. Introduction

1.1 Translational activities in everyday interaction

While translation theory has traditionally focused on the written text, considerable interest has also developed recently in oral translation or what is generally termed 'interpreting'.[1] The main focus of research in interpreting is directed towards professional settings such as conferences or the courtroom, where oral translations are required. Naturally, the emphasis in the investigation of interpreting in such settings must be placed on the quality of the service which is provided by specially trained and paid experts and the assessment and the training of their performance. Questions of fidelity and the adequacy of content remain just as important as in written translation.

Since the 1990s, research related to interpreting has largely been oriented towards the use of empirical data and the investigation of less institutionalized forms of oral translation such as semi-professional, community and dialogue interpreting; see for example Carr *et al.* (1997), Knapp-Potthoff and Knapp (1986 and 1987), Mason (1999), Wadensjö (1998), Bührig and Meyer (1998, 2004), Bührig (2001). While examining those forms of semi-institutionalized interpreting, researchers have come to regard the role of the lay interpreter and the interpreting event as an interactional event situated in a particular social context:

---

[1] For a discussion on the scope and relationship of Translation Studies (TS) and Interpretation Studies (IS) see Schäffner (2004), for example.

> This growing body of interpreting research which focuses on the micro-interactional context represents a significant shift in perspective within interpreting studies. It claims a role for interpreters as actively shaping locally produced communicative practices and characterizes interpreted events as a form of sociolinguistic activity, not merely exercises in decontextualised linguistic transfer. (Inghilleri 2004:73)

The latter, however, has long been the norm for interpreters in formal settings:

> from a normative point of view, the products of Dialogue Interpreter-activity are (or rather, should be) provided in between each and every original utterance, and are copies of these, re-corded in another language. All information explicitly expressed in a primary party's original, including the style and form in which it is expressed, is relayed as closely as possible; i.e. the propositional content explicit in the original utterance (the "what") is relayed, with approximately the same illocutionary force (the "how"). As one notes, this norm concerns only the interpreter as *text-producer*. (Wadensjö (1993/2002:357)

The strong restraints placed on the participants in a professional setting become more relaxed in an informal setting. Though it might sound trivial, this in fact has a considerable influence on the way in which informal interpreting is analyzed. First of all, it has become necessary to use data from actual encounters as the basis for an analysis in order to be able to identify the methods interactants use to establish the conversational structure of an interpreter-mediated event. Secondly, the analysis of the data shows that there are significant changes in the way language is mediated, that it moves away from strict preimposed rules towards more local and more flexible forms of interpreting:

> In professional and institutional settings, the function of an interpreter is comparable to that of a machine, rewording what is said in language A in language B and vice versa. [...] In less formal situations, the third person similarly has to process longer stretches of discourse and to render them into the other language. However, he or she is not in the same way restricted in his or her functions. Apart from transmitting what is said by the primary interlocutors, he or she within certain limits may develop his or her own initiatives, introduce new topics, give comments and explanations, present arguments etc., thus becoming a more or less true third party. (Knapp and Knapp-Potthoff 1987:182)

Nevertheless, research on interpreting is still very often based on situations for which the three-party-model of the interpreting process with more or less fixed participant roles can be applied for the duration of the encounter:

> In all situations in which interpreting occurs there are at least three parties: the primary interlocutors, i.e. those persons who want to communicate with each other, but whose respective languages A and B are mutually unintelligible. They can be referred to as speaker A (S_A) and speaker B (S_B). The third party is the interpreter. (*ibid.*)

This is also true of most of the data used in interpreting research which is based on conversation analytic methods. Conversation analysis focuses on natural data taken from everyday spoken discourse. It seeks to discover the mechanisms of organisation underlying a seemingly unorganized and chaotic activity such as everyday conversation. Unlike in most institutional settings, the roles of the interactants, the distribution of turns, the choice of the topic and the activity in everyday conversation are not predetermined externally but rather negotiated *in situ* by the interactants themselves (Sacks *et al.* 1978). This is achieved by the conversation participants by employing a turn-taking system which itself is context-free and thus functions as the basic underlying system of conversational organization. At the same time, it is context-sensitive to allow for the specific characteristics of the given conversation. In her conversation-analytic research of institutional interpreting, Apfelbaum (1998a) shows that the turn-taking system enables participants to construct some institutional features of the setting locally by contextualizing the allocation and construction of their turns. She concludes that

> mit dem Untersuchungsinstrumentarium der Konversationsanalyse auch die "Institutionsspezifik" von Instruktionsdiskursen mit Dolmetscherbeteiligung rekonstruierbar ist und damit prinzipiell die interaktive Konstruktion aktivitätstypspezifischer Teilnehmerrollen aufgezeigt werden kann. (Apfelbaum 1998a:33)
> [the specific "institutional nature" of instructional discourse can be reconstructed using the research instruments provided by conversational analysis and that the interactive construction of activity-specific participant roles can thus also be characterized]

Müller (1989) looks at natural translational activities in everyday interaction "as a member's activity and as a continued mode of interaction, introduced, organized and handled by members of bilingual or multilingual participant constellations" (1989:713). He argues that "natural lay translation modes admit a much wider variety of possible realizations and applications than do professional ones" (*ibid.*). Translation activities serve a specific purpose within an ongoing interaction and their implementation is negotiated and accomplished by the interactants according to their needs and the problems they encounter during the interaction. Müller illustrates this aspect by comparing "natural lay translation [...] with direct, unmediated conversation on the one hand and with a professional, 'monolithically' applied mode on the other" (*ibid.*:714). He shows how participants judge the level of transparence in their linguistic repertoires and adjust the mode of translational activity according to their needs. Müller points out that the features of professional translation or interpreting are

> open to negotiation and to change in natural translation: Neither must the institution of translation be installed once and for all of the span of the encounter, nor is the role of the translator invariably tied to one participant, nor must the language serving as a bridging medium and the directionality of the translations invariably remain the same, nor do translators always limit themselves to their duty and remain just 'voice' for other 'authors' without ever claiming auctorial rights as speakers contributing also on their own behalf. (*ibid.*:720).

Everyday conversation in bilingual settings not only necessitates the negotiation of the roles of the interactants, the distribution of turns, the choice of topic and activity, interactants must additionally negotiate how to employ the languages which are available. The interactants must evaluate the compatibility of the linguistic repertoires present in the group: the less compatible they are, the greater is the need for translational activities. On the other hand, if the linguistic repertoires are fairly compatible, the need for translational activities becomes less urgent. Therefore, it is not surprising that the need for translation in everyday conversations among bilinguals and thus in a combination of roles typical of an interpreter-mediated event arises spontaneously at specific points during the interaction rather than in a predetermined fashion. Furthermore, compatible linguistic repertoires allow for a greater flexibility in the creation of the translational activity itself. Such instances of translatory action in less clearly defined combinations have thus far received little attention as translation/interpreting activities in their own right; in fact, they are probably located at the very edge of the already much broadened scope of the definition of what counts as a translation.[2] Nevertheless, they are worthy of analysis as a very

[2] See, for example, Wadensjö (1993/2002:356), who poses the question of minimal criteria in order for a copy to count as a copy at all in the context of identifying renditions in dialogue interpreting.

specific and very flexible form of translatory action, as will be illustrated by the data samples discussed below.

1.2 Humorous activities in everyday interaction

For most people, the prototype of conversational humour is the orally delivered joke. The telling of a joke in a conversation, however, is only one of many different forms of humorous activities that do not occur very often and, when they do, usually only under specific circumstances. More typical of informal everyday interactions are humorous activities such as teasing, the telling of anecdotes, gossiping, etc. These are actually complex forms of interaction and are employed in order to establish and maintain social relationships. They are highly dynamic and creative and demand as a "Form der Kunst im Alltag" *Form of art in everyday life*, Kotthoff (1998:362), a high level of conversational expertise on the part of the interactants. Humorous activities range from the occasional witty remark causing others to laugh to well-constructed funny stories occupying longer stretches of conversation. Some activities can be said to have an identifiable structure and can therefore be called communicative genres. This is particularly obvious with activities such as the telling of a joke (Sacks 1974), but also teasing activities, for example, have been shown to have a distinct if more flexible interactional structure (Günthner 1996). Most humorous activities that are employed in everyday interactions, however, have a fairly open conversational structure with few fixed elements. One such element is the punch line, which is not only a necessary feature of the joke but also of a funny story or anecdote. The desired result of such a punch line is mutual laughter, one of the highest forms of interactional involvement. Shared laughter is an important event in social situations:

> Extended laughings together become memorable, reportable, and storyable events. They offer relationally potent moments which may contribute to group solidarity, developing romance, or hurt feelings. Like other social activities [...] laughings together occur, not accidentally or randomly, but through recognizable, systematic means. (Glenn 2003:53)

It is obvious that humorous activities have great social potential. Some forms may be (potentially) aggressive, such as teasing and gossiping, and need to be employed carefully if they are to contribute to group solidarity. As the perception of something as humorous or funny is highly subjective, engaging in humorous activities always involves the danger of alienating or offending certain members of the group. If mutual laughter is achieved, however, the interactants openly display their (shared) interpretation of the situation as funny, thus profoundly affecting group solidarity.

Another characteristic of successful conversational humour (and of humour in general) is the fact that it builds on shared and often implicit knowledge. It uses and exploits ambiguities, vagueness, and the poetic potential of language. It alludes to shared stocks of knowledge, refers to past experiences or evokes fictitious images. It is this feature of humour that makes its employment in intercultural encounters a frequently cited cause of miscommunication. Conversational humour in particular is highly context-bound and very group-specific and thus must be viewed as an ethno-category, i.e. the humorous value of an activity must be judged by the interactants' reactions and not by some extra-contextual definition of humour.

Finally, conversational humour is constructed interactively. Active recipient participation is typical of conversational humour, for instance in the form of anticipatory laughter while listening to a funny story or in the form of mutual laughter as a reaction to a shared humorous experience. A very typical feature of many humorous activities is the extension of this pleasurable experience by reshaping the punch line over and over again until its humorous potential is exhausted. The interactants employ prosodic, stylistic and sequential measures such as contextualisation cues (Gumperz 1982) to indicate their humorous interpretation or intention and to invite the others to share in it.

To sum up, it can be said that conversational humour is very dynamic, immediate, implicit, highly involving and demanding with respect to the level of conversational skill. It is only to be expected that such a conversational activity is regarded as critical not only in intercultural but also in mediated settings.

1.3 Translational activity and conversational humour

Humour and translation are a difficult combination. Humour is usually avoided in professional contexts and hardly ever commented on, except insofar as to advise the translator to keep clear of it. If at all, humour is either mentioned as a possible result of stylistic devices (Spillner 1980) or treated as a marginal feature not important enough to translate. If humour figures into the context at all, it appears in the traditional and written genres of jokes or puns, which are indeed difficult to translate (Koller 1992:258). As with other instances of creative language use, certain strategies exist for dealing with humour depending on the aim of the translation: if the content is the important aspect, a neutralized rendering could be a solution; if the function is the important aspect, then substituting the humorous text with a functional equivalent in the target language might be suitable. It is very difficult, however, to find a strategy that combines information transfer (neutralization) with functional equivalence (substitution).

As explained above, conversational humour is a common and important phenomenon in informal interactions and is difficult to ignore when the situation requires interpreting. The question then becomes how the interactants deal with such a task (e.g. Bührig 2004). Given a sufficient compatibility of linguistic repertoires in bilingual settings, there might be the possibility for interactants to largely avoid interpreter-mediated situations by choosing one of the languages as the language of conversation (*exolingual communication)*, Lüdi (1987). Sometimes, however, side sequences or parallel conversations develop in the other language that might have to be interpreted in order to be comprehensible for everybody. The reason why a particular stretch of conversation is selected for translation might be due to the wish to convey the information contained in the humorous activity. More often, the desire exists to share the experience of laughter with the others while at the same time pass on some, though not necessarily all, of the information. It is obvious that the interactants are faced with a formidable task: given the demands of conversational humour and the complex interactional coordination of oral translation, it seems that a combination of both can only result in chaos or, at the very least, in an unsatisfactory conversational experience, the natural flow of conversation being impeded and artificially constructed. It is therefore all the more surprising to witness bilingual conversations in which interactants converse and laugh with ease, with the fact that they have to deal with two languages seeming to enhance rather than spoil their entertainment.

2. The data

The examples to be discussed in the following section are taken from a corpus comprised of about 11 hours of mainly English-German bilingual everyday conversations. The corpus served as the basis for a qualitative conversation analytic PhD study conducted by the present author in accordance with the principles of ethnographic conversation analysis (*Ethnographische Gesprächsanalyse*) as described by Deppermann (2001). This work investigates certain aspects of the communicative behaviour of a group of people. The study identifies and analyzes specific communicative practices employed by the interactants in various interactional tasks. The interactions examined in this study are examples of everyday communication in an extended bilingual family and consist of stretches of conversation among the family members during their gatherings, usually around mealtimes. The core members of the family are MIA, a German, and BOB, an Englishman, and their two children. All four of them are bilingual, BOB and MIA having native-like competence in their respective L2s. The German side of the extended family includes MIA's parents (RIA and UWE), her brother (JAN), her aunt (IDA) and her aunt's partner (LEO). The English side includes BOB's mother (SUE), sister (ANN) and brother-in-law (TOM). Whereas the Germans display a variety of competence levels in English ranging from rudimentary to fluent, the English family members can hardly speak any German at all and are barely able to follow a conversation in German. Thus, it is only natural that the preferred language of conversation for the mixed gatherings be English, with occasional stretches or parallel conversations in German. These stretches of German conversation tend to trigger the kind of translational activity described below.

The informal table talk of the group in question was audio-recorded with the participants' consent. The tape recorder was set up as unobtrusively as possible and after a few initial comments, the participants carried on with their conversations as normal. Those stretches of conversation were then selected that displayed the features desired for analysis. This selection was guided by the sequential development of humorous activities as described by Kotthoff (1998) and by shared laughter. Humorous activities were not identified according to my own interpretation of their humorous value but as an ethno-category: a stretch of conversation was labelled 'humorous' if interactants themselves indicated their perception of humour in the interaction. The stretches selected were then transcribed according to the conventions of GAT (*Gesprächsanalytisches Transkriptionssystem*); Selting *et al.* (1998).

As mentioned before, a holistic, conversation-analytic approach was used based on ethnographic conversation analysis. This necessitated a very detailed step-by-step analysis of the data, the subsequent identification and description of conversational activities and practices, and their interpretation with the help of ethnographic knowledge about the group.

3. Interactional translation

From a conversation analytic point of view, natural lay interpreting in everyday spoken discourse exhibits a variety of translational activities which are designed to fulfil specific functions in a bilingual setting. One of those activities is the so-called *interactional translation*. Interactional translation is a conversational activity with an identifiable sequential ordering and an expandable boundary for the end of the activity. It mostly occurs over longer stretches of talk and is accomplished and used by the interactants as a multifunctional resource for achieving specific interactional goals. Interactional translation is not established as a continuous mode for the larger part or the entire length of the conversation, nor is it exclusively used in side-sequences to clarify lexical problems. Interactional translation occurs when it is specifically needed during the interaction in order to meet the particular demands of the situation. Such a demand is the recreation of a humorous activity in the other language not only with respect to the information conveyed but in particular with respect to the function of the activity for the group. With respect to the needs of the interactants in everyday spoken interactions, this kind of translational activity exhibits specific features compared to other interpreter-mediated events with respect to

(1) the role of speaker/interpreter/listener
(2) translation as a process
(3) translation as a product
(4) its suitability for the translation of humorous activities.

Although oral translation is commonly referred to as 'interpreting' in scientific research and in practice, I have chosen the more general term 'translation' for the following reasons.

Firstly, it is important to emphasize the fact that interactional translation is not a professional form of interpreting and does not follow the above-mentioned pattern (see also Knapp and Knapp-Potthoff 1985:457) of professional or even semi-professional activities. This statement is in line with Harris' reasons for terming oral translation conducted by lay people *natural translation*:

> it [language] is spoken before it is written, and the spoken form is still more widespread in the world than written texts. It follows that most *natural* translation is oral translation. It is true that there is oral translation in professional translation too. The professionals do not call it translation, they call it "interpretation"; but the name need not trouble us – it is still translation and it is taught in translation schools. (Harris 1978:422)

Secondly, the term's orientation towards the general meaning of transferring material from one state to another (translation) stresses the idea that from a conversation analytic view not only verbal content is transferred, but also conversational activity or forms of sequential organization: despite the coining of new terms such as dialogue or liaison interpreting, which can refer to less rigid forms of interpreting, the term 'interpreting' itself seems to be too narrowly confined to the transfer of oral textual material from one speaker via another speaker to a listener and vice versa.

Thirdly, it is important to conceptualize interactional translation as an ethno-category: in everyday language, people commonly ask for or offer a 'translation' of something, not an 'interpretation', although they are clearly using oral methods to accomplish their task.[3] It is therefore true that the

[3] See, for instance, Apfelbaum's title "I think I have to translate first…" (Apfelbaum

everyday term used by the lay person for the transfer of spoken discourse into another language is 'translation' and 'translate' and not 'interpreting' and 'interpret'. The choice therefore reflects the terminology of the participants themselves.[4]

A conversation analytic approach to such flexible everyday translational activities may shed light on the perception and handling of cultural differences and/or the problems of its participants in multicultural and multilingual communication situations.

3.1 Data sample Platzwahl

Consider the following example:[5]
Platzwahl (choice of seat)

001 RIA: **BOB willst du dich HIERhin setzen, neben deine [frau,**
BOB DO YOU WANT TO SIT HERE NEXT TO YOUR WIFE
002 BOB: [<<pp>
003 **ich hol-> (--) <<p>> NE; NE:, (.) um gottes willen.**
I'll get no no for god's sake
004 **nein.**
no
005 MIA: **[(ne:) das wär ja auch ne [zumutung.**
NO THIS WOULD BE AN IMPOSITION
006 RIA: **[NÄ:?**
NO
007 IDA: **[NE? (was?) wieso.**
NO WHAT WHY
008 BOB: [he he he he he he
009 RIA: <<lachend> OH gott; [JA:.> HE HE HE HE HE HE
010 IDA: [MIA. (--) he .HHHE: .HHHE: .HHE
011 .hhe (---) **[<<p> soso.>**
WELL WELL
012 MIA: **[wir HEI[raten.**
WE'RE GETTING MARRIED
013 BOB: *[RIA (was) just asking whether i*
014 *wanted to SIT down next to my wife.*
015 (---)

1998b). Other examples from the data include "you'll have to translate my joke" and "translate that into German".

[4] This is also true for the German language. Moreover, German allows for a variety of terms for translational activity as well as the slightly different use of the term translation (*Übersetzung*) itself, as pointed out by Pöchhacker (2004:108).

[5] Transcription notation GAT (Selting *et al.* 1998, see appendix)

016 SUE: [*OH.*
017 BOB: *[<<p> i said> for god=s sake NO;*
018 SUE: he [HE HE HE HE he
019 IDA: [he he he .hhe [.hhe
020 RIA: [HE HE HE
021 BOB: [he
022 RIA: *it=s early;* hm, hmhm[hmhmhm
023 IDA: *[d=ye:s.*
024 BOB: .hhm
025 MIA: *[<<f> NOT YET MARried and [already-*
026 IDA: [(XXXXX)
027 ???: [sch::::
028 IDA: *(you should think [of it)*
029 SUE: [((Räuspern)) *yeah.*
030 IDA: [‘eh
031 BOB: [.hhm .hhm
032 IDA: <<lachend> *(till) TUESday.*> [.hhe he he [he
033 BOB: [.hhm

In this stretch of conversation, RIA asks BOB whether he would like to sit down next to his wife. BOB starts to answer RIA's question by indicating that he is about to leave to get something when he interrupts himself in mid-turn to redesign his answer as an ironic refusal of RIA's offer. RIA, IDA and MIA confirm his introduction of the humorous activity by joining in themselves: they display mock understanding (line 5), indignation (lines 6 and 7), and laugh. In line 13, BOB repeats RIA's question to SUE, who is a monolingual English speaker, in English. She gives a minimal response signalling understanding in line 16. BOB then goes on to translate his own answer to RIA's question, eliciting laughter from SUE and with minimal delay from IDA and RIA, too. Having thus established the original humorous activity in the translation, it is continued and expanded upon by the previous interactants, now with the inclusion of SUE acting as a recipient.

Interactional translation displays a systematic sequential organisation. The following structures can be identified in the above prototypical example:

1) An optional introductory phrase involving a code switch (line 13). Other examples from the data include:
   - er hat erzählt (he told)
   - he says
   - hat der BEN das gesagt (did BEN say that)
   - RIA just said
2) The uptake and remodelling of some aspect of the previous interaction in the new language with a new recipient design (line 13-14)

3) The response (often minimal) of the new addressee (line 16)
4) Further development of 2), usually with co-participation of the other participants (line 17 onwards).

After the translational activity has been completed, a seamless transition to further interaction is achieved without overt translational features as the new stretch of discourse develops its own dynamic. Interactive translation has no marked ending and is specifically designed to lead into talk which is unmarked as a translation. In the following example, the translational activity occupies a considerably longer stretch of conversation:

3.2 Data sample Karnevalsprinz

The data sample ***Karnevalsprinz*** (Prince of the Carnival) is a particularly valuable sample, as it illustrates the recreation of a humorous activity by giving it a new recipient design with the help of interactional translation. It is also especially useful for the conversation analyst in that it illustrates the underlying knowledge of the phenomena discussed here and its employment in conversational humour and interactional translational activity.

Karnevalsprinz

001 RIA: **der JAN (---) hat UWES mutter eine (1.0) autogramm**
JAN SENT UWE'S MOTHER AN AUTOGRAPH
002 **geschickt vom AA:chener KA:Rnevals[prinzen.**
BY THE AACHEN CARNIVAL PRINCE
003 BOB: **[mein gott.**
MY GOD
004 RIA: [hihihi
005 UWE: **[ne: BONN ne oder?**
NO BONN WASN'T IT
006 (--)
007 RIA: **ne: BONner (.) BONner karnevals[prinzen] ja genau bonner**
NO BONN BONN CARNIVAL PRINCE YES BONN
008 BOB: [hm=hm]
009 RIA: **karnevalsprinz prinzen. (--) weil der UDO heißt.**
CARNIVAL PRINCE PRINCE BECAUSE HE IS CALLED UDO
010 (--)
011 [hihi hihihi **UDO der erste;**
UDO THE FIRST
012 BOB: [hmhmhmhmhmhmhmhmhmhm hm hhhhm hmhm
013 (-)
014 UWE: **ham se draufgesch ham se draufgeschrieben- (.) für UTA von**
THEY WROTE ON WROTE ON IT FOR UTA FROM

015 **UDO dem ersten und LIZ der ersten.**
UDO THE FIRST AND LIZ THE FIRST
016 RIA: [hmhm[hmhm
017 BOB: [hhm [hhm
018 UWE: **[der JAN** ((schluckt)) **der JAN hat mir dat schon**
JAN JAN ANNOUNCED IT TO ME
019 **vorher angekündigt- (1.0) hat erst gefragt ob er dat**
BEFOREHAND HE ASKED IF HE
020 **machen könnte.=ich sach,=ja mach ma ruhig.**
COULD DO THIS I SAID YES GO AHEAD
021 RIA: hm=hm
022 (--)
023 UWE: **die steht ja auf prominenten ne,** [hehehe
SHE LOVES CELEBRITIES DOESN'T SHE
024 BOB: [hmhmhm
025 UWE: [hehehehehehe
026 MIA: **[jaja hat se uns die (-) OHren voll erzählt da wo se den-**
YES YES SHE TOLD US ALL ABOUT HER
027 **↑wen hat se im aufzug getroffen? (--) den (-) ach den**
WHO DID SHE MEET IN THE LIFT THE THE
028 **schwarzen da nich roy black; (.) jedenfalls- (3.0) wie**
BLACK ONE NOT ROY BLACK ANYWAY WHAT
029 **heißt der denn**.
IS HIS NAME
030 RIA: **roberto blanco.**
031 MIA: **roberto blanco.=**
032 BOB: =hmhmhmhmhmhmhmhm [hhhm
033 RIA: **[der heißt**
HE IS CALLED
034 RIA: **DER heißt blanco. (.) ist aber SCHWARZ und der [und der**
HE IS CALLED BLANCO BUT HE IS BLACK AND AND
035 BOB: **[der dürfte**
HE SHOULDN'T
036 RIA: **[roy black- (.) he (.) der roy black- heißt black ist**
ROY BLACK ROY BLACK IS CALLED BLACK BUT IS
037 BOB: **[eigentlich nicht so heißen;** hehe
BE CALLED THAT
038 RIA: **aber schwarz; [ist aber weiss;** hehehehehehe
BLACK IS WHITE
039 BOB: [hehehehehehe
040 UWE: ((räuspert sich)) **ne: sie hatte damals hat se**
NO SHE HAD IN THE PAST
041 **[zum beispiel-**
FOR INSTANCE
042 MIA: **[hat se sich gefreut?**
DID SHE LIKE IT

043 UWE: **jaja sicher die fand dat unheimlich lustig. [sonst hätt-]**
YES YES SURE SHE THOUGHT IT WAS VERY FUNNY OTHERWISE
044 MIA: **[ahja.]**
045 (--)
046 UWE: **ehm damals hat se ja sogar vom- (2.0) die war ja auch mal**
IN THE PAST SHE HAD EVEN FROM SHE WAS
047 **in bayreuth da hat se [vom wolfgang wagner [und vom**
IN BAYREUTH SHE GOT FROM WOLFGANG WAGNER AND FROM
048 BOB: *[MIAs brother-*
049 ANN: *[hm:*
050 BOB: *[(who was-)*
051 UWE: **[schock(wohl n) autogramm gekricht**
SCHOCK AN AUTOGRAPH
052 MIA: **ahso.**
053 BOB: ((räuspert sich))
054 MIA: **ich hab mal [eins von hendrik martz-**
I ONCE GOT ONE FROM HENDRIK MARTZ
055 BOB: *[(XX) studying as a journalist. (.) a as a*
056 *freelance journalist.*
057 ANN: *ouh yes,*
058 BOB: *and he was sent to- (1.5) write a report about th the*
059 *(1.0) [BONN CARnival-*
060 RIA: *[(bonn) carnival-*
061 BOB: *some bonn carnival thing.*
062 RIA: *[m::h very serious.*
063 ANN: [hhhm
064 BOB: *[but eh this this-*
065 UWE: *[princess of bonn.*
066 BOB: *[is humour-*
067 RIA: [HA hmhmhm[hmhmhmhmh
068 ANN: [hhhm
069 BOB: *humour pursued with great seriousness.*
070 ANN: hhm hm hm
071 RIA: *VEry serious.*
072 BOB: *and she HE got- (1.0) a signature from- (2.0) carnival*
073 *king and queen-*
074 RIA: hmhmhm
075 BOB: *dedicated to- (---) his grandmother.*
076 RIA: [hmhmhm
077 ANN: [hmhmhmhm hm
078 MIA: *it was (his) (-) the king was called- (1.0)*
079 BOB: *called-* [UDO UDO *is the name of her*
080 MIA: [UDO UDO
081 MIA: *her ex [boyfriend-*
082 BOB: *[eSRTA:NGED boyfriend.*

083 RIA: [hehehe
084 MIA: *[who lives lives still in the same house (X) in the top*
085 *flat and gets on her nerves; [(XXX*
086 ANN: [hehe hhhm hhhm
087 BOB: [hm hm
088 RIA: [hahahahahahahaha [hha

This stretch of conversation can be divided into two phases:

Lines 1-54 contain a conversation in German (**bold**); the topic is an anecdote from the German part of the family: JAN, UWE's and RIA's son, has sent his grandmother UTA the autograph of the Bonn carnival prince. The participants seem to find this amusing and laugh about it. They also ridicule UTA for her interest in local or minor celebrities. A brief play on words is embedded in the conversation about UTA centered around the names of two well-known German folk singers.

The conversation in line 48-88 switches to English and the anecdote is translated into English by BOB, MIA and RIA.

Again, the conversational structure of interactional translation can be identified: in line 48, BOB starts his translation of the anecdote, in this instance without using an introductory phrase and overlapping with MIA, who then gives the floor to BOB entirely in line 55. ANN signals her role as a recipient in line 49 and BOB continues with his translation. RIA and MIA join in; even UWE, whose command of English is rather rudimentary, makes a contribution (line 65). The successful delivery of the punch line is indicated by shared laughter (86-88). After this point, the conversation continues in English without any translational features. This part of the conversation is not printed here for space reasons.

Karnevalsprinz is a good example of the complex interactional structure that interactants establish in their conversations. In embarking on the translation of the funny anecdote, BOB is faced with the problem of implicit knowledge that is the basis for the humorous effect in the German version. RIA delivers her punch line in two steps: first, she describes the autograph being given and sent, saving the revealing of the celebrity until the end of her turn (line 2). In a second step, she reveals that the name of the carnival king was UDO (lines 9-11) and that this name was the reason why JAN got UTA the autograph in the first place. This is highly amusing for BOB, and he and RIA continue to laugh together until UWE begins to exploit the punch line by providing additional information on the event and his own punch line in line 23. The gossiping about UTA, which has a slightly malicious edge, continues and is expanded to include the ridicule of folk singers as a cooperative realisation of a humorous activity. The reason behind the initial humorous effect of the name UDO remains obscure to the external observer. From the design of the collaborative and also partly competitive translation by BOB and MIA that then follows, it becomes clear that this obscure piece of knowledge is also not familiar to ANN: if the humorous effect is to be achieved, the information has to be delivered in a different way than it was in the German version. Interactional translation enables BOB and MIA to do just that: instead of making the revelation of the king's name the punch line, they provide this information as part of the preparatory story section (lines 78-83). MIA then delivers the previously unknown fact that UDO is the name of UTA's ex-boyfriend as the punch line. The success of this strategy is illustrated by the shared laughter of ANN, BOB and RIA (lines 86-88).

In ***Karnevalsprinz***, the interactants manage to accomplish two tasks within the same stretch of conversation: they use the flexible structure of interactional translation to render an anecdote into English, i.e. they transmit information about a notable event in the past, while at the same time reshaping the delivery of the knowledge in such a way that the previous humorous activity can be reproduced in the English version. Not only does this integrate ANN into the group and their activities, it enables the bilingual participants to re-live the humorous activity in a modified form due to the relative compatibility of linguistic repertoires. As described above (see section 1.2), this enhances the enjoyment of a humorous activity rather than boring the interactants with a mere repetition. Furthermore, the example of the ***Karnevalsprinz*** illustrates the need to include ethnographic knowledge in an in-depth analysis of humorous activities: without the information given in the English translation, it would have been impossible to fully analyze the German section as an independent part of conversation because of its hidden references to family lore. As it is not to be expected that humorous activities in monolingual conversations need to be translated or otherwise explained, one should keep in mind that such implicit knowledge might not appear on the surface of the conversation at all.

3.3 Data sample Sauerbraten

Finally, interactional translation is employed in the following stretch of talk in which the teasing activity from the previous conversation is continued. Within the translation, the speaker is able to tease with impunity. He exploits his role of mediator, using interactional translation to scaffold his teasing. Once this is achieved, the tension is dissolved and the whole activity results in shared laughter. Following the teasing, the conversation continues unmarked.

Sauerbraten

009 RIA: **MIA du wolltest doch mal sauerbraten (machen ne? oder-)**
MIA YOU WERE GOING TO MAKE SAUERBRATEN SOME TIME, WEREN'T YOU
010 BOB: `HM:,
011 MIA: <<gleichgültig> **jo=jo-**>
YEAH YEAH
012 BOB: `HM:,=
013 MIA: =<<p> **hab ich gemacht;**>
I HAVE
014 RIA: hmhmhmhmhmhm
015 BOB: **hat mich aber muß ich sagen ziemlich kalt gelassen.**
I must admit I wasn't very convinced
016 RIA: **ja? [ja nu-**
YOU WEREN'T AH WELL
017 BOB: [he (.) hehehehehehehehe
018 (1.0)
019 RIA: **s:: sis schAde drum; ja doch- da verpaßte was;** [hehehe
WHAT A PITY YOU MISSED SOMETHING THERE
020 BOB: [he
021 **ja ja Eben;** [hehehehehehehe
YES EXACTLY
022 RIA: [hmhmhmhm
023 ((Geschirrklappern und Eßgeräusche für ca. 2.0 Sek.))
024 MIA: (XXXXXX).
025 RIA: <<zustimmend> m::h,> **(wie) immer.** hmhmhm
as always
026 (1.0)
027 BOB: *let me explain that to you; there is a local delicacy*
028 *known as (.)* **SAUerBRAten;**
029 (-)
030 ANN: hm=hm
031 BOB: *this (.) this involves [leaving meat*
032 ???: *[sour roast* **ja**
033 BOB: *to ROT-*
034 (--)
035 BOB: *[a:nd-*
034 MIA: *[it does !NOT! !ROT! you pickle meat in [vinegar and*
037 BOB: [HHHE HEHEHEHEHE
038 RIA: *[OUH*
039 MIA: *[spices.*
038 BOB: [HEHEHEH[EHE
040 RIA: *[OUH*
041 BOB: *[yes and e:hm it sort of MArinates i suppose; (-) e:hm-*

042 MIA: [(XXXX)
043 RIA: *[YE:S;*
044 MIA: **[ja;**
045 BOB: *yes; (.) it MArinates and MArinates and Marinates, (-)*
046 *[and=eh-*
047 RIA: [hm=hm, (.) *for a few DA:YS?*
048 ANN: [hm=hm,
049 BOB: [hm=hm,
050 RIA: *three or four DA:YS?*
051 ((Geschirrklappern 2.0 Sek.))
052 MIA: *and then (.) you you (.) FRY it with ehm you make a*
053 *sauce with the=that BREAD that i-*
054 BOB: <<pp> *thank you*>
055 ANN: *[ouh, yeah,*
056 MIA: *[eh that you had today,*
057 ANN: hm=hm,
058 MIA: *and tomato:- (.) so it=s a nice (-) dark brown;*
059 ANN: ↑hm::.
060 MIA: *gravy.*
061 BOB: <<all> *and this is what is*> *[KNOW:N,*
062 MIA: *[with RAIsins in it and*
063 *then you have red (--) cabbage?*
064 TOM: [<<rückfragend> *red, cabbage*?
065 MIA: [(spiced)
066 *red cabbage? and ehm potato dumplings with it; (.) [and*
067 ANN: [hm
068 MIA: *ehm (.) apple: e:h* <<p> **na** *apple*> *APple sauce;*
069 (--)
070 BOB: *and this is what [is known in*
071 ANN: *[sounds good-*
072 BOB: *england as an acQUIRED TASTE;*
073 ANN: *ou(h)u right,* hee hee hee
074 BOB: *it=s not everybody=s [cup of !TEA:!-*
075 ANN: *[cup of !TEA:!-*

In this example, BOB is being teased by RIA and MIA for his dislike of a German delicacy known as *Sauerbraten*. After a pause following the teasing activity, BOB addresses a non-participating interactant, ANN, in the other language (line 27). As above, this is done with an introductory phrase: "let me explain that to you". Following this introduction, the speaker continues talking about the previous subject, *Sauerbraten*, and after ANN's minimal backchanneling (`hm=hm` in line 30), he seizes his role as mediator in order to fulfill his own interactional goals. He tells ANN that *Sauerbraten* involves leaving meat to rot, thereby addressing MIA and RIA and continuing the teasing of which he was previously the target. His comment earns a hefty response from MIA, who identifies herself as the addressee of the teasing (line 34) and reveals BOB's strategy to the English interactants. Following the translation, ANN and TOM (line 64) become active participants in the conversation. Thus, the translation serves to integrate the English participants into the interaction while at the same time continuing the teasing activity with the German speakers. The change in language does not prevent RIA and MIA from participating in the English conversation. They contribute to the now detailed description of the preparation of *Sauerbraten*. With his contributions, BOB succeeds in giving the impression that *Sauerbraten* is not liked by everyone and can elicit laughter from ANN in line 73. It is at this point that he has finally justified his position as someone who has been unfairly teased and manages to bring ANN over to his side.

4. Conclusions: A specialized form of translatory action

The above examples have shown that interactional translation has an identifiable sequential structure, that it can be used in a variety of ways, and that it seems to be particularly useful in providing functionally equivalent renderings of humorous activities. On a superficial level, interactional translation does the following:

- It changes the language of interaction;
- It considers some aspect of the previous conversation (of the content and/or of the interaction);
- It integrates an interactant who, because of language problems, was not able to participate in the previous conversation.

During this process, however, there are potential dangers that might occur, such as

- Retarding or interrupting the conversation by repeating it for another participant;
- Alienating speakers not fluent in the target language;
- Exposing differences in language competence among the participants and therefore emphasizing those differences. This is not desirable in a group in which the aim of the interaction is to unify the group on a social level, as is the case here.

The type of translational activity must therefore be designed such that these dangers are minimized. The translator must integrate the new participant, knowing that there is the danger of excluding some of the other participants. The translator must repeat some aspect of the previous conversation for the new interactant; simultaneously, he or she must reshape it in a way so that the previous interactants are still involved or at least so that the ongoing conversation is not retarded through the repetition of known information. The application of the traditional turn-for-turn interpreting model is unsuitable for fulfilling all the requirements posed by the interaction. This is one reason why it is generally avoided by participants in everyday conversation (Müller 1989:736). Such a complex translational activity displays certain characteristics in the aforementioned areas (section 3).

4.1 The roles of speaker/interpreter/listener

As explained above, models of formal interpreter-mediated events often focus on the persons involved in the translation as transmitters of information, not as social interactants in their own right. This is not surprising, as professional interpreting is regulated by external requirements and thus follows a set pattern. The translator of a written text as well as the interpreter ideally subordinates his role as a full interactional participant[6] to his task of mediating discourse:

> The interpreter's own feedback should primarily reflect his perception and understanding, but not too many of his reactions. A feedback that is too personal can make the speaker feel that it is the interpreter who is the other interlocutor. This is in fact where the main risk lies if the interpreter acts as a deputy listener giving feedback. The interpreter's feedback should, therefore, be limited to showing only perception and understanding. (Englund Dimitrova 1997:163)

The mediator is asked to withhold his own judgements, goals, opinions, etc., and – in its most ideal form – simply acts as an invisible transformer of texts. Speaker/writer and listener/reader roles are also clearly defined. The speaker directs a message intended for the listener at the interpreter, who relates it to the listener. The listener then takes over the role of the speaker and the direction of transmitting is reversed.

Going along a continuum of progressively relaxed role definitions in moving from highly institutionalized interpreting to translational activities

---

[6] The desired degree of involvement of the interpreter differs according to culture. In Japan, for instance, the interpreter takes a more active role in certain cross-cultural interactions (cf. Trompenaars 1997:110)

in informal conversations, the translator in the discussed data samples neither has a fixed role as a translator nor is his role the outcome of explicit negotiation amongst the participants of the interaction. His main role is that of a fully competent and integrated interactant who takes on the role of translator at specific points in the interaction. He or she self-selects as a translator. Moreover, if the linguistic abilities of the participants allow it, more than one participant can take on the role of translator. This role is not invariably tied to one person but can rather be distributed flexibly among participants. While acting as a translator the speaker is not bound by any constraints and can act as an author in his or her own right.

Unlike in pre-determined interpreting settings, where speakers of source utterances are observed to design their talk to be translated in the next turn, the speakers in my data are unimpeded in their formulation by what they envisage to happen in the upcoming turns-at-talk. However, the translation activity might turn previous speakers into present listeners or even objects of talk, while integrating former passive listeners into the interaction, thereby making them active recipients. Translation changes the system of personal reference: persons-to-be-talked-to may become persons-to-be-talked-about (Müller 1989:729). Often, however, the original speakers are also capable of following or even participating in a conversation in their weaker language so that they are not fully excluded from the conversation after the code-switch and continue to contribute to the talk.

4.2 Translation as a process

Numerous different definitions of translation exist, most of which acknowledge that translation (and interpreting even more so) is in some way a process. The concept of process in traditional translation theory is based on the cognitive aspects of information processing and text production.

In oral translatory action, the process of mediating has been shown to be a systematically achieved and sequentially organized social activity. In more informal interpreter-mediated settings, the interactants have various means at their disposal for coordinating and constructing their talk:

> The emphasis on the shifting role of the interpreter in interactionistic accounts highlights how agency, despite being culturally or socially inscribed, is achieved in and through local, communicative practices – even in situations of institutionalised power asymmetry between interlocutors. It emphasises discursive freedom while at the same time, recognising that, in particular contexts, certain configurations of co-presence may serve to reproduce rather than challenge social/linguistic orderliness. (Inghilleri 2004:73)

In the data analyzed above, the interactants are able to employ translational activities which are

- very flexible
- sequentially organized
- interactively accomplished
- designed to allow the conversation to progress smoothly
- highly group-specific.

in order to master the particular requirements of the bilingual nature of the interaction. They actively shape their situation according to their needs. This is true both for the translator(s) as well as for the speaker and listener as they contribute to the ongoing interaction.

4.3 Translation as a product

Traditional theoretical views on translation see the target text as the product of translation and its relation to the source text as their object of research. Questions of quality and equivalence are of central importance. Equivalence of content (i.e. the message in terms of the sender-receiver model) plays a prominent role and is often the central requirement underlying definitions of translation:

> Translation may be defined as follows: the replacement of textual material in one language (SL) by equivalent textual material in another language (TL). (Catford 1965:20)

Alongside the desired equivalence, a target language text should ideally be adequate in the target language environment.[7] In natural everyday conversation, the data samples show a very flexible and function-oriented view of equivalence and adequacy on the textual as well as on an interactional level. Exact translation of content might occur but is not required, nor does a non-equivalent translation automatically lead to problems on either of these levels. The above examples make clear that equivalence can also be achieved on an interactional level: activities like teasing, storytelling or joking can be reproduced or continued in the course of the translation process. Another aspect is the cultural embeddedness of the interaction: culturally determined elements might make it necessary in a mediated encounter to neglect high equivalence of content between original and

---

[7] See Snell-Hornby (2006:25) for a discussion of the different types of equivalence and their relationship in the history of translation studies.

translation in favour of functional equivalence. Although the data show that textual equivalence in everyday spoken discourse does not have the same importance as is often asserted in traditional translation theory, it does play at least a small role in allowing for a stretch of speech to be recognized as a translation and not simply a code switch. The text produced during an interpreter-mediated event as an oral activity is ephemeral and has immediate effect in the ongoing interaction. There is little room for correction or improvement of the final product – the utterance - unless these are made part of the interaction. The judgement of the adequacy of the product of oral translation is therefore also immediate and can be accessed through the interactants' reactions towards the translator's utterances.

4.4 Interactional translation and conversational humour

Interactional translation has been identified in the context of humorous conversational activities. It is reasonable to assume that such a translational activity is particularly suited for the translation of humorous activities in informal everyday conversations. This assumption is supported by the following observations (see also Wilton 2005):

- The interactants avoid the employment of a rigid interpreting structure. Instead, the initial humorous activity is given room to develop and take effect before a translation is begun. This indicates that the translation is not planned beforehand but rather engaged in spontaneously at a point within the development of the interaction that is found suitable by the interactants.
- The equivalent translation of propositional content is possible but is not the main aim of the translational activity. On the contrary, humour often requires the modification of content to achieve its effect. Functional equivalence is therefore much more important than equivalence of content. In interactional translation, interactants are not primarily concerned with showing who said what to whom and instead with transferring the humorous activity and its dynamics across linguistic and cultural boundaries.
- The immediacy of face-to-face oral interactions necessitates flexible structures for the interactants to orient themselves towards. The flexibility of the structure of interactional translation takes the dynamic development of humorous activities into account and can accommodate *online*-modifications of structural elements such as punch lines.

- Interactional translation necessarily duplicates some aspect of the previous humorous activity. The repetition of punch lines either with or without modification is also a feature of conversational humour in monolingual contexts. The interactants exhaust the humorous potential of the activity through repetitions and modifications and thus enhance their enjoyment of the interaction. Interactional translation achieves this effect by transferring such repetitions and extensions into the other language.
- Conversational humour and the accompanying laughter are dependent on an interactively constructed activity. Interactional translation enables participants to actively shape the course of the conversation. Particularly the seamless transition into talk, which is unmarked as translation, enables a humorous activity to continue undisturbed.

As instances of intercultural communication, the data samples show how interactants successfully handle a potentially risky communicative situation: the transfer of humour. In terms of Alexieva's (1997/2002) multi-parameter typology of interpreter-mediated events, the above highly context-bound and group-specific interactions would have to be located towards the culture-specific end of her proposed 'universal' vs. 'culture-specific' continuum This in turn has an impact on the role of the translator:

> the task of the interpreter in events located towards the "culture-specific" end of the continuum [...] is more difficult to perform, and the interpreter therefore has a more important role to play: he or she has to actively intervene in the communication to prevent misunderstanding and smooth cultural differences [...]. In other words, the more an event is embedded in a particular culture (speaker's, or hearer's, or both), the greater the role of the interpreter as intercultural mediator and "repairer" and the more visible he or she becomes. (Alexieva 1997/2002:231)

As we have seen in the above analyses, interpreted conversations are characterized by the closeness of the interactants, their high level of involvement in the interaction, the informality of the setting, the orality of the communication, and the shared goal of striving to enhance group solidarity. Although the role of the translator as 'repairer' might not feature as prominently as Alexieva states for intercultural encounters, it is nevertheless true that the role of the translator in such encounters is a very special and highly demanding one.

References

Alexevia, Bistra (1997/2002) 'A typology of interpreter-mediated events', in Franz Pöchhacker and Miriam Shlesinger (eds) *The Interpreting Studies Reader*, London: Routledge..

Apfelbaum, Birgit (1998a) 'Instruktionsdiskurse mit Dolmetscherbeteiligung. Aspekte der Turnkonstruktion und Turnzuweisung', in Alexander Brock and Martin Hartung (eds) *Neuere Entwicklungen in der Gesprächsforschung*, Tübingen: Narr, 11-36.

------ (1998b) '"I think, I have to translate first..." Zu Problemen der Gesprächsorganisation in Dolmetschsituationen sowie zu einigen interaktiven Verfahren ihrer Bearbeitung', in Apfelbaum, Birgit and Hermann Müller (eds) *Fremde im Gespräch. Gesprächsanalytische Untersuchungen zu Dolmetschinteraktionen, interkultureller Kommunikation und institutionalisierten Interaktionsformen*, Frankfurt: IKO – Verlag für interkulturelle Kommunikation, 21-46.

------ and Hermann Müller (eds) (1998) *Fremde im Gespräch. Gesprächsanalytische Untersuchungen zu Dolmetschinteraktionen, interkultureller Kommunikation und institutionalisierten Interaktionsformen*, Frankfurt: IKO – Verlag für interkulturelle Kommunikation.

Bührig, Kristin (2001) 'Interpreting in hospitals', in S. Cigada, S. Gilardoni and M. Matthey (eds) *Communicare in Ambiente Professionale Plurilingue*, Lugano: USI, 107-119.

------ (2004) '"Che devo dire?" Zu einigen Möglichkeiten und Schwierigkeiten in der Thema-Rhema-Progression in der mehrsprachigen Familienkommunikation', in Juliane House, Werner Koller and Klaus Schubert (eds) *Neue Perspektiven in der Übersetzungs- und Dolmetschwissenschaft. Festschrift für Heidrun Gerzymisch-Arbogast zum 60. Geburtstag*, Bochum: AKS-Verlag, 151-172.

------ and Bernd Meyer (1998) 'Fremde in der gedolmetschten Arzt-Patienten-Kommunikation', in Birgit Apfelbaum and Hermann Müller (eds) *Fremde im Gespräch. Gesprächsanalytische Untersuchungen zu Dolmetschinteraktionen, interkultureller Kommunikation und institutionalisierten Interaktionsformen*, Frankfurt: IKO - Verlag für interkulturelle Kommunikation, 85-110.

------ (2004) 'Ad-hoc interpreting and achievement of communicative purposes in doctor-patient-communication', in Juliane House and Jochen Rehbein (eds) *Multilingual Communication*, Amsterdam & Philadelphia: John Benjamins, 43-62.

Carr, Silvana E., Roda Roberts, Aideen Dufour and Steyn Dini (eds) (1997) *The Critical Link: Interpreters in the Community. Papers from the First International Conference on Interpreting in Legal, Health and Social Service Settings. Geneva Park, Canada, June 1-4, 1995*, Amsterdam: John Benjamins.

Catford, J. C. (1965) *A Linguistic Theory of Translation*, London: OUP.
Deppermann, Arnulf (2001) *Gespräche analysieren*, Opladen: Leske and Budrich.
Englund, D. B. (1997) 'Degree of interpreter responsibility in the interaction process in community interpreting', in Silvana E. Carr, Roda Roberts, Aideen Dufour and Steyn Dini (eds) *The Critical Link: Interpreters in the Community. Papers from the First International Conference on Interpreting in Legal, Health and Social Service Settings. Geneva Park, Canada, June 1-4, 1995*, Amsterdam: John Benjamins, 147-164.
Glenn, Phillip (2003) *Laughter in Interaction*, Cambridge: CUP.
Günthner, Susanne (1996) 'Zwischen Scherz und Schmerz – Frotzelaktivitäten in Alltagsinteraktionen', in H. Kotthoff (ed.) *Scherzkommunikation*, Opladen: Westdeutscher Verlag, 81-108.
Gumperz, John J. (1982) *Discourse Strategies*, Cambridge: CUP.
Harris, B (1978) 'The difference between natural and professional translation', *Canadian Modern Language Review* 34: 417-27.
House, Juliane and Shoshana Blum-Kulka (eds) (1986) *Interlingual and Intercultural Communication. Discourse and Cognition in Translation and Second Language Acquisition Studies*, Tübingen: Narr.
Inghilleri, Moira (2004) 'Aligning Macro- and Micro-Dimensions in Interpreting Research', in Christina Schäffner (ed.) *Translation research and interpreting research. Traditions, Gaps and Synergies*, Clevedon: Multilingual Matters, 71-76.
Knapp, Karlfried and Annelie Knapp-Potthoff (1985) 'Sprachmittlertätigkeit in der interkulturellen Kommunikation', in Jochen Rehbein (ed.) *Interkulturelle Kommunikation*, Tübingen: Narr, 450-64.
Knapp-Potthoff, Annelie and Karlfried Knapp (1986) 'Interweaving two discourses – The difficult task of the non-professional interpreter', in Juliane House and Shoshana Blum-Kulka (eds) *Interlingual and Intercultural Communication. Discourse and Cognition in Translation and Second Language Acquisition Studies*, Tübingen: Narr, 151-169.
Knapp-Potthoff, Annelie and Karlfried Knapp (1987) 'The man or woman in the middle: Discoursal aspects of non-professional interpreting', in Karlfried Knapp, Werner Enninger and Annelie Knapp-Potthoff (eds) *Analyzing Intercultural Communication*, Berlin, New York, Amsterdam: de Gruyter, 181-212.
Koller, Werner (1992) *Einführung in die Übersetzungswissenschaft*, Heidelberg: Quelle and Meyer.
Kotthoff, Helga (1998) *Spaß verstehen. Zur Pragmatik von konversationellem Humor*, Tübingen: Niemeyer.
Lüdi, Georges (1987) 'Exolinguale Konversation und mehrsprachige Rede. Untersuchungen zur Kommunikation in Sprachkontaktsituationen', in Els Oksaar (ed.) *Soziokulturelle Perspektiven von Mehrsprachigkeit und Spracherwerb*, Tübingen: Narr, 76-100.

Mason, Ian (ed.) (1999) *Dialogue Interpreting, The Translator* 5(2).
Müller, Frank (1989) 'Translation in bilingual conversation: Pragmatic aspects of translatory interaction'. *Journal of Pragmatics* 13: 713-39.
Oksaar, Els (ed.) (1987) *Soziokulturelle Perspektiven von Mehrsprachigkeit und Spracherwerb*, Tübingen: Narr.
Pöchhacker, Franz and Miriam Shlesinger (eds) (2002) *The Interpreting Studies Reader*, London: Routledge.
Rehbein, Jochen (ed.) (1985) *Interkulturelle Kommunikation*, Tübingen: Narr.
Sacks, Harvey (1974) 'An Analysis of the Course of a Joke's Telling in Conversation', in Richard Bauman and Joel Sherzer (eds) *Explorations in the Ethnography of Speaking*, Cambridge: CUP, 337-53.
------ Emanuel Schegloff A. and Gail Jefferson (1978) 'A simplest systematics for the organization of turn-taking for conversation', in Jim Schenkein (ed.) *Studies in the Organization of Conversational Interaction*, New York, London: Academic Press, 7-55.
Schäffner, Christina (ed.) (2004) *Translation research and interpreting research. Traditions, Gaps and Synergies*, Clevedon: Multilingual Matters.
Schenkein, Jim (ed.) (1978) *Studies in the Organization of Conversational Interaction*, New York, London: Academic Press.
Selting, Margaret *et al.* (1998) 'Gesprächsanalytisches Transkriptionssystem (GAT)', *Linguistische Berichte* 173: 91-122.
Snell-Hornby, Mary (2006) *The Turns of Translation Studies*, Amsterdam & Philadelphia: John Benjamins.
Spillner, Bernd (1980) 'Semiotische Aspekte der Übersetzung von Comics-Texten', in Wolfram Wilss (ed.) *Semiotik und Übersetzen*, Tübingen: Narr, 73-85.
Trompenaars, Fons (1997) *Riding the waves of culture*, London: Nicolas Brealey Publishing.
Wadensjö, Cecilia (1998) *Interpreting as Interaction*, London & New York: Addison Wesley Longman.
------ (1993/2002) 'The double role of a dialogue interpreter', in Franz Pöchhacker and Miriam Shlesinger (eds) *The Interpreting Studies Reader*, London: Routledge, 354-70.
Wilss, Wolfram (ed.) (1980) *Semiotik und Übersetzen*, Tübingen: Narr.
Wilton, Antje (2005) *"...but eh this this – is humour – (–) humour pursued with great seriousness." Eine gesprächsanalytische Untersuchung zu Scherzaktivitäten in zweisprachiger Familienkommunikation*, Unpublished Dissertation, University of Erfurt.

Appendix

GAT notation for transcription

Basic transcript

Sequential Structure

`[ ]` `[ ]`	overlapping utterances, simultaneous talk
`=`	latching

Pauses

`(.)`	micropause
`(-), (--), (---)`	short, middle, long pauses of ca. 0.25 - 0.75 sec.; up to ca. 1 sec.
`(2.0)`	estimated pause of more than one second
`(2.85)`	measured pause

Other

`und=äh`	slurring within units
`:, ::, :::`	stretched sound, according to length
`äh, öh, etc.`	hesitation
`‘`	glottal stop

Laughter

`so(h)o`	laughter during speech
`haha hehe hihi`	vocalized laughter
`((lacht))`	description of laughter

Backchanneling

`hm,ja,nein,nee`	monosyllabic signals
`hm=hm,ja=a, nei=ein, nee=e`	bisyllabic signals
`‘hm‘hm`	with glottal stop, usually used to negate

Stress

`akZENT`	main stress
`ak!ZENT!`	extra strong stress

Intonation at the end of a TCU

?	high rise
,	slight rise
-	no movement
;	slight fall
.	final fall

Other

((hustet))	para- and extralingual actions and events
<<hustend> >	para- and extralingual actions and events accompanying speech
<<erstaunt> >	interpretative comments about a stretch of speech
( )	unclear word or phrase
(solche)	guess of a word
al(s)o	guess of a word or syllable
(solche/welche)	possible alternatives
((...))	omission in the transcript
—>	marks line in the transcript which is referred to in the text

Detailed transcript

Stress

akZENT	main stress
akzEnt	secondary stress
ak!ZENT!	extra strong stress

Pitch

↑	rising
↓	falling

Change in pitch level

<<t> >	low pitch level
<<h> >	high pitch level

Changes in loudness and speed

<<f> >	forte, loud
<<ff> >	fortissimo, very loud
<<p> >	piano, quiet
<<pp> >	pianissimo, very quiet

<<all> >	allegro, fast
<<len> >	lento, slow
<<cresc> >	crescendo, getting louder
<<dim> >	diminuendo, getting quieter
<<acc> >	accelerando, getting faster
<<rall> >	rallentando, getting slower

Breathing

.h, .hh, .hhh	breathing in, depending on length
h, hh, hhh	releasing breath, depending on length

(taken from: SELTING *et al.* (1998), my translation)

Additional conventions

italics	definitely English utterances
bold	definitely German utterances
standard	neutral utterances

6. The Self-retreat of the Interpreter[1]

An Analysis of Teasing and Toasting in Intercultural Discourse

JAN D. TEN THIJE
Utrecht University, The Netherlands

Abstract. *This paper reconstructs the process of achieving intercultural understanding during the interpreting of humorous teasing in toasting situations at an international research meeting. The analysis focuses on the self-retreat of the interpreter. This self-retreat is an extreme result of the discursive handling of the interpreter's role conflict, which stems from the fact that he or she transmits the utterances of the original speakers and is at the same time an autonomous participant of the interaction. Proposals are discussed that assign certain translatory actions of the interpreter to the continuum depending on his action space. At one end of the continuum, the interpreter is regarded as a so-called translation machine; at the other end, he is considered to be an equal participant in the interaction. The self-retreat of the interpreter has not yet been extensively addressed in the research literature but can be reconstructed with respect to this continuum. The analysis also shows how interpreters reflect and act upon the achievement of functional equivalence in the tripartite discourse structure. The paper concludes in stating that the distinction between 'professional' and 'non-professional' interpreters is actually questionable.*

---

[1] I wish to thank Tatsjana Heinz, Ann Patrick, Katja Müller, Natalia Solovjeva, Carola Weise, Conny Wustmann and Bernd Müller-Jacquier for their participation and contributions in the research project at the Department of Intercultural Communication at the Chemnitz University of Technology, in which they collected, transcribed and contributed to the analyses of the data in the international project (cf. Ten Thije 1998, 2003 and 2006b). Moreover, I want to thank the participants of the workshop on intercultural discourse at the 6th International Pragmatics Conference, Reims, 19-24 July 1998 and the participants of the workshop 'Translatory Action and Intercultural Communication', which took place at the conference of the Societas Linguistica Europaea, 19-24 August 2001 in Leuven for their valuable comments on earlier drafts of this paper (see Ten Thije 1998). Birgit Apfelbaum, Kristin Bührig, Nicholas Burke and Juliane House contributed with valuable comments to an earlier version of this paper. Finally, I thank the Dutch, Russian, German and Danish participants of the international project who allowed me to record their team meetings and visits over a period of several years. The names of persons and places have been changed. Despite the support of so many people, the author remains soley responsible for all potential errors in the text.

1. Introduction

Linguistic research in the field of intercultural communication has recently changed its focus of interest. Misunderstanding no longer dominates analyses, and with self-evident and successful intercultural discourse now attracting increased attention. Moreover, it is now recognized that the mere presence of people with different linguistic and cultural backgrounds does not automatically yield an *intercultural* discourse. Individual analyses must show to what extent the discourse is institutional and to what extent it can be characterized as intercultural (Ten Thije 2006a).

This paper does not focus on intercultural misunderstandings. Rather, it reconstructs the process of intercultural understanding by reflecting on institutional and intercultural discourse structures. 'Non-professional' interpreters (Knapp-Potthoff and Knapp 1987) have a special task in mediating cultural differences, yet the potential of their translatory actions is limited. This becomes clear in cases in which interpreters resign from their position and are replaced by other colleagues. In this paper, stretches of discourse that document the interpreter's retreat are regarded as *rich points* (Agar 1994). These cases can be taken as a starting point for an analysis concentrated on the special characteristics of intercultural understanding. In fact, by reconstructing the translatory action in multilingual and multicultural constellations, one gains insight into the process of intercultural understanding conducted by interpreters in general.

In this paper I reconstruct the *internal dilation of the speech situation* (Bührig and Rehbein 2000) in which, in the specific case considered here, a 'non-professional' interpreter helps to overcome the linguistic barrier (Dutch/English/Russian) that arises during the interpretation of humorous teasing in toasting situations at an international research meeting. I will analyze the discursive handling of the interpreter's role conflict which stems from the fact that he transmits the utterances of the original speakers and is at the same time an autonomous participant of the interaction. The analysis reveals how interpreters reflect on the achievement of functional equivalence in this tripartite discourse structure.

The structure of the paper is as follows: In section 2, I begin with a clarification of different theoretical approaches to the interpreter's discourse and continue by questioning the distinction between 'professional' and 'non-professional' interpreters (Apfelbaum 1998, 2004). Proposals are discussed that place translatory actions of the interpreter on a continuum depending on his action space (e.g. Wadensjö 1998; Bot 2005). At one end of the continuum, the interpreter is considered to be a so-called *translation machine*; at the other end, he is considered to be an equal participant in interaction. The self-retreat of the interpreter has not yet been addressed in detail in the literature but can be reconstructed with respect to this continuum, as will be shown in section 3. In section 4 I present the data from an international academic project. The analyses of institutional toasting discourse and the discursive structures of teasing are delivered in sections 5 and 6, respectively. Section 7 contains the analysis of the data and section 8 the conclusions.

2. Translatory actions along a continuum

The concept of interpreter is ambiguous. In the most elementary sense, an interpreter is solely an 'in-between' between two primary speakers who do not speak or understand each other's languages (Knapp and Knapp-Potthoff 1986a:151). The task of the interpreter in a *triadic conversation* (Wadensjö 1998:10) can be realized in different modes depending on the action space the interpreters have at their disposal when translating the primary speakers.

Various analyses on interpretation refer to the role of the interpreter as a continuum. Bot (2005) uses the notions *translation-machine* versus *liberal interactive model* as the two poles of the continuum. The translation-machine model assumes that the interpreter merely translates the utterances of the primary speaker into the other language without actually participating in the interaction himself. Consequently, the interaction between the primary speakers develops following the same interaction patterns as it would in a monolingual configuration. The only difference relates to the fact that the so-called translation-machine is positioned between the two primary speakers. The liberal interactive model gives the interpreter more action space, which leads him to rely more on his own initiative. Instead of merely functioning as a translation-machine, the interpreter becomes a third participant who bridges the gap between the primary speakers by organizing turn-taking and ensuring thematic continuity, for example.

The same continuum can be found in the work of Knapp-Potthoff and Knapp (1986, 1987), who distinguish between a *professional* and a *non-professional interpreter*. The professional interpreter corresponds to the translation-machine, as he transmits the utterances between the primary speakers precisely. According to Knapp-Potthoff and Knapp (1986), the function of the non-professional interpreter moves continuously along the continuum and is situated somewhere between transmission and mediation. In his or her role as a mediator, the non-professional interpreter not only transmits the interactions of the primary speakers but also explains and explicates presumptions and can even introduce new topics to the conversation. Hence, he or she participates as an autonomous third interactant. Knapp-Potthoff and Knapp (1986:153) stress the fact that the participation of the non-professional interpreter can change its position along this continuum throughout the course of the interaction. They refer to the non-professional interpreter as "the man or woman in the middle" *(ibid)*.

Apfelbaum (2004) argues that the distinction between professional and non-professional interpretation is based on text-external criteria such as education, training and payment. Based on a conversation analytical study of the interpretation carried out during international expert communication, she concludes that the discursive means and strategies of both professional and non-professional interpreters are essentially the same and that their distinct use can be characterized in a more sophisticated manner based on a continuum that complies with the fundamental linguistic structures of authentic speech.

Wilton (this volume) also presupposes such a continuum with respect to the different roles of the interpreter in translatory action. Her analyses of the interpretation of humorous activities in informal everyday conversations confirm one extreme of the continuum. In fact, Wilton analyzes interactants whose main role is that of a fully competent and integrated participant who only takes on the role of a translator on certain occasions during the interaction. They are so-called "self-selects as translators". They switch fluently between the role of a translator and the role of a normal participant depending on the needs for the progression of the informal conversation.

Wadensjö (1998) proposes a so-called *dialogical interpretation* model. According to this model, the interpreter does not function as a translation-machine but rather participates in the interaction process on his or her own. She describes the task of the interpreter as that of *relaying and co-ordinating*. She analyzes the translations of the interpreter by focussing on the fundamental question of what relationship exists between the interpreter's contributions and the original contributions of the primary speakers. In this context Wadensjö distinguishes between *renditions* and *non*-renditions with respect to the contributions of the interpreter. The latter notion concerns all of the interpreter's contributions that do not contain a translation or reformulation of an utterance made by a primary speaker. The former notion relates to the coordinating task of the interpreter within the interaction. For instance, the interpreter may clarify turn assignments and meta-communicative comments. Wadensjö states that renditions and non-renditions can also co-occur in one contribution. She proposes a taxonomy of six renditions including close renditions, expanded renditions, reduced renditions, substituting renditions, summarizing renditions, and lack of renditions (1998, 70).

Meyer (2004) considers Wadensjö's taxonomy to be a reductive model, since it does not account for the institutional configuration in which translatory actions are carried out and the interpreter must fulfil his task of relaying. In comparing Wadensjö's model with the analyses of Bührig and Rehbein (2000), Meyer (2004) finds that both approaches analyze the interactive structure of interpretation by focusing on deletions and additions on the part of the interpreter. Wadensjö (*ibid.*) categorizes these changes in her text linguistic-based taxonomy of (non-)renditions as previously indicated. Within a functional pragmatic framework, Bührig and Rehbein (*ibid.*) reconstruct the consequences of the interpreter's changes in the propositional content for the institutional actions of the primary speakers. They assume that an interpreter is both observer as well as transmitter of the interaction of the primary speakers. Consequently, the interpreter is able to plan his or her contribution based on the mental schemata developed by primary speakers when structuring their contributions.

While Bot (2005), Knapp-Potthoff and Knapp (1986), Apfelbaum (2004), Wilton (this volume) and Wadensjö (1998) all concentrate on the external formal interactional characteristics of the interpreter's actions, Bührig and Rehbein (2000) focus on the mental dimension of the interpretation process. In their theory of *reproductive action* they assume that the interpreter's translation does not consist of the arbitrary transformation of an utterance from the source language (SL) into an utterance in the target language (TL). They assume that the interpreter's translation of speech actions results from a reproductive process in which the interpreter's knowledge is directly related to the translation process itself.

Their reconstruction is based on the following argument (see also Bührig 1999; 2004): The interpreter acts as a transmitter in an interaction in which interactants do not speak the same language. This means that the normal input and output conditions which characterize mono-lingual interaction are no longer guaranteed. The speech actions of primary speakers are characterized by a rupture between two languages, with the interpreter helping to overcome this rupture. As a consequence of this process of *going-in-between*, the speech situation of the primary speakers is dilated by the interpreter. The primary speakers receive a *mediated* rather than an *original* message. In summary, Bührig and Rehbein (*ibid.*) analyze specific characteristics of the interpreted speech situation based on the assumption that interpretation is realized within an *internal dilated speech situation*.

One of the means used by the interpreter to bridge the barrier is to *characterize* the speech action of the original speakers. Bührig and Rehbein (*ibid.*) identify the following dimensions of the interpreter's characterizations: (1) the propositional content of the action of the primary speakers, (2) their action purposes, (3) the pre-history (causes) of their actions, (4) their constellation, (5) the discourse species (the genre) of the speech actions, and finally, (6) the interactional nexus (connectivity). The relevance of these dimensions and the extent to which these characterizations are adopted by interpreters depend on the actual need to bridge the language rupture, which varies according to specific speech actions in the source language or the specific action configuration.

Not all translatory actions imply the use of characterizations. In fact, Bührig and Rehbein's six dimensions can be compared to Wadensjö's taxonomy of (non) renditions with respect to the fact that both account for the change between original and translatory action. However, the former accounts for the institutional constellation in which the change is taking place. The dimensions can be traced back to a functional pragmatic approach to discourse (Ehlich 1991; Rehbein 2001; Bührig and Ten Thije 2005).

A discursive rupture is not characteristic of the interpreter's discourse alone. This rupture occurs in all speech situations in which time and place do not correspond with one another. According to Ehlich (1984, 1991), dilation occurs whenever a textualized message is transmitted instead of the original message. Ehlich uses the notion of *text* in order to denote this transmission of knowledge in a dilated speech situation in either a written or an oral mode. Bührig and Rehbein (2000) also refer to knowledge transfer in a dilated speech situation as a form of *textualization*. Characterization is one of the possible forms of *textualization*. The way people characterize their messages depends on *textuality* – in other words the *transmissibility of the linguistic action.* Texts with a high transmissibility have a special linguistic structure, as in the case of rhymes, for instance. Rhymes can be remembered more easily than an improvised oral story, for example.

Bührig and Rehbein (*ibid.*) consider an interpreter in a face-to-face interaction to be a *messenger*. The dilation of the speech situation is *internal,* as only the temporal orientation of the transmitted speech action is dilated in a given speech situation, whereas the spatial orientation remains constant. In the case of external dilated speech actions, interactants have neither a common spatial nor temporal orientation. It is essential for both internal and external dilation that the messenger characterizes the speech actions, resulting in the textualization of the speech actions (Bührig 2004).

Bührig and Rehbein (2000) claim that the existence of an interpreter as a translation machine is impossible. Changes always occur as a consequence of translatory action, these not being arbitrary but rather dependent on the systematic translation process that takes place in the mind of the interpreter. This translation process is determined by the interpreter's mental activities. He or she does not repeat the utterances of the primary speakers but rather reproduces them. The interpreter produces an utterance in his or her L2 that is already available via his or her L1 knowledge, embedding utterances in the ongoing discourse while also realizing his or her own purposes.

Primary speakers – in contrast to interpreters – must organize and structure their knowledge before producing an utterance. Their production requires a speaker plan that differs from an interpreter's speaker plan. When a primary speaker realizes an utterance, the interpreter becomes subject to the following situation: The utterance of the primary speaker is available in the source language (SL), while the utterance in the target language (TL) is unknown for the primary hearer (H). This utterance is *Rheme* for the (primary) hearer; it contains new knowledge. Since the interpreter understands the source language, it becomes *Theme* of his knowledge (known). The interpreter thus has the task of transmitting the utterance from SL to TL for the hearer, i.e. from *Rheme* to *Theme* of H's knowledge. Hence, the translatory knowledge relation concerns the relation of *Rheme* to *Theme*.

The interpreter in consecutive[2] translation has a double task. First, he or she transmits knowledge from Rheme to Theme for the hearer by realizing translatory actions. At the same time, the interpreter functions as the third speaker in the discourse by realizing speech actions on his or her own accord. Hence, the interpreter is simultaneously translator and third interactant. With respect to the interpreter's translatory actions, this means that he or she reproduces these actions second hand. Consequently, the illocutions of the primary speaker are not reproduced as *actions* themselves, but rather as *perceptions of the primary speaker's actions*. The utterance *'bon voyages'* in the first fragment below is translated by '*he wishes you bon voyages*'. According to Austin (1962), this distinction can be seen as a change from *phatic* to *rhetic* speech.

In summary, face-to-face translatory discourse can be considered from a functional pragmatic approach to be realized in an internal dilated speech situation. The interpreter characterizes the original speech action with the purpose of delivering a textualized speech action. The interpreter always participates in a double role, both as transmitter and as third participant. The resulting tripartite discourse structure is constituted by interrelated mental and discursive dimensions. The analysis aims at a reconstruction of this interrelatedness.

---

[2] Bührig and Rehbein (2000), like many other researchers (Pöchhacker and Shlesinger 2002), distinguish between three constellations, specifically translations on the one hand and simultaneous and consecutive interpretations on the other hand. When translating a written text, the translator is able to oversee the complete text structure including the underlying knowledge structure in SL before transferring the text into the other language (TL). However, in the case of *simultaneous interpretation,* the interpreter must anticipate this overall knowledge structure based only on parts of the linguistic structure, as these are uttered in a linear sequential manner. Consequently, the interpreter transfers pieces of utterances from language (SL) into pieces of utterances in language (TL) by presupposing an overall plan on the part of the original speaker. Finally, in the case of *consecutive interpretation* or so-called 'turn related interpretation', the interpreter is able to oversee a completed turn and therefore understands the utterance and the underlying knowledge structure before the actual transmission into another language is executed. This overall insight into the mental plan of the original speaker enables the interpreter in consecutive interpretation to translate the utterances from language SL into language TL having already acquired an overall understanding of the discourse purposes of the original speakers.

3. The end points of the continuum: constellations for retreat

In light of this functional pragmatic theoretical framework I introduce the question of which constellations can lead to the interpreter's retreat. The retreat of an interpreter is characterized by the interpreter ending his or her translatory actions. This issue has not yet been the subject of intensive consideration in translation studies. Various constellations can lead to a retreat of the interpreter. Only some of these are discussed in the literature on translatory action:

- The interpreter determines that the primary speakers understand each other even without his translations, making translatory actions redundant. Bronsdijk (2006) analyzes interrogations of asylum seekers by Dutch functionaries. The presence of an interpreter is legally required during these interrogations. However, since some asylum seekers have lived in the Netherlands for a long time prior to these interrogations, they already understand Dutch and are capable of answering the questions of the functionary directly. Consequently, the interpreter often retreats.
- Interpreters retreat because primary speakers start to use a language that they cannot translate appropriately. Ten Thije (2007) reports on the interpreter's practice in interviews in which asylum seekers must display their language competencies in all language varieties of their region of origin. The assigned interpreter is not always capable of translating all these different varieties and languages. As a result, the interpreter retreats.
- Interpreters are requested to stop their translatory actions due to the fact that they create a communicative breakdown between the primary speakers, who are then no longer content with the suggested translations. Bührig (1999) analyzes the retreat of a conference interpreter as a consequence of the discontent of the primary speakers.
- The interpretation is linked to a very specific discourse species (e.g. a humorous genre). Wilton (this volume) illustrates in her analyzes the *self-select* and, consequently, the *self-retreat* of the interpreter in informal conversation depending on the specific need to explain a punch line. The interpreter retreats after the translation of the punch line.
- The interpreter becomes tired and thus physically and mentally incapable of fulfilling his or her translatory actions in the appropriate manner and thus retreats.
- The primary speakers structure their interaction in such a way that translatory actions cannot be realized at all by realizing turns that last for too long without a pause, for instance.
- The interpreter retreats because the primary speakers talk about a topic

that requires professional expertise or specific inside knowledge that he or she ostensibly lacks.

– The interpreter retreats because he can no longer handle the double involvement as both a translator and third discourse participant. Subsequently, a changeover of the interpreters takes place in order to guarantee the continuation of the interaction.

This paper focuses especially on the last constellation of self-retreat. Hence, the paper focuses on the question of how the double involvement of an interpreter may become contradictory. This double involvement is inherent in translatory actions. Consequently, the reasons for contradiction can be reconstructed from the two extreme ends of the continuum: (1) from the role of the interpreter as a translator and (2) from his or her role as a third interactant. From the first perspective, one could imagine that the interpreter characterizes speech actions of the primary speaker in such a way that the translated speech action pattern is abandoned and another pattern is adopted in which the interpreter his- or herself is addressed as primary speaker. The resulting translatory actions cannot be combined with his or her actions as a third actor. From the second perspective, one could imagine that primary speakers discuss a topic in which the interpreter is addressed directly as a primary speaker. Consequently, the interpreter must realize speech actions on his or her own account in order to continue the interaction between primary speakers and thus fails to realize the translatory actions.

Based of authentic data, I will examine in detail how these contradictions are dealt with in discourse. It is important to begin this case study by analyzing the institutional and intercultural constellation (see also Ten Thije 2002) in order to be able to reconstruct the specific institutional qualities of the interpreter's contradictions.

4. The data

The data for this paper were collected in the context of an international academic project in which Germans, Dutch and Danes worked together with Russians (see also Ten Thije 1998, 2003, 2006b). The main purpose of the project was to develop a curriculum for new forms of training in the field of 'social work' in post-Soviet-Union society. Russian colleagues were trained at Western European universities by Western European colleagues in order to become acquainted with the theory and practice of social work in Western European countries. The coordinating team consisting of representatives from each of the countries involved in the project met regularly in Russia. The team worked together for a long period of time and experienced a large number of administrative difficulties in accomplishing their tasks.

The goals of the project needed to be reached within a strict time schedule. In this respect, the project resembles many other cooperative supranational projects which can be seen as a result of the Eastern European expansion of the European Community and the rebuilding of societal systems in Eastern Europe (De Stefani *et al* 2000). The core of the Russian team consisted of six women, whereas all of the members from the Western European countries were men, meaning that gender also played a role in shaping the institutional and intercultural teamwork.

Although English was used as a *lingua franca,* the restricted language competencies of the Russian team members did not always guarantee mutual understanding. Certain team members therefore took up the role of 'non-professional' interpreters (Knapp and Knapp-Potthoff 1985) in order to facilitate the intercultural understanding for their colleagues. This type of communicative situation created a transparent constellation (Müller 1989), since half of the Russian team members were already moderately proficient in English and could understand the foreigners speaking English directly. Emerging intercultural misunderstandings were sometimes dealt with and sometimes neglected, with team members often discussing assumed expectations tied to linguistic and cultural knowledge. Consequently, team discussions reflected the process of reorganization of fixed expectations and the emergence of a common ground. Ten Thije (2003) analyzes this process as the genesis of a *discursive interculture* within the international project.

The multilingual Dutch-English-Danish-Russian constellation offered all parties the opportunity to use their own language for internal consultations, even during official meetings. When using their Dutch or Russian mother tongue, participants could be sure that non-Dutch speaking or non-Russian speaking team members were not able to understand what was being said. Müller (1989) characterizes these constellations as non-transparent constellations. Obviously, these non-transparent constellations also affected the interaction in English. This group-specific manifold communicative potential contributed to a type of *discursive interculture* which Fienemann and Rehbein (2004, 264) refer to as a "lingua franca interculture with a multilingual base".

Each the meetings of the multicultural coordination team were audio-recorded over the course of three years. During working visits in Russia, the delegation visited many different social institutions. Consequently, the recordings included meetings, receptions, presentations, guided tours, general small talk, preliminary consultations, conversations during dinner and the proposing of toasts. The total length of the corpus is about 40 hours. For this paper, a subset of the corpus containing the toasts proposed during a team visit to Russia was extracted, transcribed and analyzed in detail. Ten Thije (1998) presents a first analysis of the discourse species of toasting.

This paper expands upon this study by means of an analysis of institutional and homileic (i.e. phatic) discourse while focusing on translatory actions.

5. Toasting as institutional discourse

Frake (1972) has shown in his classic sociolinguistic study that proposing a toast in other cultures can be seen as an elaborate institutional discourse species: among the Subanum, the procedure of toasting establishes social hierarchy and administers justice. Kotthoff (1995; 1997) presents an extensive analysis of the thematic, interactive and institutional structures of toasting in Georgia.

In Western European cultures, the discourse of toasting is not as significant as in Georgia. Nonetheless, the discourse of toasting can be considered an expression of a polite action in many cultures. Fienemann and Rehbein (2004:225) state that by using polite forms of speaking and acting, interactants express a certain courteous goodwill by acting in accordance with the respective social measures, i.e., their – potentially – incompatible control field (i.e. their sphere of command) is 'neutralized' and their respective 'action fields' (i.e. power dispositions) are calibrated. Subsequently, the authors (*ibid.*) state that by acting politely, speakers usually undergo a process of reflexivity in which they view the constellation from the perspective of a third party, i.e. they take on a 'bystander-role' (Goffmann 1981).

By proposing a toast in intercultural discourse, interactants demonstrate their 'courteous goodwill' towards one another. They act according to social conventions in order 'to neutralize' potential threats stemming from their different social and cultural standards, while their courteous words simultaneously reveal to what extent they take existing power relations into account. In fact, the analysis will assess how the toasts express these mutual estimations. Moreover, verbalization of the reflective activities from a 'bystander position', as suggested by Fienemann and Rehbein (*ibid.*), may provide insight into the interculturality of their interactions. Consequently, whenever a toast is realized in a multilingual constellation in which an interpreter is needed, the interpreter's translatory actions result in specific discourse structures. Thus, one may gain specific insights into the process of intercultural understanding conducted by interpreters by means of reconstructing translatory action of toasting in multilingual constellations.

As guests of the Russians, the Western European team members became familiar with Russian toasts and learned to respond appropriately to this verbal expression of hospitality. The Russian toast is less literal or stylized than the Georgian one, yet nonetheless represents a part of everyday discourse (cf. Kotthoff 1995, 1997). Toasts are often proposed when people drink vodka or champagne together (cf. Jatzkowskaja 1994) and rules the pertaining to the content, form and order of toasts are expected to be adhered to (Richmond 1992).

As an example of a Russian toast, I will present the following text excerpt in which a Russian official, Vladimir, proposes a toast to the Dutch delegation at the end of their working visit at the Russian institution (see also Ten Thije 1998). In his toast, the director of the department addresses the two Dutch team members. Hans is the project coordinator and has already been to Russia several times, whereas Otto is visiting Russia for the first time. The Russian official thanks the Dutchmen for their participation in the international project. Fienemann (2006) describes the speech action pattern of *rendering thanks* as a reflective communicative process that interrupts the exchanges of gifts. Rendering thanks is not only an expression of emotional feelings, but also a reflection of the social means that constitute courteous goodwill whereby the speaker enables the hearer H to act in accordance with this goodwill. (Fienemann and Rehbein 2004:256). The toast below displays both courteous goodwill as well as reflections on social measures of the international cooperation.

Since I begin with an analysis of the discursive structures of toasting, the translatory actions of the interpreter are left out in the first two fragments. The deletion of the translation actions is marked with the signs (***). The toast of the Russian host official is as follows:

Fragment 1: Toast of the host

Participants:

RV: Vladimir (Russian official)
NH: Hans (Dutch delegation leader)
NO: Otto (Dutch team member)
RW: Wera (Russian team member, non-professional interpreter)
All: six Russian team members

RV: [1] Now my dear friends I would like to thank you from all our heart for / for the splendid work you've done here.
[2] We'll wish you bon voyage. nach / nach Holland. (***)
All: [3] laugh
RV: [4] Well for just for Hans, while Hans is quite a different situation because he's been part of our teaching staff already. (***)
[5] He is / As for / as for / as for Otto to whom I would like to have him as our constant member in the future. (***)
[6] So for our future cross cultural contacts for many many years ahead. (***)
[7] So happy return home. (***)

This toast includes typical characteristics of a Russian toast, e.g. standard formulations such as *from all our hearts*, *splendid work*, *so for our future*

... *contact for many, many years ahead*, and even the required creative expressions, such as the double code-switching *'bon voyage nach Holland'*, which alludes to the special multilingual framework of the project. The toast expresses praise for the activities carried out during the working visit, respect towards the individual members of the delegation, a certain satisfaction with the international company, the hope of continuing the cooperation, and the wish for a safe return home. According to Fienemann (*ibid.*), this toast reflects social measures that constitute courteous goodwill within an international team, whereby the host enables the Dutch partners to act according to the social measures of academic colleagues.

The second example of a toast was proposed by the Dutch delegation leader, Hans, during the same working visit to an old people's home. After proposing an initial toast in which he thanks the director of the home for his hospitality, he proposes a second toast in which he specifically addresses the six female Russian team members, as the visit to the home coincided with International Women's Day (March 8th). This second toast from the Dutch project co-ordinator is presented as follows:

Fragment 2: A toast on International Women's Day

Participants:
NH: Hans (Dutch delegation leader)
NO: Otto (Dutch team member)
RS: Stanislav Stanislavovitsch, forename Alec (Russian, director of the rest home)
RB: Boris (Russian student, non-professional interpreter)
RZ: Zina (Russian team member)
RW: Wera (Russian team member)
RN: Natasha (Russian team member)
RA: Anna (Russian team member)
RI: Ida (Russian team member)
RT: Tanja (Russian team member)
RX: an unnamed Russian team member

NH: [1] Alec, may I bring another toast?
[2] In Holland I am not used to bring so many toasts. (***)
[3] But now I got a special reason for it. (***)
[4] It's äh/ the first was about the visit to this (institution). (***)
[5] My second goes to äh the fact that it is the eight of March today (***)
[6] and we are glad that we have six of such beautiful examples of the female human nature among us (***)
RW: [7] *laughs* (***)
RZ: [8] it's compliment (***)
RB: [9] it's joke (***)
NH: [10] Some / some/ äh sometimes äh our compliments are a bit doubted (***)

[11] But this is a very serious one (***)
[12] I am very glad to be here with you and
[13] I äh I wish you everything good in your life, all the things that you as a woman deserves to have in you life. (***)
RA: [14] Good said
NH: [15] (*raising his glass*) Tanja, Zina, Ida
RI: [16] Thanks. You are the right / you are the right gentlemen.
All: [17] *Clinking of glasses*

After asking for permission from the director to propose another toast in segments s1 and s2, the Dutchman announces the special reason for his second toast (s3). Subsequently, he reminds the audience of his first toast (s4) and refers to the actual date, the eighth of March (s5). In s6, he compliments the female team members on their beauty. The compliment provokes different reactions: Wera laughs (s7) and Zina explains that the toast is meant as a complement (s8), whereas Boris, the non-professional interpreter, remarks that it is a joke (s9). The Dutchman seems to recognize the various interpretations, as he hesitates at the beginning of his utterance in s10 and subsequently confirms that his compliments are not always taken seriously by the Russian team members. However, he states in s11 that this time his complement should be taken seriously, he reinforces the compliment, expresses his pleasure with respect to the present company (s12) and he wishes all of the women "all the things they deserve in life" (s13).

The reactions in s14 and s16 clearly show that the translatory constellation in this discourse fragment is partially transparent (Müller 1989), since at least two Russian team members obviously understand English and are capable of responding directly in English. The compliment is accepted and appreciated. In s16, the Russian team member first thanks and then compliments her Dutch colleague by addressing him as "the right gentlemen". According to Fienemann and Rehbein (2004:225), this fragment shows various polite forms of speaking and acting, as the male and female actants demonstrate mutual courteous goodwill by acting according to standards of mutual politeness. Both refer to particular female standards on the occasion of International Women's Day that are regarded as high social values both in Russia and in Western European countries.

To sum up, the toast shows that the Dutch team member is capable of proposing a toast in an adequate and appreciated form and is even capable of repairing possible misunderstandings. Moreover, the toast shows that the relationship between men and women in the team is respected and addressed in an honourable manner. These observations are important since the relationship between men and women is one of the issues addressed in the next toast. The teasing within the next toast is responsible for the replacement of the interpreter (see the fragments below). Accordingly, the next section focuses on the discourse structure of teasing.

6. Teasing as homileic discourse

Humour is often regarded as very important for the success of intercultural understanding (cf. Hofstede 1991). Although research on humour in general is extensive, little work has been carried out in the field of intercultural communication. Although Chiaro (1992), for instance, has discussed problems in translating humour and Kotthoff (1998) has presented different analyses of humour in interaction, the matter of how humour shapes intercultural discourse is scarcely analyzed. Lee's work (1994) contains an example in which he discusses how jokes can cause considerable conflicts in intercultural communication due to the fact that hidden cultural knowledge is often presupposed. He presents some discourse strategies developed especially for coping with these problems in achieving intercultural understanding. While Lee (*ibid.*) focuses on the intercultural understanding of cartoons and Dimova (2000) investigates the translation of jokes, Wilton (this volume) analyzes conversational humour and the interactive translation of punch lines. Bührig (2004) analyzes the interpretation of persiflaging discourse. Persiflaging and teasing can both be regarded as features of homileic discourse. According to Ehlich and Rehbein (1979), homileic discourse refers to discourse forms such as small talk, telling stories, jokes, etc., which function primarily in establishing a community but can also be functionalized for institutional purposes. In everyday language, one could speak of *applied humour* (cf. Mulkay 1988, cited in More 1993).

According to Eder (1993) and Günthner (1996), teasing exhibits a double actant's structure: on the one hand, the speaker, i.e. the *teaser*, makes a provocative remark – which can include mock challenges, negative commands or even hostile threats, if taken literally – towards another person, the *teased person*. The teasing remark can contain exaggerations, contradictions and implausible expressions, or it can be accompanied by para-verbal or meta-communicative comments, signalling to the teased person that he or she should take the remark in a playful manner. The success of teasing depends to a large extent on the reactions of the *audience*. As long as the audience laughs, the teasing is successful. As soon as the audience quiets down or agrees with objections raised by the teased person, teasing has then failed. The best possible reaction for the teased person is to turn the situation around and to tease the teaser.[3] According to Alberts (1992), the positions of teaser and teased person cannot be as easily reversed in the context of

---

[3] Bührig (2004) differentiates between *persiflaging* and *teasing*. She argues that while teasing starts with the teaser making a negative remark towards the teased person, persiflaging is also concerned with the communicative prehistory of the negative remark and aims at the reflection of the teased person towards the exaggerated comments made by the teaser.

male-female communication in the workplace. Thus, when a man teases a woman in the context of workplace communication, this may result in an allegation of sexual harassment.

The toast presented below is proposed by the Dutch leader of the delegation in response to the farewell toast offered by the official Russian host (see fragment 1). In his response toast, the Dutchman initially pays respect to the institutional toasting conventions discussed in section 4. Subsequently, he realizes certain speech actions and addresses topics which belong to the discourse of teasing. The embedding of the teasing in the toast results in contradictive provocative claims by the Dutchman towards the interpreters, resulting in their retreating twice.

7. The self-retreat of an interpreter

In the following, I will take a closer look at the self-retreat of the interpreter. The complete fragment of the response toast proposed by the Dutchman can be found in appendix 2. Fragment 3 below contains the discourse stretches in which the interpreter, Wera (RW), retreats resulting in her colleague Vladimir (RV) taking over. This exchange occurred as the result of a teasing remark made by the Dutchman, who states that he himself has been harassed. The exchange of interpreters takes place after RW confesses that she was the subject of the teasing. In section 3 above, I concluded that an interpreter can occupy two possible positions: translator and third participant. The thesis suggests that the interpreter can retreat when these two positions contradict each other. In the following fragment, the primary speaker indirectly mentions a topic in which the interpreter is addressed as primary speaker.

This fragment begins after the Dutchman expresses his thanks towards the Russian official for his hospitality in accordance with the conventions of toasting. He then makes the following remark in his toast.

Fragment 3: T4/20-33; 'Toast to say goodbye'

RV: Vladimir (Russian official, second interpreter during toast)
RB Boris, (Russian student, interpreter during working visit)
NH: Hans (Dutch delegation leader, proposer of the toast)
NO: Otto (Dutch team member)
RW: Wera (Russian team member, first interpreter during toast)
All: six Russian team members

```
   >
   NH[ [37And I have to tell you one problem we had to deal with.
20
```

21
NH [[38]There was really one serious problem.
RW [[39] одна очень серьезная
one very serious

22
NH [[40]Except from the harrassment of some of your employees.
RW проблема
problem.

23
NH [[42]There was an/ [[43] You can translate as well
[[41]*coughs*
RW [[44] и и
and and

24
NH [[45](At/At)Apart from the harrassment by one of your employees.

25
RV [[47]harrassment это значит вот помимо, значит,
that means / that by the way means
RW [[46] чё такое?
What exactly?

26
RB [[48]ну вот о чём мы говорили, смеялись в воскресенье ...
well, that's what we talked about,laughed about on Sunday.
RW [[49] ага, ага
uh-huh, uh-huh

27
RV [[50]помимо значит беспокойства,которое представл/которое представляла
Apart from the bother
RW [[51] повышенный интерес
intense interest

RV: для него одна из работниц нашего университета.
caused for him by one of the employees of our university.

RW: [52 ну это я
Well, that was me.

28

NH: [56 There was really one serious problem that

RV: [53да
yes

RW: [54*laughs*

R?: [55*laughs*

29

NH: [57was the problem of trust. [58It was not possible for Otto and me to

30

NH: know when we can trust people or not.

RV: [59 Ага, значит, он сказал,
Uh-huh, that means, he said

31

RV: что была одна проблема , мы с Отто тут обговорили, в общем
That there was one problem, Otto and I have already discussed this, in general

32

RV: мы не знаем , кому можно доверять, кому нельзя
We don't know, who we can trust and who not.

33

The analysis below is structured according to the following three argumentative steps: the first step is related to the question of how teasing is realized within this multilingual discourse fragment. The second step concerns the translatory actions of the interpreter, while the third step refers to the self-retreat of the interpreter.

The realisation of the teasing phases can be reconstructed as follows: In s37-38 the Dutchman (NH) addresses the Russian official, Vladimir (RV) as the representative of the institution and announces that the Dutch delegation has had a serious problem during their working visit to the Russian university. The interpreter, Wera (RW), summarizes this announcement in s 39 by reproducing that a problem exists. Subsequently, NH formulates in s40 a side sequence (cf. Jefferson 1972) starting with *apart from*, followed by *the harassment by one of your employees*. Within the pattern of teasing, this remark can be considered as a provocative one. The remark is directly addressed at the official by making use of the deictic procedure *your* and, therefore, his institutional responsibility is engaged which makes the allegation even more severe. No translation is formulated by RW. In s41 NH coughs, and begins to repeat his remark, but stops and addresses the interpreter RW directly by asking her to translate *you can translate as well*. This direct request to translate is remarkable in a constellation in which RW has been the interpreter from the very beginning of the toast. Within the pattern of teasing, this request could be interpreted as an indication that something uncommon or unexpected is at hand, in which the addressed person plays a special role. The interpreter (RW) hesitates in s44 uttering *and and* in Russian. Subsequently, NH repeats his remark in s45, and rephrases his allegation more precisely by stating that not *some* but *one* of the Russian employees has behaved impolitely. According to the teasing pattern (Günthner 1996), the teased person is always addressed directly. It is striking that in this stretch of discourse the teased person is addressed by way of an allusion. Wilss (1988) notes that allusions can only be understood if the alluded knowledge is available to all participants involved in the discourse. In this case, the teaser creates a specific group-bound communicative task of discovering the person intended by his remark regarding the harassment.

The reproach of the teaser is not translated immediately. Rather, it initiates an internal non-transparent (Müller 1998) Russian discourse, in which the speech situation is no longer dilated, instead creating an interaction space of its own. The language rupture between English and Russian is not bridged. Consequently, the Russian discourse cannot be understood by the Dutch participants. It is striking that the interpreter (RW) does not formulate a clarification turn by asking the primary speaker to explain his speech, something which happens quite often in non–professional interpretation (Knapp-Potthoff and Knapp 1987). In that case the interpreter would have asked NH what he means by *harassment*. Instead, she indicates to her English speaking Russian colleagues RV and RB that she does not understand this notion. The subsequent Russian discourse s47-s55 includes the clarification of the notion *harassment*, but also the realisation and completion of the teasing pattern. In s47 the Russian official (RV) starts to describe the word *harassment* and is interrupted in s48 by RB. The latter is the Russian student who was responsible for interpretation during the entire working visit. He refers, in s48, to a common humorous experience at an earlier stage of the working visit. Within the teasing pattern his remark can also be considered a *meta-communicative comment*. RW acknowledges this humorous event in s49 and confesses in s51 that she herself is the person who is being blamed for the harassment. This means that she accepts being the teased person. The official (RV) accepts RW's confession in s53 and, subsequently RW and an unidentified person (R?) start *laughing* (s54, s55). This laughter can be considered the positive audience reaction within the teasing pattern by at least part of the audience.

Within the monolingual teasing pattern (cf. Günthner 1996), this laughter indicates the success of the intended teasing. One must observe, however, that most members of the audience do not react verbally to the teasing remark and remain silent, meaning that the teasing was not successful for everybody in the audience. Moreover, in the multilingual constellation in which the Russian discourse is not being translated, we can conclude that the teaser (NH) has formulated a provocative remark in English. This initiated a teasing pattern that led to the Russian-only speech situation. RW accepts the position of the *teased person* in the newly initiated Russian speech situation. The teased person (RW) and part of the audience (R?) begin laughing in s54 and s55 as a reaction to the confession of the teased person. Her confession is not translated to the teaser himself. Nonetheless, the non-verbal reactions of laughing can be observed and interpreted by the teaser. Although the speech situation in Russian is not internally dilated at this moment, laughing may overcome the language rupture, i.e., the teaser (NH) might conclude that his teasing was at least partially successful. From the subsequent discourse during the remaining part of the toast it becomes clear that after her confession of being the teased person, RW does not verbally react to the Dutchman's provocative remark. She only comments on the toast at the end by saying *Ah, what a joke* (s91).

On the basis of the reconstruction of teasing, we can now progress to the next step of the analysis by asking the question of how the interpreter translates the utterances made by the primary speaker. The answer to this question will shed light on the question of how the non-transparent Russian discourse functions in the overall translation and also help us to understand what caused the self-retreat of the interpreter. Interestingly, the dimensions of the characterization presented by Bührig and Rehbein (2000) can be used to analyze the speech actions in the Russian discourse. In s46 the interpreter (RW) indicates that she does not understand the *propositional content* of the primary speaker's speech action (i.e. the meaning of the word *harassment*). RW can consider NH's utterance as a *Rheme* of her knowledge. RV begins to characterize the propositional content by using his linguistic knowledge of English. He is interrupted by RB who, in s48, characterizes the propositional content by mentioning the *prehistory* of the speech situation and realizing the *common group knowledge* with respect to the discussion and laughter on the previous Sunday. In fact, RB characterizes the common experiences as a *discourse species* with homileic qualities. His characterization clarifies the potential *action purpose* of the speech action of the primary speaker (NH), both for the interpreter (RW) and for the rest of the Russian audience. From the common knowledge of the prehistory, the indirect realization of NH's reproach can be interpreted as a provocative remark directed at RW. Subsequently, RV translates the notion of *harassment* in s50 with the notion of *bother.* RW accepts and reformulates this characterization in s51 as *intense interest*. Furthermore, RV changes *one of your colleagues* in s48 into *one of the employees of our university* in Russian. Hence, RV changes the deictic and symbolic procedures of NH's speech action. He redirects the personalized address of the remark initially directed at himself as the academic official in charge of the project by indicating that some member of the general academic community of the university is responsible for the harassment. In the utterance made by the primary speaker (NH), RV is addressed in his institutional position. RV's reformulation *of the institutional constellation* in the actual speech situation is adequate because he splits his roles of the interpreter (RW) and primary speaker (RV). He thereby indicates that he can handle the potential contradiction of the interpreter's double role.

The successful *functional equivalence* of RV's translation can be seen in the reaction of RW in s52, in which she confesses that she is the member of the university that NH is referring to. In sum, NH's reproach is translated for the Russian audience by referencing (1) the *prehistory* and (2) the *propositional content* as well as through (3) the *constellation* in the actual speech situation and (4) the *discourse species* (i.e. genre) of the speech actions. Although (5) the *purpose* of the speech action (i.e. reproach) is not explicitly *textualized*, the different dimensions of characterization as a whole clarify the reproach of NH. The confession made by RW in the Russian discourse makes it clear that RV's translation is also successful from another perspective, i.e. that the speech action pattern of a reproach is conventionally followed either by a denial or a confession. RW's confession removes the potential threat of NH's reproach for the whole Russian delegation. If the accusation had remained unanswered, these courteous words would indicate that the power relations between the Dutch and Russian delegations could end up out of balance.

One might observe that the translatory actions of RV and RB do not characterize (6) the *interactional nexus* (e.g. connectivity) of NH's speech action in s40/s45. In fact, the connectors *'expect from'* in s40 and *apart from* in s45 are not actually translated. The side sequences that these formulations would normally initiate create a new speech situation here in which the speech pattern of teasing is not only translated but also realized and completed.

This completion seems reasonable in the constellation of the international cooperation in which one of the employees of the responsible official is being accused of acting impolitely. The translatory actions can be considered to be functionally equivalent.

Finally, in the third step of the analysis, the self-retreat of the interpreter RW will be analyzed: RW does not know the Rheme of the speech action of the primary speaker in s40 and s45. As soon as she realizes what is meant by *harassment* as a result of the clarification by her colleagues (RV and RB), she understands that she is actually being addressed as the primary speaker herself. In the discourse species of toasting, in which the toaster has the right to speak for a longer period of time, she accepts that it is not possible to react to the primary speaker immediately as a third speaker. However, in the Russian non-transparent speech situation, she openly takes responsibility for the presumed impolite action and also publicly admits that she is the person being teased. The Russian discourse is not translated for NH. Consequently, he cannot understand that RW has confessed to her colleagues in Russian. Due to the non-verbal laughing of RW and R?, NH might conclude that his teasing has been acknowledged by the teased person RW and by some other members of the audience (R?). The self-retreat of the interpreter is the result of the contradiction of her double role. Through her self-retreat, she also contributes to the successful continuation of the toast. The Russian official (RV) takes over the position of the interpreter in s59.

In the next fragment we see how the toast continues. RW has retreated and RV has taken over the interpretation, but the latter also hands over his role. In fact, the subsequent interpretation is carried out in tandem, with two interpreters being involved. Wilton (this volume) illustrates the same reason for a change of interpreter within interactive translation. The interpretation in the next two fragments contains a cooperative narrative in which additional participants work together in order to recall and display common group experiences (Quasthoff 1980). The exchange between the interpreters reveals discourse structures that are fundamental to translatory actions. Self-retreats in our data nicely show how the double role of the interpreter as both transmitter and third participant can be coped with successfully.

Fragment 5 is taken from the last part of the same toast shown in fragment 4. After the critical remarks concerning the sexual harassment, the Dutchman addresses other precarious topics that for space reasons cannot be analyzed in this paper in detail. I will therefore merely mention the subsequent speech actions. NH reveals that the Dutch team members did not know whether they could trust their Russian colleagues. He explains this statement by asserting that the Dutch made compliments during their working visit which the Russians did not accept or take seriously. NH continues by stating that the Dutchmen had agreed to reduce the number of compliments and to only tell the truth. Afterwards, he begins to tell a story that is shown in the fragment below.

The speech actions of the proposer of the toast can be considered reflections on polite actions and courteous goodwill within this type of international cooperation. Again, their provocative formulations comply with the teasing structure, in which the teased person is not addressed personally – here, the Russian team members are addressed – and teased – as a group. The Russian official (RV) is the interpreter of the toast. It is striking that RV comments on the toast during his translatory action (see s69 in the annex) by saying in Russian that the proposer of the toast (NH) expresses himself in a very complicated manner. This comment indicates to the audience that the speech actions of the toast might be ambiguous.

The second self-retreat can be observed in s79, shown in fragment 5 below. The interpreter (RV) notes that he was not present at the described event and therefore retreats. Subsequently, the previous interpreter (RW) again takes over by translating this utterance (s80). Afterwards, RV continues translating until the end of the recording.

Fragment 5: T4/47-56: Continuation of the 'toast to say goodbye"

```
NH [74 We got a toast. [75It was during one of the evenings.
46
```

```
NH [76We got a toast and it was said: [77 'we are coming to the end
47
```

```
NH  of the evening'.

RV                [79 я в этом не участвовал
                     I was not present there.

                      [80 (laughing)
RW [78   [3 (                )говорит как раз3] в один из вечеров один
                                Now he says, one of evening at
48
```

[3 lauging

```
RW  из товарищей, у кого мы были в гостях,   сказал:
    the home of one of our friends,          he said:
49
```

50
RW так, ну вечер подходит к концу [81 ((2 sec.))
'*So, now* the evening is coming to an end'.

51
NH [82 So of course again we thought this is honest. [83 So we/ we shamed/

52
NH we felt shamed and we packed our things and run out of the door.

53
RV [84 но они восприняли это серьёзно естественно э э они подумали, что
But of course, they took it seriously and they thought, that

54
RV действительно значит что вечер подошёл к концу
it did indeed mean that the evening was coming to its end.
RW [85 всё честно по честному
Everything the honest truth

55
RV [86 и мы так сказать уже собрали свои вещи и покраснели
and we so to gathered our things and we blushed.

56
NH и нам было неудобно и мы собрались уходить.
We were uncomfortable and we wanted to leave.

In s79 the Russian official (RV), instead of translating the previous utterance of the primary speaker (NH), states that he was not present at the event referred to in the toast. In professional interpretation, not being present would not be a valid argument for a change of the interpreter, but this fragment indicates that personal involvement and knowledge of the prehistory of the communicative events addressed by the primary speakers are important prerequisites for effective interpretation. From ethnographic sources we know that the Dutchmen never left the house, nor did the hostess scream out of the window. In fact, this story represents a 'persiflage' of what actually took place. The formulations used by the proposer of the toast correspond to the kind of exaggerations that are characteristic of teasing.

The story of the toast made by the toast giver refers to the repair of a misunderstanding that can be traced back to a lack of cultural knowledge on the part of the Dutch with respect to the social sequence of Russian toasting at home. The penultimate toast is reserved for the hostess to praise her guests and thank them for their presence. The last toast should be proposed by the guests themselves (cf. Kotthoff 1995, 1997). Although the penultimate toast functions as an initiation of the leave taking process, the visitors are expected not to leave immediately. A group may stay seated after the meal for a moment to avoid a rash farewell, as this would be very unusual for many Russians.

Due to the premature ending of the (audio) recording, the audience's final reaction to the toast is unfortunately not documented. The question as to whether the toast was successful, however, can be answered as follows: The fact that teasing was embedded in the toast raised the expectation on the part of the Russians that the formulations would correspond to speech actions such as praise, mutual respect, satisfaction and hope for future co-operation – actions that had also been uttered in previous toasts between team members and thus constituted part of their common team knowledge (see fragment 1). As soon as the audience recognized that the Dutch toast contained playful exaggerations, which became clear during the funny story, the other critical remarks could be retrospectively reinterpreted. The doubt expressed with respect to Russian reliability (s58, in the annex) could also be interpreted as an apology for impolite actions, while the reproach concerning sexual harassment (segments 40 and 45) could be interpreted as an exaggerated compliment. Such a positive interpretation of the compliment could be based on the association of the toast on International Women's Day (see fragment 2). Finally, these re-interpretations can be confirmed with reference to ethnographic information revealing hearty laughter and the joyful raising of glasses by all of the interactants at the end of the encounter.

Fragment 6 shows the last part of the recorded toast in which the Russian team members comment on the teasing and toasting.

Fragment 6: T4/57-61: Final part of the toast to say goodbye

```
   >
   NH [ [87But then they shout from out of the window:[82 'No no,
57
```

```
   >
   NH [ it's /it's not honest. [88Come back.'
   >
   RV [                          [89 потом,когда мы собрались,
                                     Then, as we got going,
   >
   RW [                                        [90   (
58
```

```
RV  он он закричал и сказал, что нет это не честно,
    he called out and said, that no, it was not meant seriously,
RW                                                        )
59
```

```
RV  в общем-то это не правда, заходите назад.
    'It's not true, come back'.
RW                    [91   ну это такая шутка.
                             Ah, what a joke.
60
```

```
NH  [92 So                 it is not / we don't know when you have
RX    [93  ну они и шутят
           So, that's how they make jokes.
61
```

(end of the tape)

The comments made in s91 and s93 are highly important for the overall analysis of the toast since they show that at least two interactants actually interpreted the teasing in the toast as humour. In fact, the formulation of the second comment (s93) firmly categorizes the toast as a joke. The utterance made by RX contains a generalization in which the Dutchman's joke is qualified as a group characteristic of how *they make jokes*. However, one does not know whether she is referring to *that's the way men joke* or *that's the way the Dutch joke* or *that's the way Western Europeans joke*. In any case, according to Barth (1969), one could note that a cultural boundary has been interactively constructed, separating an in-group and an out-group. In summary, one can conclude that intercultural understanding does not mean that all participants agree on the same values; rather, they seem to recognize and respect them.

It should also be noted that these comments are not actually transferred to the Dutch speaker, i.e., the proposer of the toast and teaser does not know whether the teasing contained in his toast has actually been understood. The ultimate grounds for my diagnosis of successful mutual understanding are based on ethnographic sources.

8. Conclusions

This paper has described a case study of institutional, intercultural and translatory discourse. The analysis exemplifies the functional pragmatic approach to translatory action by focussing on an extreme action of the interpreter, namely his self-retreat.

In a survey of different theories of translatory discourse, I have shown that the distinction between professional and non-professional interpreters should be rejected and replaced by the concept of a continuum of the interpreter's action space. On one pole of this continuum the interpreter is considered as a sole transmitter of utterances between the original speakers and on the other pole is regarded as an autonomous (third) participant equal to the original speakers. The action space of the interpreter can be conceptualized by an internal dilated speech situation in which the language rupture between the original speakers is bridged by the reproduction of their speech actions in various translatory modes. The stages of this continuum can be reconstructed as different forms of textualization by the interpreter. The characterization of the primary speaker's utterances is one means of reproduction.

The analysis of the translatory actions has been reconstructed in recurrent analytical phases that can be summarized as follows (cf. also Ten Thije 2002).

Firstly, the institutional constellation of the cooperation of an international team is analyzed in order to determine the institutional positions of the Russian and Dutch officials and their functionaries. The reconstruction reveals different language competencies in English, Russian and Dutch with respect to the various team members. These differences in language competency explain the need for interpretation for some of the Russian team members. This language constellation also explains the occurrence of non-transparent speech situations both in Dutch and Russian; both parties can speak their own language without being understood by the others. This multilingual constellation appears to be an important factor in international cooperation and the establishment of a discursive interculture (Koole and Ten Thije 1994, 2001, 2003).

Secondly, the discourse species (or genre) of toasting is reconstructed as a form of polite action in which courteous goodwill is formulated while paying respect to social measures. Certain standards of this discourse species could be identified on the basis of the Russian discourse species of toasting. The characteristics of an intercultural realization of this discourse species could then be reconstructed based on these cultural standards. This intercultural realization was determined by embedding the speech action pattern of teasing in the toasting. The proposer of the toast simultaneously acts as the teaser, while the interpreter is addressed as the teased person and the other participants are treated as the audience of the teasing.

The analysis of the embedding of teasing (Günthner 1996) in toasting (Kotthoff 1995, 1997) led in a third analytical phase to the conclusion that this concurrence of discourse structures provided the Dutch with the opportunity to playfully reflect on differences in Russian and Dutch social measures of polite action. The main topic of the toast refers to the problem of giving compliments and showing personal interest in male – female international cooperation. The issue wittily addressed by the toast giver refers to the question of to what extent giving compliments must to be taken seriously, when such compliments actually support effective team cooperation, and when they are overdone and hence might be considered personal harassment. The analysis demonstrates the characteristics of the complexity of gender discourse in intercultural communication. Although this case study may only hint at the importance of gender discourse, it is quite clear that gender should not be considered as a language external factor but should rather be incorporated in the discourse analysis from the beginning (Eckert and McConnel-Ginet 2003).

Finally, I wish to summarize the conclusions with respect to the analysis of translatory action. By presupposing an internal dilated speech situation for translatory action, I was able to reconstruct the manner in which the teasing pattern was initiated in a dilated speech situation and completed in a non-transparent Russian interaction space. In fact, the problem of translating the notion of *harassment* was resolved by initiating a clarification turn that was not directly addressed at the original speaker, as one would expect, but rather at the Russian audience. As soon as her Russian colleagues explain the notion and the interpreter understands the propositional content of the speech action of the Dutch primary speaker, she displays her understanding by realizing the hearer-side of the illocution of his reproach in the target language. The interpreter confesses that she was the person involved in the harassment. The analysis reveals the collapse of the two roles of the interpreter, which subsequently leads to her withdrawal from the position of interpreter.

The constellation of the self-retreat of an interpreter has scarcely been discussed in translation studies. This case study reconstructs in great detail how the roles of an interpreter as a transmitter on the one hand and as an independent third participant on the other contradict each other and result in the retreat of the interpreter. At first glance this conclusion corresponds to the common sense rule that interpreters should not be actively involved in the discourse they are interpreting. However, as I concluded from a review of the state of the art of translation studies, interpreters are always more or less involved in the discourse, a phenomenon that can be described on the basis of a continuum. Consequently, paying more attention to the constellation of self-retreat increases our understanding of translatory action in general. This case study shows one case of self-retreat caused by an excessive degree of personal involvement and one caused by a case of too little involvement on the part of the interpreter. The theoretical impetus of this case study thus relates to the reconstruction of the everyday notion of the personal involvement of the interpreter.

References

Agar, Michael (1994) *Language Shock Understanding the Culture of Conversation,* New York: Morrow.

Alberts, Jess K. (1992) 'Teasing and Sexual Harassment. Double-Bind Communication in the Workplace', in Linda A. Perry, Lynn H. Turner, and Helen A. Sterk (eds) *Constructing and reconstructing gender,* Albany: SUNY Press, 185-97.

Apfelbaum, Birgit (1998) '"I think, I have to translate first..." Zu Problemen der Gesprächsorganisation in Dolmetschsituationen sowie zu einigen interaktiven Verfahren ihrer Bearbeitung', in Birgit Apfelbaum and Hermann Müller (eds) *Fremde im Gespräch. Gesprächsanalytische Untersuchungen zu Dolmetsch-Interaktionen, interkultureller Kommunikation und institutionalisierten Interaktionsformen,* Frankfurt: IKO – Verlag für interkulturelle Kommunikation, 21-46.

------ (2004) *Gesprächsdynamik in Dolmetsch-Interaktionen. Eine empirische Untersuchung von Situationen internationaler Fachkommunikation unter besonderer Berücksichtigung der Arbeitsprachen Deutsch, Englisch, Französisch und Spanisch,* www.verlag-gespraechsforschung.de, [last visited: 15 July 2007].

Austin, John L. (1962) *How to Do Things with Words*, Oxford: Oxford University Press.

Barth, Fredrik (1969) 'Introduction', in Fredrik Barth (ed.) *Ethnic Groups and Boundaries. The Social Organisation of Cultural Difference*, Bergen & Oslo: Universitetsforlaget, 9-39.

Bronsdijk, Myrthe (2006) *Interpreter in the language analysis interview. Translation machine or second interviewer?* Master thesis Communication studies Utrecht: Utrecht University.

Bot, Hanneke (2005) *Dialogue interpreting in mental health,* Amsterdam & Atlanta: Rodopi.

Bührig, Kristin (1999) 'Konsekutives Übersetzen Englisch-Deutsch', in Heidrun Gerzymisch-Arbogast, Daniel Gile, Juliane House and Annely Rothkegel (eds) *Wege der Übersetzungs- und Dolmetschforschung*, Jahrbuch der deutschen Gesellschaft für Übersetzungs- und Dolmetschwissenschaft, Tübingen: Narr, 241-66.

------ (2004) '"Che devo dire?" – Zu einigen Möglichkeiten und Schwierigkeiten in der Thema-Rhema-Progression in der mehrsprachigen Familienkommunikation', in Juliane House, Werner Koller and Klaus Schubert (eds) *Neue Perspektiven in der Übersetzungs- und Dolmetschwissenschaft. Festschrift*

für Heidrun Gerzymisch-Arbogast zum 60. Geburtstag, Bochum: AKS-Verlag, 151-72.
------ and Jochen Rehbein (2000) *Reproduzierendes Handeln. Übersetzen, simultanes und konsekutives Dolmetschen im diskursanalytischen Vergleich*, Arbeiten zur Mehrsprachigkeit, Folge B 7, Hamburg: SFB.
------ and Jan D. Ten Thije (2005) 'Diskurspragmatische Beschreibungsmodelle', in Ulrich Ammon, Norbert Dittmar and Klaus Mattheier (eds) *Sociolinguistics – Soziolinguistik. An international Handbook of the Science of Language and Society*, Berlin: Mouton, 1225- 250.
Chiaro, Delia (1992) *The Language of Jokes. Analysing verbal play*, London: Routledge.
De Stefani, Elwys, Johanna Miezcnikowski and Lorenza Mondada (2000) '"Können sie vielleicht kurz übersetzen". les activités de traduction dans des reunions de travail plurilingues', *Revue Française de Linguistique Appliquée* 5(1): 25-42.
Dimova, Anna (2000) 'Humor zwischen Sprachen und Kulturen: Läßt sich Humor übersetzen?', in Elias Canetti (ed.) *Internationale Zeitschrift für transdisziplinäre Kulturforschung* 2(2): 40-56.
Eder, Donna (1993) '"Go Get Ya a French". Romantic and sexual teasing among adolescent girls', in Deborah Tannen (ed.) *Gender and conversational interaction*, Oxford: Oxford University Press, 17-30.
Eckert, Penelope and Sally McConnel-Ginet (2003) *Language and Gender*, Cambridge: Cambridge University Press.
Ehlich, Konrad (1984) 'Zum Textbegriff', in Annely Rothkegel and Barbara Sandig (eds) *Text – Textsorten – Semantik. Linguistische Modelle und maschinelle Verfahren*, Hamburg: Buske, 9-25.
------ (1991) 'Funktional-pragmatische Kommunikationsanalyse. Ziele und Verfahren', in Dieter Flader (ed.) *Verbale Interaktion. Studien zur Empirie und Methodologie der Pragmatik*, Stuttgart: Metzler, 127-43.
------ and Jochen Rehbein (1979) 'Sprache in Institutionen', in Hans Peter Althaus, Herbert Ernst Wiegand and Helmut Henne (eds) *Lexikon der Germanistischen Linguistik*, Tübingen: Niemeyer, 338-45.
Fienemann, Jutta (2006) *Erzählen in zwei Sprachen. Diskursanalytische Untersuchungen von Erzählungen auf Deutsch und Französisch*, Münster: Waxmann.
------ and Jochen Rehbein (2004) 'Introductions: Being polite in multilingual settings', in Juliane House and Jochen Rehbein (eds) *Multilingual Communication*, Amsterdam & Philadelphia: John Benjamins, 223-78.
Frake, Charles (1972) 'How to ask for a drink in Subanum', in Pier Giglioli (ed.) *Language and Social Context*, Harmondsworth: Penguin, 87-94.
Goffman, Ervin (1981) *Forms of Talk*, Oxford: Blackwell.
Günthner, Susanne (1996) 'Zwischen Scherz und Schmerz - Frotzelaktivitäten in Alltagsinteraktionen', in Helga Kotthoff (ed.) *Scherzkommunikation. Beiträge aus der empirischen Gesprächsforschung*, Opladen: Westdeutscher Verlag, 81-108.

Hofstede, Geert (1991) *Cultures and organizations. Software of the mind*, London: McGraw.

Jatzkowskaja, G. (1994) 'Russisch-deutsche Tischgespräche und Essgewohnheiten', in Richard Brutting and Günter Trautmann (eds) *Dialog und Divergenz. Interkulturelle Studien zu Selbst- und Fremdbildern in Europa*, Frankfurt am Main: Lang, 235-42.

Jefferson, Gail (1972) 'Side Sequences', in David Sudnow (ed.) *Studies in Social Interaction*, New York: Free Press, 294-328.

Knapp, Karlfried and Annelie Knapp-Potthoff (1985) 'Sprachmittlertätigkeit in der interkulturellen Kommunikation', in Jochen Rehbein (ed.) *Interkulturelle Kommunikation*, Tübingen: Gunter Narr, 450-64.

Knapp-Potthoff, Annelie and Karlfried Knapp (1986) 'Interweaving two discourses – The difficult task of the non-professional interpreter', in Juliane House and Shoshana Blum-Kulka (eds) *Interlingual and Intercultural Communication. Discourse and Cognition in Translation and Second Language Acquisition Studies*, Tübingen: Narr, 151-69.

------ (1987) 'The man or woman in the middle. Discoursal aspects of non-professional interpreting', in Karlfried Knapp, Werner Enninger and Annelie Knapp-Potthoff (eds) *Analyzing Intercultural Communication*, Berlin, New York & Amsterdam: de Gruyter, 181-212.

Koole, Tom and Jan D. Ten Thije (1994) *The construction of intercultural discourse. Team discussions of educational advisers*, Amsterdam & Atlanta: Rodopi.

------ (2001) 'The reconstruction of intercultural discourse. Methodological considerations', *Journal of Pragmatics* 33: 571-89.

Kotthoff, Helga (1995) 'The social semiotics of Georgian toast performances. Oral genre as cultural activity', *Journal of Pragmatics* 24: 353-80.

------ (1997) 'Rituelle Trinksprüche beim georgischen Gastmahl: Zur kommunikativen Konstruktion von Vertrautheit und Fremdheit', in Annelie Knapp-Potthoff and Martina Liedke (eds) *Aspekte interkultureller Kommunikationsfähigkeit*, München: iudicium, 65-93.

------ (1998) *Spaß verstehen. Zur Pragmatik von konversationellem Humor*, Tübingen: Niemeyer.

Lee, W.-S. (1994) 'Communication about humour procedural competence in intercultural encounters', in Larry A. Samovar and Richard E. Porter (eds) *Intercultural communication: A reader*, Belmont: Wadsworth, 373-82.

Meyer, Bernd (2004) *Dolmetschen im medizinischen Aufklärungsgespräch. Eine diskursanalytische Untersuchung zur Wissensvermittlung im mehrsprachigen Krankenhaus*, Münster: Waxmann.

More, E. (1993) 'The role of humour in workplace communication – Training implication', Paper presented at International Conference 'Communication in the Workplace: Culture, Language and Organisational Change', Sydney, 1-4 September.

Müller, Frank (1989) 'Translation in bilingual conversation. Pragmatic aspects of translatory interaction', *Journal of Pragmatics* 13: 713-39.

Pöchhacker, Franz and Miriam Shlesinger (eds) (2002) *The Interpreting Studies Reader,* London: Routledge.

Quasthoff, Uta M. (1980) *Erzählen in Gesprächen. Linguistische Untersuchungen zu Strukturen und Funktionen am Beispiel einer Kommunikationsform des Alltags*, Tübingen: Narr.

Rehbein, Jochen (2001) 'Das Konzept der Diskursanalyse', in Klaus Brinker, Gerd Antos, Wolfgang Heinemann and Sven F. Sager (eds) *Text- und Gesprächslinguistik. Linguistics of Text and Conversation. Ein internationales Handbuch zeitgenössischer Forschung. An International Handbook of Contemporary Research.* Halbband. Vol 2, Berlin & New York: de Gruyter, 927-45.

Richmond, Y. (1992) *From Nyet to Da. Understanding the Russians*, Yarmouth: Intercultural Press.

Thije, Jan D. Ten (1998) 'Proost Pieter, Een toast op de interculturele communicatie', in Adriene Bruyn and Jacques Arends (eds) *Mengelwerk voor Muysken. Voor Pieter C. Muysken bij zijn afscheid van de Universiteit van Amsterdam* [Publicaties van het Instituut voor Algemene Taalwetenschap 72], Amsterdam: Universiteit van Amsterdam, 35-40.

------ (2002) 'Stufen des Verstehens in der Analyse interkultureller Kommunikation', in Helga Kotthoff (ed.) *Kultur(en) im Gespräch. Studien zur Fremdheit und Interaktion*, Tübingen: Narr, 57-97.

------ (2003) 'Eine Pragmatik der Mehrsprachigkeit: Zur Analyse diskursiver Interkulturen', in Rudi De Cillia, Josef Krumm and Ruth Wodak (eds) *Die Kosten der Mehrsprachigkeit – Globalisierung und sprachliche Vielfalt / The Cost of Multilingualism – Globalization and Linguistic Diversity / Le Cout du Plurilinguism – Mondialisation et diversité linguistique,* Wien: Akademie der Wissenschaften, 101-125.

------ (2006a) 'Beyond Misunderstanding; Introduction', in Kristin Bührig and Jan D. Ten Thije (eds) *Beyond Misunderstanding. The linguistic analysis of intercultural communication*, Amsterdam & Philadelphia: John Benjamins, 1-11.

------ (2006b) 'The notion of 'perspective' and 'perspectising' in intercultural communication research', in Kristin Bührig and Jan D. Ten Thije (eds) *Beyond Misunderstanding. The linguistic analysis of intercultural communication,* Amsterdam & Philadelphia: John Benjamins, 97-153.

----- (2007) 'Meertaligheid in de asielprocedure' *Toegepaste Taalwetenschap in Artikelen, 71-85.*

Wadensjö, Celia (1998) *Interpreting as Interaction,* Linköping: Linköping University.

Wilss, Wolfram (1988) *Anspielungen. Zur Manifestation von Kreativität und Routine in der Sprachverwendung,* Tübingen: Niemeyer.

Appendix 1: Transcription conventions

Score transcription conventions

The score format follows musical notation. Each speaker is given three lines:

- a verbal communication line (indicated by speaker initials in capitals; e.g. RI);
- a non-verbal communication line (indicated by italics);
- an intonation line (indicated by >).

Verbal and non-verbal communication transcribed above each other within a score indicates simultaneity.

In addition, the following conventions are used:

verbal communication line

/	Repair
( )	not understood
(walks)	good guess
((1 sec.))	pause of 1 second
.	pause of less than 1 second
((laughs))	naming a verbal activity
? Hm	not certain which speaker uttered 'Hm'
$[_1$ Hm $_1]$	information on the section between brackets is given under the score
$[^1$	number of segment
$[^{1a}$	number of subsegment
.	(full stop) sentence final falling intonation
,	non sentence final rising intonation
?	Sentence final rising intonation

intonation line

!	Stress
-	Lengthened
/	rising intonation
\	falling intonation
V	Doubling
^	Shortened

Toasts to say goodbye (March 9th 1996)

NH	Hans
NO	Otto
RV	Vladimir
RZ	Zina
RW	Wera
RN	Natascha
RA	Anna
RI	Ida
RT	Tanja
RX	Unknown

```
1
>NH  [1 I'am very glad I have had the opportunity to see VXXXXXXXX

2
>NH  NH by snow.     [3 Thas was the first time.        [5 Yeah
>NO                                                 [4 Yeah?
>RV             [2 Hm

3
>RW  [5 Ганс вчера Вxxxxxxxx снежным видел в первый раз [6 ((2 sec.))
     Hans saw Vxxxxxxxx covered in snow for the first time yesterday

4
>NO  [7 You don't bring a toast (      ) Hans?  [8 You're just answering?
>RX                                            [7 ah

5
>NH  [9 I'll/ I was a bit answering. [10 Shall I?
                                         laughs
>NO                                        [11   Yes.
>RW                                  [12  чуть-чуть нальём!
                                          Let's have a top-up!

6
>NH                                               [15 So please
>NO  [13 Yes, please.  You are the head of the team.
                                              laughs
>RX     [14. (                          )

7
>NH  take glasses again.     [17 this is yours.
                    puts new sekt in the glases
>XX               [16 all laugh                    laughing
>RW                                       [18  не допивайте!
                                           Don't drink it all!
```

8
RX [19 ( )

9
NH [20 I'am not such a good drinker, so ( )
RW [21 [1 так ну все по-братски 1]
Sooo. That's it.just like brothers.

[1 laughing

10
RV [22 ( ) That's the problem. [23 He doesn't drink, so

11
RV anything he drinks has a very big influence. !
NO [24 *laughs*

12
NH [25 So uuuhh, Vladimir. [26 Thank you foruuhh confirming my position
RX [27 ( )

13
NH in your staff and inviting Otto to be in the staff here.
RV [29 Hmhm.
RW [28 Владимир, спасибо большое
Vladimir, thank you very much,

14
NH [30 I promise you we will best / I'll do my/
RW за то, что ты подтвердил свою роль в университете
for confirming your position at the university.

15
NH: We will do our best . to involve them so much in Holland, that
RW: и за то, что ты развернул
and for developing that.

16
NH: *they won't come back here* *[[32][$_{2}$that they will be in our staff$_{2}$].*
RX: [[31] и . и (lachen)
and . and

[$_{2}$ laughing slightly

17
RW: [[33]я начало прослушала и [[34]так надеемся, что да что вам так
I missed the start and therefore we hope, that yeah, that you

18
RW: понравится, что вы туда не вернётесь,
will like it so much, that you won't go back there,

19
NH: [[36] ((2 sec.))
RW: ! сюда не вернётесь
won't come back here.
RX: [[35]. вернётесь
return.

20
NH: [[37]*And I have to tell you one problem we had to deal with.*

21
NH: [[38]There was really one serious problem.
RW: [[39] одна очень серьезная
one very serious

22
NH: [[40]Except from the harrassment of some of your employees.
RW: проблема
problem.

23
NH [42 *There was an/* [43 *You can translate as well*
[41 *coughs*
RW [44 и и
and and

24
NH [45 (At/At) Apart from the harrassment by one of your employees.

25
RV [47 harrassment это значит вот помимо, значит,
that means / that by the way means
RW [46 чё такое?
What exactly?

26
RB [48 ну вот о чём мы говорили, смеялись в воскресенье ...
well, that's what we talked about , laughed about on Sunday.
RW [49 ага, ага
uh-huh, uh-huh

27
RV [50 помимо значит беспокойства,которое представл/которое представляла
Apart from the bother
RW [51 повышенный интерес
intense interest

28
RV для него одна из работниц нашего университета.
caused for him by one of the employees of our university.
RW [52 ну это я
Well, that was me.

29
NH [56 There was really one serious problem that
RV [53 да
yes
RW [54 *laughs*
R? [55 *laughs*

30
NH [[57]was the problem of trust.[[58]It was not possible for Otto and me to

31
NH know when we can trust people or not.
RV [[59] Ага, значит, он сказал,
Uh-huh, that means, he said

32
RV что была одна проблема , мы с Отто тут обговорили, в общем
That there was one problem, Otto and I have already discussed this, in general

33
RV мы не знаем , кому можно доверять, кому нельзя
We don't know, who we can trust and who not.

34
NH [[60]*We gave a lot of compliments and they were not taken for serious*
RX [[61] *inhale*

35
RV [[62]и мы/ мы/ мы значит говорили много комплиментов,
and we/ we/ we have voiced many compliments

36
RV но их не воспринимали серьёзно, как нужно было воспринимать,
but they were not taken seriously like they were meant
RW [[63] ( )

37
NH [[64]*So we agreed to reduce the number of compliments, but to be*
RW [[65] (*hi*)

38
NH very honor/ honest.
RV [[66] поэтому мы решили сократить количество
therefore we decided to reduce the number

39
RV: комплиментов и тем самым быть очень э искренними.
of compliments and consequently be very sincere.
RW: [67 искренними
very sincere

40
NH: [68But immediately on that very point that we started to be

41
NH: honest and s/ and start to believe that everything that was said

42
NH: was / would be honest as well.
RV: [69 значит э как сложно говорит-то он,
so, he expresses himself in a very complicated manner.
RW: [70 хм
Hm

43
RV: и поэтому, когда мы стали значит говорить меньше мы полагаем,
and therefore, as soon as we began to talk less, we assumed that,

44
RV: что это всё будет воспринято так как полагается.
everything would be taken as it was meant.

45
NH: [72 exactly/ exactly on that very moment.
RV: чё-то там крутит мм
Something like that.
RW: [71 Hm (laughs) ( )
R?: [73 *laughs loudly*

46
NH: [74 We got a toast. [75It was during one of the evenings.

NH [76We got a toast and it was said: [77 'we are coming to the end

47

NH of the evening'.

RV [79 я в этом не участвовал
I was not present there.

RW [78 [3([80 *(laughing)*)говорит как раз3] в один из вечеров один
Now he says, one of evening at

48

[3 lauging

RW из товарищей, у кого мы были в гостях, сказал:
the home of one of our friends, he said:

49

RW так, ну вечер подходит к концу [81 ((2 sec.))
'So, now the evening is coming to an end'.

50

NH [82 So of course again we thought this is honest. [83 So we/ we shamed/

51

NH we felt shamed and we packed our things and run out of the door.

52

RV [84но они восприняли это серьёзно естественно э э они подумали, что
But of course, they took it seriously and they thought, that

53

RV действительно значит что вечер подошёл к концу
it did indeed mean that the evening was coming to its end.

RW [85 всё честно по честному
Everything the honest truth

54

RV [86и мы так сказать уже собрали свои вещи и покраснели
and we so to gathered our things and we blushed.

55

NH и нам было неудобно и мы собрались уходить.
We were uncomfortable and we wanted to leave.

56

NH [87*But then they shout from out of the window:* [82 *'No no,*

57

NH it's /it's not honest. [88Come back.'

RV [89 потом,когда мы собрались,
Then, as we got going,

RW [90 (

58

RV он он закричал и сказал, что нет это не честно,
he called out and said, that no, it was not meant seriously,

RW)

59

RV в общем-то это не правда, заходите назад.
'It's not true, come back'.

RW [91 ну это такая шутка.
Ah, what a joke.

60

NH [[92 So it is not / we don't know when you have

RX [93 ну они и шутят
So, that's how they make jokes

61

(end of the tape)

7. Interpreting in Hospitals
Starting Points for Cultural Actions in Institutionalized Communication[1]

KRISTIN BÜHRIG
University of Hamburg, Germany

Abstract. *To what extent is multilingual discourse characterized by intercultural incidents? This question has been widely discussed in current research on translation and intercultural communication, especially as multilingual discourses take place in institutionalized contexts. This chapter aims to contribute to this debate by focusing on interpreted briefings for informed consent in hospitals. By analyzing questions typically posed by medical staff to multilingual patients such as "Do you have any questions?" as well as patients' reactions to these questions, I hope to reconstruct starting points and forms of cultural actions. The discussion of these actions will shed light on how to optimize not only multilingual but also monolingual communication in institutions.*

1. Intercultural and institutionalized communication

In the current literature, the term **intercultural communication** refers most frequently to face-to-face interactions in intercultural situations (cf. e.g. Knapp and Knapp-Potthoff 1990). Situations are understood as **intercultural** when multilingual individuals, i.e. interactants with different linguistic backgrounds communicate with one another. Only in-depth analyses, however, can show to what extent actants' multilingual potential is actually responsible for actions to be called 'intercultural' (cf. Rehbein 1985, 2006; Blommaert 1991; Sarangi 1994; Koole and Ten Thije 1994; Hinnenkamp 1995; Ehlich 1996; Hartog 2005, 2007; Ten Thije 2002, amongst others).

It seems to be not only the presence of different languages, the multilingual background of actants and their ability to access a language of verbal understanding which are characteristic of the phenomenon of intercultural communication, but also specific action-oriented stores of knowledge, assessments, value judgements, etc. (e.g., Goodenough 1964; Geertz 1973;

[1] I would like to thank Claudia Böttger, Juliane House, Bernd Meyer und Jan Ten Thije for their helpful comments on this article. I would additionally like to thank Juliane House, Claudia Böttger, Audrey McDaugall, Maren Schiefke and Oludele Botchway for their assistance in translating this article into English.

Redder and Rehbein 1987; Sperber 1996; Günthner and Luckmann 2002 and many others). These categories are regarded as culture-specific, while the concept of **culture** is not used correspondingly and instead seems to be tied to the idea of a nation, a language area, a social group, etc. (for a summary cf. Bolten 2001).

Considering the specific distribution of stores of knowledge in a given society and the resultant combinations of verbal actions, Koole and Ten Thije (e.g. Koole and Ten Thije 1994, 1994b, 2001, Ten Thije 2002) claim that many of the so-called 'intercultural incidents' in discourse that have been evaluated and documented in the literature can be attributed to the fact that they took place within the 'action space' (Rehbein 1977) of an institution. Verbal interaction in institutions is based on the actants' unequal stores of knowledge (cf. Ehlich and Rehbein 1977, 1980, 1986): In contrast to the **clients,** the **agents** of the institution have a knowledge advantage that is not limited to functional content, but also encompasses the purpose of particular forms of verbal action (**Institutional knowledge Level 2**, cf. Ehlich and Rehbein 1977). Misunderstandings in conversations between the agents of the institution, who are native speakers as well as clients who are non-native speakers (e.g. consulter and consultant) and have been described as examples of intercultural communication, should be viewed first and foremost as manifestations of the difficulties typical of institutional communication.

This brief overview alone shows that the correlation between verbal action and knowledge can be seen as a key issue in exploring both intercultural and institutional communication. In contrast to the literature cited above, which understands **culture** as an ensemble of action-instructing values in the sense of artefacts, I will focus on cultural actions (Rehbein 2006). Based on Gramsci (1983) as well as Redder and Rehbein (1987), cultural actions are understood here as the actants' critical reflections on their own actions. With the category of cultural actions – as opposed to the dichotomy of institutional and intercultural actions implied by Koole and Ten Thije – I wish to pursue the question of to what extent institutional communication comprises the starting point for cultural actions.[2] In the following, the category of **cultural actions** (Rehbein 2006) and its individual steps will be briefly described in order to capture intercultural instances in verbal actions that may appear in multilingual as well as monolingual [3] communication and especially often in institutions.

---

[2] These features are not identical to misunderstandings – as Koole and Ten Thije rightly remark.

[3] It is often pointed out in the literature that subcultures exist within a culture characterized by shared moral concepts, assessments and action-oriented stores of knowledge (Bolten 2001; Maltz and Borker 1982). Tannen (1990) goes as far as to claim that communication between women and men should be regarded as intercultural communication. However, this assumption was fundamentally critiqued by Günther (1992), among others.

1.1 Cultural action

The research literature (for an overview see e.g. Knapp and Knapp-Potthoff 1990) differs in its view of how action-oriented stores of knowledge, assessments and particularly moral concepts are understood to be connected to language, how they occur in language, and how they are organized through language. Within the framework of **functional-pragmatic discourse analysis** (cf. Ehlich 1991; Rehbein 2001; Bührig 2005), which also provides the theoretical-methodological framework of this article, Rehbein (2006) summarizes the mental categories mentioned above with the term **technai.** These include **action-practices, forms of imagination, thinking-structures** and specific processes of perception and evaluation as well as societal knowledge. As shared **presuppositions** (Ehlich and Rehbein 1972), these **technai** are made up of action systems between actants, which are constitutive of various groups.

According to Rehbein (2006), individual **technai** are related differently to verbal action: While forms of imagination, for example, are mostly revealed in symbolic field expressions (stems of verbs, nouns, adjectives, etc.) and are connected to wishes and motives, action practices adapt forms of realizations of verbal and non-verbal actions to the deep-structures of verbal action patterns and cultural apparatuses. In this way they contribute to the creation and strengthening of habits and contribute in (communicative) practice to the assessment of situations and the way action processes come into being. They are often routinized forms of actions and carry a **cultural load:**

> Once, however, an action practice has become commonplace, i.e. as soon as set phrases and speech formulae have crystallized into a generally known stock of language (here the language of the authorities), these can no longer be termed cultural. Rather, the action practice has become reified and is thus no longer a creative mental process. Evidence for this is the way in which such phrases are so routinely used, without any sense of the problems or reflection on the institutional constellations with which they are tightly bound. Thus the communicative forms which are tied to a constellation based on an action practice are to be regarded as having "cultural load". (Rehbein 2006:49).

Critical instances in communication which occur, for example, as a consequence of the use of various technai by the actants, can cause the **cultural apparatus** to emerge in discourse. The cultural apparatus ensures that current presuppositions and therefore the present action system of an actor can be reflected and restructured when necessary. In the actual course of discourse, the cultural apparatus normally emerges in fourth position. It is preceded by (1) a cultural loaded action, (2) **a negating action,** i.e. a reaction to the first step of the action by another actor, as well as (3) a partial restructuring of one's own presupposition (3rd position), which may result in changes to the initial problematic verbal action (4th position). According to Gramsci (1983), the use of the cultural apparatus can therefore be seen as a critique of one's own action and its premises (see Rehbein and Redder 1987). Rehbein (2006) refers to **intercultural communication** as a case in which both actants involved in an interaction sequentially complete the stages outlined above. If only one of the actants completes this process, however, the outcome will be a **one-sided application of the cultural apparatus.** According to Rehbein (2006), the cultural apparatus only becomes effective when an actant's presuppositions of the action system are affected in the course of communication and when this circumstance is of relevance to the interaction. Therefore, not all follow-up requests for additional information, for example, can be traced back to the emergence of a cultural apparatus. Requests that serve to ensure comprehension (see also Kameyama 2004) might instead be based on different levels of knowledge that are not constitutive for an action system.[4] Only a detailed analysis of verbal action can show in which way certain utterances can be understood as **cultural actions**.

If the analysis shows that these utterances are instances of a negating action (step 2) or an action of restructuring one's own presuppositions (step 3) related to a change of the initial verbal action (step 4), then the utterances can be understood as cultural action. Even within a given society or ethnic group, the technai mentioned by Rehbein are not distributed consistently. Instead, different action systems may exist that make use of varying technai. In this regard, even monolingual conversations in institutions between agents and clients may contain the potential for intercultural moments (see also Rehbein 2006:91).

Assuming that agents and clients belong to different ethnic groups and/or linguistic communities, the differing stores of knowledge which result from the actants' different institutional roles may become relevant in specific ways

---

[4] Not every problem with reception (such as a quiet voice) necessarily leads to a negating action. The action practice appears to be interactional starting at step three. That means that two fundamental options exist: i. the action practice is used in the standardized form (–> as a culturally loaded form), but remains inactivated, reified and unrecognized; ii. the action practice is reflected upon and/or reorganized (–> cultural apparatus). With the non-reflective use of the action practice, the reception problems linked to its surface forms become firmly established and thus perpetuate the misunderstanding. In the ensuing steps (i.e. the "post-history"), the discourse is either broken off or a clarification of a different quality is achieved. (Rehbein 2006:51)

(cf. Meyer 2002). In medical communication, ideas concerning the emergence of illness or even what is perceived as 'ill' in general may very well differ between doctor and patient. Furthermore, different names for perceptions of the body or the underlying purpose of a specific discourse type can be signs of differently distributed or differently shaped knowledge. [5]

1.2 Cultural action as optimization of institutional communication

When research results have been used to prepare for intercultural communication, the emphasis thus far has mainly been placed on cultural differences and the resulting problems in communication. The analysis of monolingual data often provides the basis for comparative analysis methods of culture and language. These findings are frequently adapted for use in different forms of cultural training (see Bolten 2001; Liedke *et al.* 1999; Müller-Jaquier and Ten Thije 2000).

In the following section, the typical direction of applying research results to the practice of communication will be reversed. We will look at doctors' questions and patients' reactions in pre-operation medical discussions in which an interpreter is co-present. These phenomena may be reconstructed as **rich points,** in the sense of Heringer's (2004) expansion of the term originally introduced by Agar (1994): questions posed by doctors may lead to irritation on the part of the patients or the interpreter and are the subject of discussion during the conversation.

Following a description of the data, the doctors' questions will be analyzed in order to explore how questions such as "Do you still have any questions?" can be systematically located in the process of pre-diagnostic discussions in German hospitals. In the ensuing step, the structure of these questions will be discussed in order to illustrate where potential problems may occur. By reconstructing the course of action followed by the patients and the interpreter in dealing with these questions, I will show the extent to which the actants' verbal actions are culturally determined and how their application of the cultural apparatus can lead to an optimization of doctor-patient communication under certain circumstances.

2. Data basis

The following section contains exemplary analyses of selected excerpts from interpreted pre-operation conversations in a hospital in Germany

[5] The extent to which diverging perceptions of appropriate verbal action for clients and agents are of interactive relevance for the interpretation of conversations is nicely shown by Apfelbaum (1997).

conducted with Portuguese and Turkish patients. These patients often speak German but are not usually proficient enough to allow them to understand the medical personnel's comments on the planned procedure. For this reason, interpreters are appointed in order to ensure understanding between the doctor and patient. At present, no institutionalized interpretation services exist in German hospitals. Multilingual nursing staff or the patients' relatives therefore often assume the task of interpreting. They are not specially educated or prepared for this task. The data for the present analysis stem from the project "Interpreting in Hospitals/ Dolmetschen im Krankenhaus".[6] The corpus of the project is comprised of 100 doctor-patient conversations from German, Turkish, and Portuguese hospitals. Pre-diagnostic discussions, anamneses, and conversations regarding the findings and results of medical examinations were recorded. 50% of the 100 recorded conversations show a high degree of involvement on the part of the interpreter, while the other 50% contain monolingual comparative data. The data were transcribed according to the semi-interpretive transcription model (HiAT) (cf. Ehlich and Rehbein 1976).[7] The use of this system allows for the detailed description of the ongoing interaction between actants involved in the conversation: Notes positioned below one another within the same score area (PF) run simultaneously within conversation. The speech sigles mark the roles of the actants: (A) stands for doctor, (D) for interpreter, (P) for patient and so on. A translation is also included in the score. The score areas are consecutively numbered (outside of the graphic frame) to serve as a reference for the analysis. Furthermore, the particular verbal contributions have been divided (cf. Rehbein 1995) into individual utterances to enable the precise identification of the particular steps of action. The numbering of the segments can be found inside the score areas above the tracks of the respective speaker.

3. Questions in doctor-patient-communication

Rehbein (1993) shows that questions are an integral structural element of

---

[6] This project was supported by the German Research Foundation (Deutsche Forschungsgemeinschaft) from 1999 to 2005 as part of the Sonderforschungsbereich 538 "Mehrsprachigkeit" (Multilingualism) at the University of Hamburg.

[7] The individual comments are noted in the literary transcription. Further, certain HiAT-conventions using special characters are used to display prosodic and verbal-interactional characteristics: pauses are noted with full stops (•) with one full stop indicating a duration of 0.25 seconds. Pauses lasting longer than one second are noted in double brackets with a number, e.g. ((1.5s)). Emphatically pronounced portions of the utterances are underlined. For interjections, the course of the pitch is marked with diacritical signs: (Jà) falling, (Já) rising, (ja) falling-rising, (ja) progressive, etc. Furthermore, comments are provided to describe certain modes of speaking. Interrupted utterances will be marked with three dots (...), repairs within an utterance with a slash (/).

doctor-patient conversations. Questions tend to be used one-sidedly[8] by the doctor to obtain information; therefore, doctor-patient interactions are comparable to interviews. Doctors' questions are often either open questions or yes/no questions posed in a 'multiple-choice-format' (West 1984), both of which heavily restrict the patient's verbalizations of his or her knowledge (cf. also Ten Have 1993; Mazeland 1992). A doctor's conventional asking of questions does not leave the patient's verbal action unaffected: Often, patients do not verbalize relevant experiences and perceptions. West (1984) even goes as far as to point out that standard questions such "Is there anything else?" or "Do you have any questions?" fail to realise their original purpose of encouraging patients to ask further questions.[9] Determining why such (unsuccessful) questions continue to occur in doctor-patient communication is an important research desideratum (Rehbein 1993:313). In other words, the functional role of these questions in interactive and institutional contexts needs to be clarified.

4. Pre-operation discussions in hospitals

Standardized doctor's questions such as those cited by West (1984) often occur at the end of the doctor's explanation of the impending procedure in pre-operation discussions. Based on Meyer's (2004) study on monolingual and interpreted pre-operation discussions in German hospitals, such questions can be characterized more precisely, namely functionally. Discussions preceding operative procedures exhibit a clear division into certain phases (see fig. 1): In the first phase, the doctor explains the medical procedure in some detail as well as the medical equipment to be used. In the second phase, the doctor outlines potential complications that may arise during the procedure, checks whether the patient has any questions and asks the patient for his approval for the scheduled procedure. The patient documents his or her approval by signing a *clarification form*.

Figure 1. Meyer (2004:100)

According to Meyer, these phases are based on the specific purposes of pre-operation discussions (see Figure 2): While Phase I is concerned with

[8] Quantitative surveys have clearly shown that questions are almost exclusively asked by the doctors (cf. e.g. Fehlenberg 1985, West 1984)

[9] Under this assumption, one can assume that patients may understand doctors' questions as a procedure that Schegloff and Sacks (1973) have described as 'opening up closings'.

introducing the patient to the scheduled procedure and securing his or her cooperation, Phase II serves to fulfil the necessary legal requirements underlying pre-medical discussions. The overall purpose of the pre-operation discussion is to gain the patient's approval for the medical procedure after having been made aware of the risks involved (cf. Meyer 2004:100,).

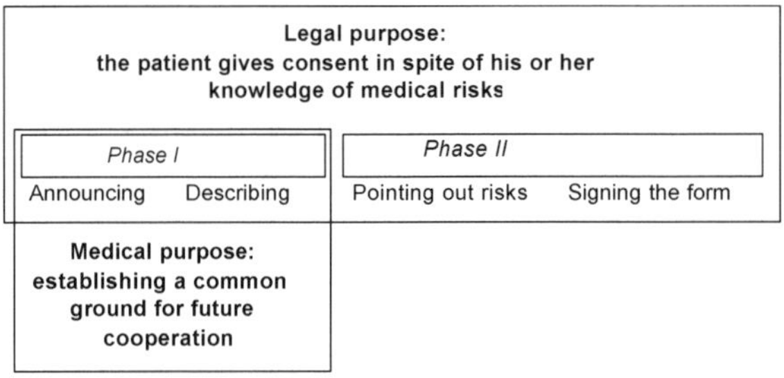

Figure 2. Adapted from Meyer (2004:102)

With regard to the patient's right of self-determination, the decision making is shifted from a legal perspective towards the patient: The doctor transmits certain information regarding the scheduled procedure to the patient which he or she must then evaluate. Generally, however, patients are not aware of the specific purpose of the pre-medical discussion. Instead, the doctor, after having informed the patient, asks by means of a question-answer pattern whether the patient needs further clarification. This is often initiated by a question such as "Do you have any questions concerning the examination?". Following Rehbein (1977), Meyer calls this action **monitoring** (2004:97). **Monitoring** is the basis for providing patients with the necessary explanation of their medical situation, following which the doctor must ensure that the patient's need for further information is met, even when patients cannot properly articulate these needs themselves. (cf. Geiß 1993:171).

If the patients express difficulties in understanding the doctor, the conversation cannot yet move to the next point and the doctor must try to explain the matter all over again. According to Meyer, by requesting that patients verbalise their need for clarification, doctors control the conditions for further verbal actions and fulfil a legal norm (cf. Meyer 2004:97).

In 18 of the 21 interpreted pre-operation discussions considered for this study, the medical personnel asks whether the patient has any further questions concerning the scheduled diagnostic procedure. But how do patients actually handle this request by the doctors? Consider three examples from our corpus that show typical reactions by patients.

5. No questions?

The first example is taken from a conversation between a German Doctor (A) and a Portuguese patient (P) who is scheduled to undergo a colonoscopy in the course of a differential diagnosis. The patient has fallen ill while on vacation in Germany and a Portuguese relative, who lives in Germany, takes on the task of interpreting. After the doctor has informed the patient of the course of action and possible complications, he asks in PF 147 if the patient requires further clarification (segment 1).

(B1) Colonoscopy

[147]

			/1	/2
A [v]		Hm˙	Hm˙	Hat sie denn
A[en]		Hm		Does she have
D [v]	Äh • • die äh von da unne sind • rübergegangen, nech?			

[148]

A [v]	noch Fragen • jetzt zu der Untersuchung • selber?	
A[en]	any questions on the examination itself?	
		/3
D [v]		Tens mais alguma
D [en]		Do you have a question, that you

[149]

				lengthened	
D [v]	pergunta a fazer	agora sobre este/ esta ehm,	((holt Luft))	eh	esta
D[en]	want to ask	now, to this, this uh	takes breath	uh	This

[150]

D [v]	diagnóstica que vão fazer contigo com o, o/ • • eh	a espelhagem?	
D [en]	examination, they are going to do with you, the uh	colonoscopy?	
P [s]		/4	/5
P [v]		Eu não tenho…	Eu não
P[en]		I don't have any	I have

[151]

		/6
D [v]		Podias perguntar alguma coisa se
D[en]		You could ask something else, if you
P [v]	tenho perguntas a fa/ nenhumas a fazer.	
P[en]	no questions to as/don't ask	

[152]

		/7	/9	
D [v]	quisesses.	Se não tens, então pronto.	Nein, die hat, ((räuspert sich)) die hat	
D[en]		If you don't have any, ok	No, she has ((cough))she has	
			/8	/11
P [v]			(Não, eu sei lá.	Eu sei lá).
P[en]			No, I don't know	I don't know.

[153]

		/13	/14		/15	/16	18
D [v]	keine äh • spezifische Frage…	Ja,	ja?		Ja,	jà.	Is
D[en]	N o•specific question…	Yes,	Yes?		Yes,	Yes.	Is
	/12						/17
P [v]	Eu sou que, eu sou que/ eu,	eu sei é		que estou nas mãos deles.			Eles
P[en]	I am (that), I am (that)/I,	I know		that I am in your hands			You are

[154]

		/19	/20	
D [v]	klar.	Is klar.	Ela/	Äh die hat keine
D[en]	clear	clear	She	uh she has no
P [v]	é que têm que fazer aquilo que/ qualquer • coisa.			
P[en]	it, they have to do that, what/ something.			

[155]

D [s]		/21
D [v]	Frage,	äh weil sie erstens einmal keine medizinisch äh äh keine
D[en]	question,	uh cause she first of all has no medical uh, uh , no

[156]

		/22		
A [v]		Hm̀hḿ		
A[en]				
		/23		/24
D [v]	Vorkenntnisse hat.	Und	sie is in Ihre Hände.	• Und äh Sie sind jetzt ihr
D[en]	has prior knowledge.	‿And	she is in your hands.	• And uh now you are her

[157]

		/26	/27		/28
A [v]		Nein,	bin ich	ja nich.	Ich möchte es • • lieber besprechen, dass
A[en]		No,	I am	not.	I rather want• • to discuss, that
		/25			
D [v]	Lieber Gott.	((lacht, 3s))			
D[en]	dear God.	((laughs,3s))			

[158]

A [v]	sie auch/		dass sie weiß, was, was,	was geplant	ist, ne?
A[en]	she too/		that she knows,what,what,	what is planned,	right?
		/29		/30	
D [v]		Is klar.		Eh o	médico diz que
D[en]		Yea		uh the o	doctor says that he

[159]

		/31
D [v]	também não te quer ensinar,	mas quer falar contigo • para ter uma
D[en]	doesn't want to tutor you,	but, he wants to talk to you, to build trust,

[160]

D [v]	confiança	para as pessoas poderem entregar umas às outras	e saberes o
D[en]		so that the people can come together	and you know, what

[161]

		/32
D [v]	que é que vai acontecer contigo,	mais nada.
D[en]	will happen to you	That's it.

After the interpreter has translated the doctor's question into Portuguese, the patient answers by saying that there is no need for further clarification (segments 3, 4). The patient repeats her negative response even after the interpreter broaches the subject again (segments 5, 6). While the patient initially claims that she has no further questions as she requires no further information, she later expresses a view that reveals her attitude towards medical institutions: She sees herself as in the doctor's hands and leaves the responsibility for the scheduled procedure completely to him (segments 8, 10, 11, 12, and 16). In so doing, she indicates that she will definitely follow through with the procedure, though without weighing the potential pros and cons of the scheduled colonoscopy.

Her explicit use of speaker deixis *eu* (I) in segments 10, 11 and 12 additionally reveals how she feels about the doctor's question. In Portuguese, the personal ending of the finite verb suffices to allocate the actant. The use of explicit speaker deixis serves to emphasize the speaker's role as an actant, for example when the speaker sets herself apart from the rest of the group or places special emphasis on her statement (e.g. Hundertmark-Santos Martins 1998:80; Neves 2000:452). In this discourse excerpt, the reason for the fact that the patient marks herself as the speaker may be that she is surprised by the doctor's question. Furthermore, as can be seen in comments 10 and 11, she feels ignorant or at a loss in this situation. This reaction may result from confronting the doctor's actions with her own anticipated actions. She is obviously not planning on evaluating the doctor's knowledge in order to arrive at her own decision and seems set to accept the doctor's plan. She is not aware of the fact that a pre-diagnostic medical discussion has an important function in the decision-making process.

In extract B2, taken from an informational dialogue preceding an intended biliary endoscopy, the patient again does not feel the need to be further informed after the doctor has described the treatment procedure (PF 90, segment 3). Here it is her daughter (D) acting as an interpreter, who asks a question in PF 90/91 (segment 7).

(B2) Biliary Endoscopy

[89]

		/1	
A [v]		Ham Sie, ham	Sie spezielle Fragen hierzu, zu dieser
A [en]		Do you, do you	have particular questions on this, on this
P [v]	viel • spreche, oh…	((lacht kurz))˙	

[90]

		/2							/6	
A [v]	Untersuchung?	Oder zu der Er	kran	kung?					Ja?	
A [en]	examination?	Or on the illness?								
								/5		/7
D [v]								Ich aber.		Wiesa/
D[eng]								But I do.		Why
					/3		/4			/8
						lengthened				
P [v]					• • •	Nee,	nee.			Ab…
P[en]						No, no				But...
P [k]						zögernd				

[91]

		/9
A [v]		Das is uns auch
A [en]		We don't really
D [v]	äh wieso sind denn die Gallenwege denn jetzt erweitert?	
D [en]	um why are the bile ducts widened?	

[92]

		/10	/11
A [v]	nich ganz klar.	Eigentlich dürften sie das nich sein.	• • • Es kann aber
A [en]	know either.	In fact, they shouldn't be.	It could be, though,

[93]

		accentuated			
A [v]	sein, dass • • einfach, weil die Gallenwege weit	waren,	• •	dass	es n bisschen
A [en]	that simply, because the bile ducts were wide,			that it	it takes a little
				/12	
D [v]				Jă˙	
D [en]					

[94]

		13
A [v]	länger dauert, bis sie wieder schmal werden, • • nich?	• • Denn wenn die
A [en]	longer till they tighten again, right?	Cause when they are

[95]

A [v]	aufgestaut sind		und selbst wenn der Stau nich	mehr da is, nich mehr da
A [en]	dammed up		and even when the damm isn't	there anymore, isn't there
		/14		
D [v]		• Al	so dadurch, dass die mal…	
D[en]		Well	due to the fact that they...	

[96]

A [v]	is, kann es • ein, zwei Wochen dauern, bis die wieder kleiner werden,	
	anymore, it can take one or two weeks till they get smaller again,	/15
D [v]		Hmhm˙

[97]

		/16			/18
A [v]	nech?	Da/ • und da war ja sehr viel Druck auf den Gallenwegen.			Und
A [en]	right?	There/ and there was a lot of pressure on the bile ducts.			And
				/17	/19
D [v]				Ja˙	Hmhm˙
D [en]				Yes,	ummmm

[98]

			/20		
A [v]	dieser	Druck ist zwar jetzt weg,	aber die Gallenwege		brauchen ein
A[en]	this	Pressure is gone now,	but the bile ducts		need
				/21	
D [v]				Ja˙	
D[en]				Yes	

[99]

		/22	
A [v]	bisschen, bis sie wieder n bisschen kleiner geworden sind.	Hm˙	
A[en]	some time till they get a little bit smaller.	Um	
			/23
P [v]			• • Und äh
P[en]			And um

[100]

			/24	/25
A [v]			Es so:	Wenn wir davon ausgehen, dass •
A[en]			This is how it is:	If we assume that is
P [v]	muss operiert	oder nich?		
P [en]	does it need to be operated on	or not?		
P [k]	instead of: does it need to be operated			

[101]

A [v]	wirklich Steine • von der Gallenblase in den Gallengang abgerutscht sind,
A [en]	the bilestones really slipped from the gall bladder into the bile duct,

[102]

A [v]	und da in der Gallenblase immer noch Steine drin sind, dann sollte man die
A[en]	and there are still bilestones in the gall bladder, then it would be better

[103]

					/27	
		more low voice				
A [v]	Gallenblase	raus	nehmen.		Ja.	
A[en]	to remove	the	gallbladder		Yes.	
				/26		/28
D [v]				• • Ganz rausnehmen?		Das Ding brauch man
D[en]				Totally remove it?		You don't really need

[104]

		/29	/30	
A [v]		Nein. • •	Das braucht man nicht.	
A[en]		No.	You don't need it.	
D [v]	eigentlich auch nich?			
D [en]	the thing, do you?			
P [v]				Sò ( ) hab ich heute
				So ( ) do I have

It is only in PF 99 (segment 23) that the patient finally asks a question, which is, however, not concerned with the planned surgery but with the very necessity of the surgery, i.e. the possible removal of her gall bladder. Characteristically, she formulates a yes-no question. The patient's lack of knowledge is verbalized by means of the modal verb 'must' in combination with the participle 'operated'. The linguistic means that are used show that the patient is in no way considering questioning with the planned procedure. She sees her action space as defined by obligations (e.g. medical necessities) that she is not capable of influencing. Moreover, B2 shows that the patient does not believe the planned examination to be relevant to the possible surgery so that one gets the impression that the doctor's information about the scheduled examination is not evaluated by the patient.

The next conversation excerpt (B3) shows the reaction of a Turkish patient who is being informed about a planned bronchoscopy. His foremost concern is that his state of health improves (PF 127, segment 7).

(B3) Bronchoscopy

[126]

					/1 lauter	
A1 [v]	auch aufstehen.		((1s))Ja?		• • • Haben Sie noch Fragen?	
A1[en]			Yes?		Do you still have questions?	
						/2
D [v]		• • Hm̌˙		Okay.		• • •
D[en]		Um.		Okay.		
[nn]	*Hintergrund))˙*		*((Geräusch))˙*			
[nn] [en]	*Background))*		*((sound))*			

[127]

	/2		/5	/6	
D [v]	Sorun var mi, diyor.		Nein.	((schmunzelt))˙	
D [en]	Do you have a question, she says.		No	((smirking))	
P [s]		/3 /4			/7
P [v]		Yok. (Sorum yok).			İyi (olmak
P[en]		No. (I don't have a question).			(I want) to

[128]

		/8	/9	/10	/11	/12
AU [v]						((1s))
A1 [v]					• • Ja.	
A1[en]					Yes.	
D [v]			Er will • nur besser sein.	((schmunzelt))˙		
D [en]			He just wants to get better.(	(smirking))		
P [v]	istiyorum).	Sorum bu.				
P [en]	get well.	That is my question.				

[129]

			/13	/14	/15
AU [v]	((schmunzelt))˙				
AU [en]	((smirking))				
A1 [v]		• •	schmunzelnd Kann ich ver	stehen.	((1,5s)) Gut.
A1 [en]			I understand that.		Good.
D [v]				((lacht kurz))˙	
D [en]				((laughs briefly))	

These three examples show that the patients do not wish to be further informed. When asked by the doctors whether they have any further questions, their reply is "no". Prompted by the interpreters' insistence, the patients ask the doctors about the further course of treatment (possible operations) or about their ultimate goal, namely a quick recovery. Their comments, however, are not a result of the evaluation of the knowledge they have been given about a planned diagnostic procedure, which would be typical of the constellation of decision making. In contrast to the doctors, who are oriented towards making a diagnosis, the patients' statements show that they primarily concerned with the doctors' prognosis (B2: possible removal of the bile) or their own quick recovery.

It is interesting from an interactional and/or an institution-analytical point of view to note that the patients are prompted by the doctors' monitoring to enter into a sequential action pattern (question – answer) (Ehlich and Rehbein 1979, 1986). However, the patients obviously do not detect a **starting point** relevant for a sequential action pattern in the ongoing speech situation or, to be more precise, in their knowledge. Therefore, they fill the designated local position in the adjacency-pair simply by answering the doctor's question. Their type of answer, or to be more precise, their negation, however, marks a disruption of the expectations, at least on the part of the interpreters, which they then handle communicatively. In order to further explore the way in which doctors' questions (paradoxically) contribute to the patients' denying the need for further information, the following section will analyze doctors' questions in the source and target language in greater detail.

5.1 Doctors' questions as 'action practices'

As discussed above, the doctors' questions in our corpus can be found in the monitoring phase of a briefing for informed consent. The doctors' questions employ linguistic means similar to those used when addressing either a patient's possible knowledge deficit or the knowledge that the doctors have already established.

		Patient's knowledge deficit		**Reference to the examination/ to previously verbalized knowledge about the examination**
(B1)	(S1)	Does she	still have questions	• about the examination itself?
(B2)	(S1)	Do you have	particular questions	About this, about this examination?
	(S2)			Or about the illness?
(B3)	(S1)	Do you still have	questions?	

The doctors address the patients' possible knowledge deficits by means of prepositional phrases in B1 and B2. Only question B3 does not include this information. Moreover, the doctor's questions B1 and B3 include the term 'noch' (English: 'still'). In German, the grading particle 'noch' marks an "excess over an assumed endpoint" (cf. Zifonun *et al.* 1997:885), i.e., "what is still going on, one would have expected to be over at this point in time" (Zifonun *et al.* 1997:884). The expression 'particular' in B2 is also worth commenting on: 'particular questions' classify the patient's possible knowledge deficit concerning the doctor's information as particular or abnormal. By using the expressions 'still' and 'particular', the doctors give the impression that they feel that they have already contributed all relevant information regarding the scheduled examination to the discourse. Thus, possible questions on the part of the patient are considered to be unexpected. In this way, the doctors' questions seem to be routine forms of linguistic action realized as diagnostic pre-operation discussions used to fulfil legal requirements. Most importantly, however, they are treated by doctors as a mere formality. Doctors obviously fail to reflect upon the complexity of the knowledge they transmit to the patients and the relatively high demand placed on patients' reception processes or their personal involvement in such a multilingual communicative situation. Given the systematic positioning of doctors' questions in the course of the discourse, the choice of linguistic means and the reconstructed communicative characteristics can thus be seen as an argument for interpreting them as specific **action practices** undertaken by the agent (cf. Rehbein 2006).

5.2 The need for clarification: reflections of patients and their interpreters

As discussed above, patients tend to express no need for being given further information. If a doctors' questions are to be analyzed as **action practices** revealing a **cultural load**, a patients' negative answers can be understood as **negating actions,** especially when considering the following explanatory actions. Explanatory actions are often not verbalized until the negative statement they refer to is translated into German. They can therefore be analyzed as a **supplement** (Rehbein 1976; Bührig 1996) to the respective negating reference statement. The mere fact that these statements are 'add-ons' to the preceding reference statements suggests that a person's actions have been reflected upon, as these reflections display a partial revision of a speech action plan influenced by a preceding comment. Moreover, these addenda contain realization forms of certain **technai** that are further reflected upon when the interpreter translates them into German. I will explain this procedure in the following paragraphs.

The patient's comments in B1 are probably initiated by the interpreter's insistent questioning. After the patient's initial negation (segments 3, 4), the interpreter points out that the patient can, but need not, ask questions (segments 5, 6). The patient insists that she does not have any questions (segments 8, 10, 11). In segments 12 and 13, the patient goes on to explain why she does not ask questions ("I am (that), I am (that)/ I, I know that I am in your hands. You are the one who will have to do it/ something."). Simultaneously, the interpreter begins to speak. After an initial translation of the patient's negative answer in segments 3, 4, 8, 10, and 11, the interpreter stops interpreting (segment 9) and reacts to the patient's explanations using hearer signals realized in German. From segment 18 onwards he translates the patient's explanation into German. While he further explains the lack of questions in segment 18 by adding another reason ("um because first of all she doesn't have any previous um medical knowledge"), he translates the patient's explanations in segments 20 and 21 ("And she is in your hands. And um you are her good god now."). By means of 'and' as well as the parallel construction of both statements, the interpreter subordinates the patient's explanation to the explanation scheme composed in segment 18 of his German interpretation. Through this procedure, the patient's statement is provided with an illocution[10] that expresses a greater commitment to the action system and the doctor. Moreover, segment 21 contains an intentional exaggeration ("And um you are her good god now.") – compared to the patient's utterance – conveying a particular 'form of imagination'. This corresponds to the stereotype of the *white demigod*, a well-known idiom in German. There is no such term with reference to doctors in Portuguese; however, a person who thinks of himself or herself as omnipotent can be

[10] The action pattern of **reasoning** is usually realized when an action system is jeopardized due to an imminent misunderstanding of an utterance (cf. Ehlich and Rehbein 1986; Redder 1990).

referred to derogatively by a comparable word. By being addressed directly, the doctor is referred to as the responsible person unquestionably and completely in charge. This happens in an ironic way, however, as is revealed by the interpreter's laughter in segment 22.[11] In addition to the independently phrased explanation, the interpreter uses another form of 'cultural action', which can be found in the ironic exaggeration of the patient's form of imagination[12] and causes the doctor to reflect on his action practice (see below §5). In B3, the patient's daughter acting as an interpreter manages to clarify the patient's negation of the need for further information. She translates her father's answer (segments 3, 4) "Yok. (Sorum yok.)" (No. I don't have a question.) using the German 'nein' (segment 5).

Her subsequent smile (segment 6) might be understood as a comment on the patient's remark which – considering its brevity – can be interpreted as an abrupt refusal of the doctor's suggestion to continue the discussion. The patient's negative response to the doctor's monitoring might well be classified as a 'rich point' in the discourse.

The father also seems to realise that his brief answer is a little out of line. He states explicitly states his interests in segments 7 and 8 "Iyi (olmak istiyorum). Sorum bu." (I want to get well. That is my question.), which are not focused on the details of further treatments but rather on his desire for a speedy recovery. With her translation "He just wants to get better" (segment 9), the daughter highlights her father's comments in the target language by combining the remarks in the source language into an utterance frame on the one hand and communicating the patient's focus on *recovery* using the grading particle '*nur*' (English 'just') on the other. The subsequently repeated smile (segment 10) can be interpreted as a comment with an apologetic tone. Both interpreters support the patients' approaches by using pointedly **reproductive utterances** (Bührig and Rehbein 2000) as well as independent remarks in the target language. Both groups of actants apply the cultural apparatus by conveying their own understanding or rather the way they understand the patient's actant role. Cultural action is thus triggered by the doctors' action practice and a monitoring process realized in the form of a question and the linguistic action of the interpreters.

---

[11] Moreover, the hyperbolic form of the interpreter's remark and the direct addressing of the doctor convey an invasion of the doctor's "zone of integrity" (Rehbein 1977). His subsequent chuckle indicates that he tries to negate the potentially impolite character of the remark by means of an additional ascription of a **jocular interaction modality** (Kotthoff 1996, 1998).

[12] One might be able to determine in an interview whether the interpreter thinks of this Topos as similarly well known in Germany and Portugal If this were the case, the selection of the Topos can be interpreted as another instance of a 'cultural action' through which the interpreter hopes to achieve **common ground**. For an inclusion of interview data in the analysis cf. Ten Thije (2002).

6. Reflections on the communicative events on the part of the doctor

The interpreting daughter's approach in B3 is successful: The ward manager as well as the doctor begin smiling. In segment 13, the doctor smiles as he expresses his empathy for the patient – "I understand that". With this remark, the doctor lessens the pressure in the communicative situation by adopting the patient's perspective after a pause of half a second. It is at this moment that the doctor first takes the patient's values into consideration, even if he then continues with his usual action practices as an agent of the institution. And it is at this point in the interaction that the doctor reflects on the **post-history** (Rehbein 1977) of the patient's question. In so doing, he performs a selective cultural action. In the ensuing course of the pre-operation discussion, however, the doctor informs neither the patient nor the daughter about the background to his question, i.e. the function of his question in segment 1.

B1 shows another meta-communicative revision of the rich point: As a response to the interpreter's remarks in the target language German "And she is in your hands. And you are her good god now." (segments 20, 21), the doctor rejects the patient's evaluation by saying "No, I'm not." (segments 23, 24). In his subsequent remark, the doctor explains to the patient what he had meant by the question "I should rather discuss it, so she knows what is planned, right?" (segment 25). The doctor does not, however, explain the legal purpose behind this question, which would reflect his action practice. However, he does explain the medical purpose of the treatment, so that this example can be seen as an instance of cultural action.

7. Conclusion: 'Cultural action' as a starting point for improving communicative practice

Neither monolingual nor multilingual pre-operation discussions properly inform the patients of the purpose of the discussion. Patients are usually not aware that they are the ones who need to decide whether a scheduled procedure should be conducted. The doctors' questions, which are typical of medical monitoring and serve to clarify the patient's need for information in multilingual discourse, often turn out to be sources of confusion. As the function of the questions is not clear to patients, they lack a starting point for posing their own questions about the planned procedure or about possible complications that might arise. The patient's interest is mainly focused on their quick recovery, not on how this recovery can be achieved. Patients seem to merely take note of the information they are given, but their remarks do not reflect an evaluation of this information with respect to possible risks or negative side effects.

Although this conclusion conflicts with the patients' legal right of self-determination in pre-operation discussions, the actants' course of action reconstructed in the above extracts seem to shed light on how this communicative practice can be improved. Neither patients nor interpreters stop at the confusion which doctor's questions analyzed in this paper have created. Instead, they work on the rich points of the interaction, the doctor's questions, as well as on their own actions as starting points for cultural action: The patients try to explain why they do not ask any questions when requested to do so and in so doing reveal forms of imagination and wishes in their linguistic actions that are probably not specific to multilingual patients. In extracts B1 and B3, the patients' forms of imagination and values were communicated by an independent explanation or through the pointedly performed reproduction and the interpreter's smile. This in turn led to an existing action practice being reflected, i.e. to the monitoring practice on the part of the doctor. The fact that the patients' add-ons are initiated by the interpreter's actions both in B1 and in B3 clarifies the extent to which the **internally dilated speech situation** (Bührig and Rehbein 2000), which is characteristic of interpreting, can encourage the course of actions taken by patients and interpreters.

In order to improve not only multilingual but also monolingual institutional communication, it seems necessary to explain both the procedure of a given operation as well as the purpose of the pre-operation discussion itself. This applies particularly to the interpreter's reproduction of the doctor's remarks in the target language. Only when interpreters know the purpose of the discourse can they make an informed choice about the medical terms to be used in the target language (Meyer 2005). Training medical staff members for pre-medical discussion could help to identify their routinized action practices and encourage them to inquire about the patients' perspectives. Moreover, training programmes in interpreting should take the patients' countries of origin into consideration as well as whether or not it is common practice in these countries to have briefings for informed consent. It would be important for the medical staff to know that in Portugal, for example, pre-operation discussions are common, whereas pre-diagnostic discussions are not.

References

Agar, Michael (1994) *Language Shock. Understanding the Culture of Conversation*, New York: Morrow.

Blommaert, Jan (1991) 'How much culture is there in intercultural communication', in Jan Blommaert and Jeff Verschueren (eds) *The Pragmatics of International and Intercultural Communication*, Amsterdam & Philadelphia: John Benjamins, 1-13.

Bolten, Jürgen (2001) *Interkulturelle Kompetenz*, Erfurt: Landeszentrale für politische Bildung Thüringen.

Bührig, Kristin (1996) *Reformulierende Handlungen. Zur Analyse sprachlicher Adaptierungsprozesse in institutioneller Kommunikation* , Tübingen: Narr.

------ (2005) 'Speech action patterns and discourse types', *FOLIA LINGUISTICA* XXXIX(1-2): 143-71.

------ and Jochen Rehbein (2000) *Reproduzierendes Handeln. Übersetzen, simultanes und konsekutives Dolmetschen im diskursanalytischen Vergleich*, Arbeiten zur Mehrsprachigkeit, Folge B, Nr 6.

Ehlich, Konrad (1991) 'Funktional-pragmatische Kommunikationsanalyse. Ziele und Verfahren', in Dieter Flader (ed.) *Verbale Interaktion. Studien zur Empirie und Methodologie der linguistischen Pragmatik*. Stuttgart: Metzler, 127-43.

------ (1996) 'Interkulturelle Kommunikation', in Hans Goebel, Peter H. Nelde, Zdenȩk Starý and Wolfgang Wölck (eds) *Kontaktlinguistik / Contact Linguistics/Linguistique de contact*, HSK12.1, Berlin, New York: de Gruyter, 180-93.

------ and Jochen Rehbein (1972) 'Erwarten', in Dieter Wunderlich (ed.) *Linguistische Pragmatik*, Frankfurt/M.: Athenäum, 99-114.

------ (1976) 'Halbinterpretative Arbeitstranskriptionen (HIAT)', *Linguistische Berichte* 45: 21-41.

------ (1977) 'Wissen, kommunikatives Handeln und die Schule', in Herma C. Goeppert (ed.) *Sprachverhalten im Unterricht*, München: Fink, 36-11.

------ (1979) 'Sprachliche Handlungsmuster', in Hans-Georg Soeffner (ed.) *Interpretative Verfahren in den Sozial- und Textwissenschaften*, Stuttgart: Metzler, 243-74.

------ (1980) 'Sprache in Institutionen', in Hans Peter Althaus, Helmut Henne and Herbert Wiegand (eds) *Lexikon für Germanistische Linguistik*, Tübingen: Niemeyer, 338-45.

------ (1986) *Muster und Institution. Untersuchungen zur schulischen Kommunikation*, Tübingen: Narr.

Fehlenberg, Dirk (1987) *Kommunikation zwischen Arzt und Patient. Gesprächsstrukturen der psychosomatischen Krankenvisite*, Bochum: Brockmeyer.

Geertz, Clifford (1983) *Dichte Beschreibung. Beiträge zum Verstehen kultureller Systeme,* Frankfurt/ M.: Suhrkamp.

Geiß, Karlmann (1993) *Arzthaftpflichtrecht,* München: Beck.

Goodenough, William H. (1964) 'Cultural Anthropology and Linguistics', in Dell Hymes (ed.) *Language in Culture and Society. A Reader in Linguistics and Anthropology*, New York: publishing house missing, 36-39.

Gramsci, Antonio (1983) *Marxismus und Kultur. Ideologie, Alltag, Literatur,* edited and translated from the Italian by Sabine Kebir. Hamburg: VSA.

Günthner, Susanne (1992) 'Sprache und Geschlecht: Ist Kommunikation zwischen Frauen und Männern interkulturelle Kommunikation?', *Linguistische Berichte* 138: 124-34.

------ and Thomas Luckmann (2002) 'Wissensasymmetrien in interkultureller

Kommunikation', in Helga Kotthoff (ed.) *Kultur(en) im Gespräch*, Tübingen: Narr, 213-43.

Gumperz, John J. (1982) *Discourse strategies*, Cambridge: University Press.

Hartog, Jennifer (2006) 'Beyond misunderstandings and cultural stereotypes. Analysing intercultural communication', in Kristin Bührig and Jan D. Ten Thije (eds) *Beyond Misunderstanding. Linguistic Analyses of intercultural communication*, Amsterdam: Benjamins, 175-88.

------ (2007) 'Das "Kulturelle" in der interkulturellen Kommunikation: Die Möglichkeit ihrer Analyse', in Konrad Ehlich and Susanne Scheiter (eds) *Interkulturelle Kommunikation analysieren*, Münster: Waxmann.

Heringer, Hans Jürgen (2004) *Interkulturelle Kommunikation*, Tübingen, Basel: Francke.

Hinnenkamp, Volker (1990) 'Wieviel und was ist "kulturell" in der interkulturellen Kommunikation? – Fragen und Überblick', in Bernd Spillner (ed.) *Interkulturelle Kommunikation. Kongreßbeiträge zur 20. Jahrestagung der Gesellschaft für Angewandte Linguistik GAL e.V*, Frankfurt/M.: Lang, 46-52.

Hundertmark-Santos Martins, Maria Theresa (1998) *Portugiesische Grammatik*, Tübingen: Niemeyer, 2nd edition.

Kameyama, Shinichi (2004) *Verständnissicherndes Handeln. Zur reparativen Bearbeitung von Rezeptionsdefiziten in deutschen und japanischen Diskursen*, Münster: Waxmann.

Knapp, Karlfried and Annelie Knapp-Potthoff (1990) 'Interkulturelle Kommunikation', *Zeitschrift für Fremdsprachenforschung* 1: 62-93.

Koole, Tom and Jan D. Ten Thije (1994) *The Construction of Intercultural Discourse. Team Discussions of Educational Advisers*, Amsterdam & Atlanta: Rodopi.

------- (1994b) 'Der interkulturelle Diskurs von Teambesprechungen', in Gisela Brünner and Gabriele Graefen (eds) *Texte und Diskurse. Methoden und Forschungsergebnisse der Funktionalen Pragmatik*, Opladen: Westdeutscher Verlag, 412-35.

------- (2001) 'The reconstruction of intercultural discourse: Methodological considerations', *Journal of Pragmatics* 33: 571-87.

Kotthoff, Helga (1996) 'Witzige Darbietungen als Talk-Shows. Zur konversationellen Konstruktion eines sozialen Milieus', in Helga Kotthoff (ed.) *Scherzkommunikation. Beiträge aus der empirischen Gesprächsforschung*, Opladen: Westdeutscher Verlag, 145-91.

------ (1999) 'Coherent Keying in Conversational Humour: Contextualising Joint Fictionalisation', in Wolfram Bublitz and Uta Lenk (eds) *Coherence in Spoken and Written Discourse*, Amsterdam & Philadelphia: Benjamins, 125-50.

Liedke, Martina, Angelika Redder and Susanne Scheiter (1999) 'Interkulturelles Handeln lehren – ein diskursanalytischer Ansatz', in Gisela Brünner, Reinhard Fiehler and Walther Kindt (eds) *Angewandte Diskursforschung.*

Band 2: Methoden und Anwendungsbereiche, Opladen: Westdeutscher Verlag, 148-79.

Maltz, D. and R. Borker (1982) 'A subcultural view on male/female misunderstandings', in John J. Gumperz (ed.) *Language and Social Identity*, Cambridge: Cambridge University Press, 52-75.

Mazeland, Harrie (1992) *vraag/antwoord-sequenties*, Amsterdam: Stichting Neerlandistiek VU.

Meyer, Bernd (2002) 'Untersuchungen zu Aufgaben interkulturellen Mittelns', in Sylvia Kalina and Joanna Best (eds) *Übersetzen und Dolmetschen in Praxis und Lehre. Eine Orientierungshilfe,* Tübingen: UTB, 51-59.

------ (2004) *Dolmetschen im medizinischen Aufklärungsgespräch. Eine diskursanalytische Untersuchung zur Wissensvermittlung im mehrsprachigen Krankenhaus*, Münster: Waxmann.

------ (2005) 'Bilingual Risk Communication', in John Cohen *et al.* (eds) *ISB4: Proceedings of the 4th International Symposium on Bilingualism*, Somerville, MA: Cascadilla Press, 1602-13.

Müller-Jacquier, Bernd and Jan D. Ten Thije (2000) 'Interkulturelle Kommunikation: interkulturelles Training und Mediation', in Michael Becker-Mrotzek *et al.* (eds) *Linguistische Berufe. Ein Ratgeber zu aktuellen linguistischen Berufsfeldern*, Frankfurt/M. etc.: Lang, 39-57.

Neves, Helena de Moura (2000) *Gramática de usos do português*, São Paulo: Editora Unesp.

Redder, Angelika (1990) *Grammatik und sprachliches Handeln. Denn und da*, Tübingen: Niemeyer.

------ and Jochen Rehbein (1987) 'Zum Begriff der Kultur', *Osnabrücker Beiträge zur Sprachtheorie (OBST)* 38: 7-24.

Rehbein, Jochen (1976) *Planen II: Planbildung in Sprechhandlungssequenzen*, Trier: Linguistic Agency Universität Trier (LAUT).

------ (1977) *Komplexes Handeln. Elemente zur Handlungstheorie der Sprache*, Stuttgart: Metzler.

------ (1985) 'Einführung in die interkulturelle Kommunikation', in Jochen Rehbein (ed.) *Interkulturelle Kommunikation*, Tübingen: Narr, 7-39.

------ (1993) 'Ärztliches Fragen', in Petra Löning and Jochen Rehbein (eds) *Arzt-Patienten-Kommunikation. Analysen zu interdisziplinären Problemen des medizinischen Diskurses*, Berlin & New York: de Gruyter, 311-64.

------ (2001) 'Das Konzept der Diskursanalyse', in Klaus Brinker, Gerd Antos, Wolfgang Heinemann and Svend F. Sager (eds) *Text- und Gesprächslinguistik. Linguistics of Text and Conversation. Ein internationales Handbuch zeitgenössischer Forschung. An International Handbook of Contemporary Research*, Vol. 2, Berlin & New York: de Gruyter, 927-45.

------ (2006) 'The Cultural Apparatus. Thoughts on the relationship between language, culture and society', in Kristin Bührig and Jan D. Ten Thije (eds) *Beyond Misunderstanding. Linguistic Analyses of intercultural communication*, Amsterdam & Philadelphia: John Benjamins, 43- 96.

Sarangi, Srikant (1994) 'Intercultural or not? Beyond celebration of cultural differences in miscommunication analysis', *Pragmatics* 4(3): 409-427.

Schegloff, Emmanuel A. and Harvey Sacks (1973) 'Opening up closings', *Semiotica* 8: 289-327.

Sperber, Dan (1996) *Explaining culture: a naturalistic approach*, Oxford: Blackwell.

Tannen, Deborah (1990) *You just don't understand – Women and Men in Conversation*, New York: Morrow.

Ten Have, Paul (1993) 'Fragen von Ärzten. Erste Bemerkungen', in Petra Löning and Jochen Rehbein (eds) *Arzt-Patienten-Kommunikation. Analysen zu interdisziplinären Problemen des medizinischen Diskurses*, Berlin & New York: de Gruyter, 373-83.

Ten Thije, Jan D. (2002) 'Stufen des Verstehens bei der Interpretation von interkulturellen Diskursen', in Helga Kotthoff (ed.) *Kultur(en) im Gespräch*, Tübingen: Narr, 61-98.

West, Candace (1984) *Routine complications. Troubles with talk between doctors and patients*, Bloomington: Indiana University Press.

Zifonun, Gisela, Ludger Hoffmann and Bruno Strecker (1997) *Grammatik der deutschen Sprache*, Berlin & New York: de Gruyter.

Notes on Contributors

Kristin Bührig is Professor of German Linguistics at the University of Hamburg. In research and teaching, her main focus is on institutional, intercultural and multilingual communication, community interpreting, translating, language acquisition/bilingualism, teaching German as a foreign language and functional grammar.

Heidrun Gerzymisch-Arbogast is Professor of Translation and Interpreting and Head of the Advanced Translation Research Centre (ATRC) at Saarland University. She has published widely on translation and interpreting science with a focus on LSP translation, translation methodology, translating culture, text linguistics and multidimesnional translation.

Juliane House is Professor of Applied Linguistics at Hamburg University. Her research interests include translation theory, contrastive discourse analysis, politeness theory, misunderstanding, English as a lingua franca and intercultural communication.

Alexandra Kallia holds a PhD in English Linguistics from the University of Tübingen. Her research interests include pragmatics (especially irony, politeness and speech acts), intercultural communication and conversation analysis.

Dorothée Rothfuß-Bastian holds a PhD in Translation Science at Saarland University. Her research interests include coherence in translation, topic/rheme relationship in translation and female and male translators' aptitud, motivation and engagement.

Jan ten Thije is Associate Professor at the Departement of Dutch Studies at Utrecht University. His research interests include intercultural and institutional discourse, non-professional interpretation, receptive multilingualism, biographic narratives and intercultural training.

Antje Wilton is an Assistant Professor of English and Applied Linguistics at the University of Erfurt. Her research interests include translation abilities of untrained natural bilinguals, humour in bilingual conversation, conversation analysis, native/non-native interaction, multilingualism from a historical perspective and lay theories of bilingualism.

Index